Foreign Investment in Southeast Asia in the Twentieth Century

J. Thomas Lindblad
Senior Lecturer in Economic History
University of Leiden
The Netherlands

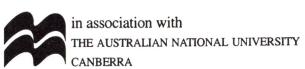

in association with
THE AUSTRALIAN NATIONAL UNIVERSITY
CANBERRA

First published in Great Britain 1998 by
MACMILLAN PRESS LTD
Houndmills, Basingstoke, Hampshire RG21 6XS and London
Companies and representatives throughout the world

A catalogue record for this book is available from the British Library.

ISBN 0–333–55851–0 hardcover
ISBN 0–333–72062–8 paperback

First published in the United States of America 1998 by
ST. MARTIN'S PRESS, INC.,
Scholarly and Reference Division,
175 Fifth Avenue, New York, N.Y. 10010

ISBN 0–312–17755–0

Library of Congress Cataloging-in-Publication Data
Lindblad, J. Thomas.
Foreign investment in Southeast Asia in the twentieth century / J.
Thomas Lindblad.
p.   cm.
Includes bibliographical references and index.
ISBN 0–312–17755–0 (cloth)
1. Investments, Foreign—Asia, Southeastern—History—20th
century.   I. Title.
HG5740.8.A3L56 1997
332.6'73'0959—dc21   97–26517
                                                              CIP

This book is printed on paper suitable for recycling and made from fully managed and
sustained forest sources.

10   9   8   7   6   5   4   3   2   1
07   06   05   04   03   02   01   00   99   98

Printed in Great Britain by
The Ipswich Book Company Ltd
Ipswich, Suffolk

FOREIGN INVESTMENT IN SOUTHEAST ASIA
IN THE TWENTIETH CENTURY

A MODERN ECONOMIC HISTORY OF SOUTHEAST ASIA

The Australian National University is preparing a multivolume economic history of Southeast Asia, which will for the first time place the remarkable economic changes of the late twentieth century within a broader historical framework. This series is at once a work of pioneering scholarship, since nothing remotely comparable has previously been attempted, and a work of synthesis, since hitherto discrete literatures in several disciplines and on ten countries must be integrated. The series will include several volumes on the economic history of the principal countries of Southeast Asia over the past one hundred and fifty years, and a larger number of volumes integrating the whole region in terms of major themes in economic history. Each volume will be accessible to students and specialists alike, aiming to make coherent a history which has been fragmented or ignored.

The Economic History of Southeast Asia Project has been supported by the Research School of Pacific and Asian Studies of the Australian National University, and by the Henry Luce Foundation.

General Editors: Anthony Reid (Chair), Professor of Southeast Asian History, the Research School of Pacific and Asian Studies, the Australian National University, Canberra; **Anne Booth**, Professor of Economics, School of Oriental and African Studies (SOAS), London; **Malcolm Falkus**, Professor of Economic History, University of New England, Armidale, Australia; and **Graeme Snooks**, Coghlan Professor of Economic History, Research School of the Social Sciences, the Australian National University, Canberra.

Other titles in the series include:

Anne Booth
THE INDONESIAN ECONOMY IN THE NINETEENTH AND TWENTIETH CENTURIES: A History of Missed Opportunities

R. E. Elson
THE END OF PEASANTRY IN SOUTHEAST ASIA: A Social and Economic History of Peasant Livelihood, 1800–1990s

Contents

List of Tables

List of Figures

Preface

It is singularly rewarding to write about a topic in economic history that is of immediate relevance to the economic situation and development today. This is certainly the case with a topic such as foreign investment in Southeast Asia during the twentieth century. The other side of the coin is that the literature about such a topic is likely to increase almost exponentially. To his dismay the researcher soon discovers that a slowdown in the writing means so much has appeared in the meantime that substantial parts of what was already on paper will have to be revised. This overabundance of information, together with the wide geographical area and long time period covered, forms the major constraint to what a study such as this can hope to achieve. This monograph derives its ambition from the relatively uncommon combination of contemporary economic issues with experiences dating back to the prewar decades of this century. It is one of the volumes in the series of publications brought out under the auspices of the Economic History of Southeast Asia (ECHOSEA) Project at the Research School of Pacific and Asian Studies of the Australian National University in Canberra.

The Biblical seven years of gestation have come to a close. On 24 November 1989 I was formally invited to join the ECHOSEA Project and agreed to write this book. A workshop organized by the ECHOSEA Project at Canberra on 16–17 March 1991 was, among others, devoted to the conception of this book. Much of the documentation needed was collected during research trips which took me to London, Paris, Tokyo, Osaka, Kyoto, Manila, Bangkok, Penang, Singapore and Jakarta. A first and still incomplete draft of the book was prepared during a four-month stay at Canberra in the first half of 1994. This manuscript was discussed in detail during a small ECHOSEA workshop held in Canberra on 19 May 1994. A brief presentation anticipating the final draft was given at the Fourth Convention of the East Asian Economic Association at Taipei on 26–27 August 1994. It has been a privilege for me as author to draw on the constructive criticism from colleagues and experts on so many occasions.

Numerous individuals have contributed in various ways to the book. I benefited from the cooperative support and good advice given by Professor Anne Booth and Dr Ian Brown at the School of Oriental and African Studies in London, Professor Cathérine Coquery-Vidrovitch at the Université Paris VII, Dr Norio Mihira at the Institute of Developing

Economies in Tokyo, Dr Suehiro Akira, then at the City University of Osaka, Professor Yoshihara Kunio at Kyoto University and Dr Mari Pangestu at the Centre for Strategic and International Studies in Jakarta. I am also indebted to the staff at the Centre for Transnational Corporations at the United Nations ESCAP in Bangkok, Hitachi Semiconductors in Penang, the Japan External Trade Organization and the Hitachi head office, both in Tokyo. Drs Remko Blom at Leiden assisted me with processing quantitative information, and, together with my colleagues Dr Boudien de Vries and Drs Doreen Arnoldus, then at the University of Leiden, furthered my work on this book by loyally taking over several teaching tasks.

Several persons read parts of the manuscript and I benefited greatly from their comments. These people include Professor Jamie Mackie, Dr Colin Barlow and Dr Hal Hill, all at the Research School of Pacific and Asian Studies in Canberra, as well as Professor Anne Booth in London and Dr Thee Kian Wie in Jakarta. Needless to add, I alone am responsible for all remaining errors.

Financial support was given by the ECHOSEA Project, the Henry Luce Foundation, the Netherlands Organization for Scientific Research and the Japan Society for the Promotion of Science. A special word of acknowledgement is due to Professor Tony Reid and other participants in the ECHOSEA Project who made my stay at Canberra in 1994 such a memorable and pleasant experience.

J. THOMAS LINDBLAD
Leiden

List of Abbreviations

ASEAN — Association of South East Asian Nations
BKPM — Badan Koordinasi Penanaman Modal [Capital Investment Coordinating Board] (Indonesia)
BPM — Bataafsche Petroleum–Maatschappij [Batavian Petroleum Company] (colonial Indonesia)
DPV — Deli Planters Vereniging [Deli Planters' Association] (colonial Indonesia)
DRAM — Dynamic Random Access Memory
EC — European Community
EPZ — Export Processing Zone
FDI — Foreign Direct Investment
FEER — *Far Eastern Economic Review*
FMS — Federated Malay States
FTZ — Free Trade Zone (Malaysia)
GDP — Gross Domestic Product
HISEM — Hitachi Semiconductor (Malaysia) Sdn. Bhd. [Sendirian Berhad]
HVA — Handels–Vereniging Amsterdam [Trading Association Amsterdam] (Indonesia)
IMP — Industrial Master Plan (Malaysia)
IPTN — Industri Pesawat Terbang Nusantara [Domestic Aircraft Industry] (Indonesia)
JETRO — Japan External Trade Organization
KPM — Koninklijke Pakketvaart Maatschappij [Royal Packet Company] (colonial Indonesia)
LNG — Liquid Natural Gas
LTC — London Tin Corporation (Malaya)
MIDA — Malaysian Industrial Development Authority
MITI — Ministry of International Trade and Industry (Japan)
MMC — Malaysian Mining Corporation
NDP — National Development Policy (Malaysia)
NEP — New Economic Policy (Malaysia)
NHM — Nederlandsche Handel–Maatschappij [Netherlands Trading Company] (colonial Indonesia)
NIAM — Nederlandsch-Indische Aardolie–Maatschappij [Netherlands-Indian Petroleum Company] (colonial Indonesia)

NIC	Newly Industrializing Countries (Hong Kong, Korea, Singapore, Taiwan)
PNB	Permodalan Nasional Berhad [National Capital Corporation] (Malaysia)
REPELITA	Rencana Pembangunan Lima Tahun [Five Year Development Plan] (Indonesia)
SFFC	Société Financière Française et Coloniale
SIJOR	Singapore-Johor-Riau Growth Triangle
SMC	San Miguel Corporation
Socfin	Société Financière (Malaya, colonial Indonesia)
UMNO	United Malays National Organization (Malaysia)
UNIDO	United Nations Industrial Development Organization
VOC	Verenigde Oost-Indische Compagnie [Dutch East India Company] (colonial Indonesia up to 1799)

1 Introduction

McDonald's in Manila, karaoke in Kalimantan, cricket in Kuala Lumpur, fashion stores in Singapore. The list could easily be extended. The foreign element is conspicuously present in today's quest for rapid economic growth and modernization in Southeast Asia. A comparison with the colonial past, only a couple of generations ago, is illuminating. Then, as now, foreign direct investment (FDI) poured into the region exerting a profound influence, for better or worse, on the prospects for subsequent economic development. Much has been written about foreign investment under the aegis of colonial rule and there is already a vast literature on contemporary foreign investment in Southeast Asia. Yet few have fully appreciated the long-run continuity in the key part played by foreign investment capital in this region. This is where this book fits in. It links past and present in the foreign investment experience of Southeast Asia during the twentieth century. It argues, among other things, that FDI was as important in the late colonial period as it is today.

Our concern is with foreign *direct* investment. The discussion is confined to private capital flows and excludes portfolio investment. This is done so as to be able to focus more sharply on foreign capital flows with an immediate impact on productive capacity in the host country economy. In principle, the analytical distinction between FDI and portfolio investment is rather clear cut. In practice, however, the distinction easily gets blurred as a broader range of financial instruments are applied in transactions with the host country, for instance in local stock markets. It remains difficult fully to incorporate such nuances in a global analysis of the kind offered here.

FDI is defined as 'an investment involving a long-term relationship and reflecting a lasting interest of a resident entity [individual or business] in one economy [direct investor] in an entity resident in an economy other than that of the investor [host country]' (United Nations 1992: 45). Qualifications such as 'long-term relationship' and 'lasting interest' convey that the direct investor wishes to have a say in the management of the enterprise in the host country. This is generally not the case with portfolio investment or foreign commitments of government capital. Even if such distinctions may on occasion become somewhat blurred, they do serve here as a convenient device to focus on those flows of capital most likely to have an impact on the economic development of the host country.

FDI in Southeast Asia must be considered within the wider context of capital flows at large. We distinguish between three levels of observation: investment flows in the world at large; capital flows between Southeast Asia and the rest of the world; and the process of capital formation in Southeast Asia itself. Each will be touched briefly upon.

Capital has become very mobile in today's world. One phone call or electronic message is sufficient to move immense funds back and forth and across borders. FDI is becoming more important than ever before, especially to host country economies among the 'developing countries'. This expression is itself somewhat anachronistic as it also embraces the four East Asian Newly Industrializing Countries (NICs), i.e. Hong Kong, Korea, Singapore and Taiwan. The world total of average FDI flows per year rose from $157 billion in the second half of the 1980s to $225 billion by 1994. The slice received by 'developing countries' increased from some $26 billion (17%) to almost $85 billion (38%) during the same period. Southeast Asia, grouped together with South and East Asia and the Pacific, is the most important region among the 'developing countries'. This region has experienced the most rapid increase in recent years in the accumulation of FDI. In 1993 it accounted for nearly one-half of the total FDI stock in 'developing countries' (UNCTAD 1995: 51–2; cf. UNCTAD 1994: 75).

Southeast Asia, represented here by the six major member states of the ASEAN (Indonesia, Malaysia, the Philippines, Singapore, Thailand and Vietnam), claims a substantial proportion of the total destined for 'developing countries'. In 1993 this proportion amounted to $13.5 billion or 18% out of a total for 'developing countries' of $73 billion. The expected total for 1995 was $15 billion. With hindsight this expectation turned out to be far too conservative (ASEAN 1994: 6; UNCTAD 1995: 52). The FDI flows entering Southeast Asia have continued to swell in volume. Nevertheless, the increase in FDI is quicker elsewhere within the wider region of Asian 'developing countries'. This reflects the intensification in the competition among recipients of investment capital since the ending of the Cold War, in particular the opening-up of China (*Far Eastern Economic Review* [*FEER*] 12/10 1995).

Southeast Asia is important to the world's investors. So are FDI flows within the aggregate of capital flows between this region and the rest of the world. The share of FDI in total receipts on the capital account of the region's balance of payments increased in the 1980s reaching 45% by 1990 (ASEAN 1994: 20–1). The high mobility of capital across borders in this region is also expressed by the so-called capital flow ratio, i.e. the average of inflows and outflows calculated as a percentage of gross domestic product (GDP). During the 1980s the capital flow ratio averaged 5–10% in all major ASEAN member states with one striking exception, Singapore. Here the ratio exceeded 20% (Montiel 1994: 324–5). Singapore is indeed a special case among its neighbours. Its economy is geared towards interaction with the world market to an extreme degree. It is also the region's only capital exporter of significance. This is of particular relevance when calculating a ratio between capital flows and GDP.

The current economic growth and industrialization in Southeast Asia implies much capital formation within the region itself. This was a major bottleneck in the colonial and immediate post-colonial periods when the savings gap was substantial. FDI then, for all intents and purposes, formed the sole source of capital needed for large-scale capital investment. Today capital formation is occupying an ever larger share of GDP. In the early 1980s only Singapore and Malaysia achieved a ratio between gross fixed capital formation and GDP in excess of about 25%, but in 1992 all major ASEAN member states (except the Philippines) reported that at least one-third of GDP was used for capital formation. These are impressive percentages but the foreign proportion appears strikingly low. This is particularly the case considering all the attention given to the necessity of attracting FDI and safeguarding the benefits to be had from FDI. The share of FDI in gross fixed capital formation in the late 1980s and early 1990s was confined to the range of 2–7% in Indonesia, Thailand and the Philippines. It oscillated around 11% in Malaysia and only reached a high level such as one-third or more in Singapore (UNCTAD 1994: 421–6; cf. ASEAN 1990: 113). The casual observer might even wonder whether FDI is such an interesting topic after all if it does not contribute more to laying the foundations for future economic growth in the host country.

But the share of FDI in total capital formation does not tell us the whole story. A large economy with a sizeable domestic population, as in Indonesia, Thailand and the Philippines, needs much capital formation only for residential construction and improvements of the physical infrastructure. Such capital formation may not directly affect the pace of economic development. FDI, however, is likely to be concentrated in industries at the forefront of development that are capable of producing for exports and employ other techniques than those already available in the host country economy. Gaining access to new technology usually constitutes the very rationale of a host country for inviting FDI in the first place. FDI can, therefore, have a disproportionately large impact in terms of export revenues, skilled employment and technological sophistication. In the ideal case FDI can function as a spearhead of economic growth. Yet FDI does not perform this function automatically but only under the appropriate conditions. The potential impact of FDI and the uncertainty whether the impact will materialize or not both make FDI an exciting and worthwhile topic of study.

FDI today is gaining a new respectability, certainly in Southeast Asia. Few would now be inclined to deny the possible benefits to the host country. The anti-FDI rhetoric that was voiced up to the 1970s is now seldom invoked. Liberalization has become a major weapon in the rivalry about incoming foreign capital (cf. Brittan 1995). Still FDI remains controversial. It is linked to the prospects of economic development and the potential to pursue a sovereign foreign policy. Southeast Asia possesses a rich tradition of responses to FDI among the region's non-Communist countries, ranging from much resentment despite little incoming investment in the Philippines to a warm welcome to the massive influx shaping Singapore's destiny. Our intention here is to abstract as far as possible from ideology and to consider FDI in Southeast Asia in terms of what it looks like and what it has meant to the host countries in the region.

This book has a twofold aim: to identify patterns of FDI in Southeast Asia and to indicate the impact of FDI in host countries. By implication it does not cover other capital flows of a comparable order of magnitude nor does it discuss the consequences of FDI for the foreign investor. Economic development in host countries will only be touched upon to the extent that it is directly linked to FDI. The same holds true for economic policies pursued by the host country. The geographical area covered is large: all of Southeast Asia from the shores of the Irrawaddy in Burma to the mountain peaks in the Indonesian province of Irian Jaya. This precludes an in-depth comprehensive treatment of each individual country. The focus on private investment compels us to leave out the Communist regimes in the region, i.e. Burma, Vietnam, Laos and Cambodia, as long as they were effectively sealed off from movements of international private capital. The time-scale is long and finds its starting-point in the late nineteenth and early twentieth centuries when FDI began to flow in under the protective umbrella of colonial rule. Such a long time-scale is exceptional in studies on this topic.

FDI comes in many shapes and it is crucial that we know how to recognize it. The three most common forms of FDI are: equity capital, reinvestment of profits and intercompany loans (i.e. between parent company and subsidiary). Of these three forms, equity capital is the one most easily detected and most readily associated with the ultimate intention of the foreign investor. But the list is not exhaustive. New forms of non-equity investment are becoming increasingly important. Examples include subcontracting and various arrangements for original equipment manufacturing, management contracts, turnkey arrangements, franchising, leasing, licensing and production- or profit-sharing. This study is biased towards use of the most easily accessible data. Such data are likely to refer to equity capital in particular.

When should investment be classified as FDI? This depends on the nationality of the investor and the extent to which equity in particular is foreign-held. The matter is clear-cut when we deal with wholly- or majority-owned subsidiaries of foreign multinationals. Difficulties of interpretation only arise when nationality as such does not provide a sufficient key to the identity of the investor or when a foreign parent company with a minority holding of equity can still exercise a substantial influence on the subsidiary. Problems arise in both the colonial economy and with the so-called 'overseas Chinese' in Southeast Asia.

The colony almost automatically became the destination for FDI from the mother country. Indeed, according to orthodox imperialist theory, overseas political expansion was principally undertaken in the interest of presumptive capital investors from the colonial mother country. These investors possessed a comparative advantage above other foreign investors since they operated within the same legal and institutional framework as at home. In addition, they could often count on a preferential treatment from the colonial authorities. Besides, as colonial rule was elaborated and pro- longed, yet another group of investors emerged consisting of the perma- nent metropolitan residents in the colony, a group that became locally entrenched in the colony while retaining close links with their country of origin. We cannot speak of one foreign investor in the colonial economy. We need to differentiate between various shades of foreignness. On this scale we find, in order of least to most foreignness, first permanent metro- politan settlers in the colony, then investors from the colonial mother country and, finally, investors from third countries (Lindblad 1991: 184–5).

There is a line of continuity running from Loke Yew in Malaya and Oei Tiong Ham in Java during the late colonial period up to Robert Kuok and Liem Sioe Liong in today's Malaysia and Indonesia respectively. The group of entrepreneurs known by the clumsy but unavoidable term of 'overseas Chinese' tended to invest vigorously in the host country. Their commercial success under virtually any political regime forms one of the most spectacular but also one of the least well documented facets of busi- ness history in Southeast Asia. Overseas Chinese are usually nationals of the host country. On occasion this may be at variance with their cultural identity. Some of them were born in the host country and scarcely speak any Chinese. Others, for instance Liem Sioe Liong in Indonesia, arrived there at a young age. Despite their close connections with Chinese business communities elsewhere in the region, the overseas Chinese seem to fit very well into the category of domestic investors (Yoshihara 1988: 37–40).

The United Nations definition of FDI, reproduced above, is unambiguous about how to treat FDI by overseas Chinese. It must be considered as domestic investment since the investor is not a resident of a country other than the one in which the investment is taking place (United Nations 1992: 45). Application of this definition compels us generally to exclude investment by overseas Chinese, as far as such investment can be isolated from other investment in the first place. In Indonesia, Thailand and the Philippines many of the overseas Chinese use non-Chinese names which obviously makes it extremely difficult to spot investment undertaken by Chinese businessmen. Nevertheless, the resident criterion remains debatable. It does not allow us to account properly for the 'alien' character of investment by overseas Chinese as it is often perceived by both themselves and others. Therefore, occasional mention shall be made of investment by overseas Chinese. This is necessary to at least indicate its importance against the background of total FDI.

When does a minority-owned subsidiary qualify for the classification as FDI? Or, to put it differently, how much equity is required to gain effective control over operations in a minority-owned subsidiary? There are two lines of thought in the literature. One refuses to fix a minimum percentage of foreign-owned equity, whereas the other stipulates that the foreign investor alone must possess at least 10% of the ordinary shares in order to let its influence be felt (Balance of Payments 1977; Detailed Benchmark 1983). Both schools emphasize that the important thing is the voting power of the foreign owner. An equity share of 10% can prove insufficient, i.e. if there are other very large shareholders, or more than enough, i.e. if all shareholders are small. In actual practice it is mostly not necessary to choose between these two criteria for minority-owned FDI since the available statistics incorporate the criterion already applied by the authorities collecting the information. It must, however, be kept in mind when discussing the relative bargaining power of foreign versus domestic partners in joint ventures.

Patterns of FDI can only be identified if FDI is measured properly and this is often more easily said than done. FDI is commonly measured in one of two ways, either as annual flows of incoming funds or as a stock of assets built up over time. Ideally, the two should tally since a cumulative total by definition equals the stock value. In practice they do not: one reason for this lies in the very concepts of stocks and flows. Stocks incorporate reinvested profits and adjustments in book value that are not likely to be included in incoming flows. Another reason concerns the method of valuation. Flows are at current prices and exchange rates whereas stocks usually reflect historical prices and exchange rates, i.e. assets valued at acquisition rather than at replacement. A third reason refers to the source of data. Flows are primarily drawn from the balance of payments statistics of the host country, whereas stock forms the outcome of company surveys in the host country. The student of foreign investment has to resign himself to the discrepancy between stock and flow representations, two different images of the same phenomenon.

The discrepancy between stock and flow is illustrated by the case of late colonial Indonesia. Contemporary spot estimates indicate that the accumulated stock of FDI in the late 1930s amounted to 3.5 billion guilders or $1.4 billion. The official balances of payments for the period 1925–1939 display incoming private flows of capital averaging 71 million guilders per year or 2% of the existing stock value which is improbably low. The same result is obtained if we compare annual incoming flows with stock estimates reconstructed from the compensation claims of Dutch-owned business enterprises after having being nationalized under Sukarno in 1957/58 (Lindblad 1991: 187–8; Creutzberg 1977: 44–6, 77–9). Much FDI is realized through reinvestment of profits which induces us to put more confidence in stock figures than in flow figures. FDI flows are to be used here only sparingly. They serve primarily to supplement the impression gathered from stock data.

A separate technical matter with the measurement of FDI concerns prices. It is common usage in economic studies to convert money values into equivalents at constant prices so as to separate real and pure monetary changes over time. The problem with FDI stock data is that stock figures in fact reflect neither current nor constant prices but rather something in between. The only option, which is also adopted in the literature, is to give values in current prices. This makes comparisons over long periods of time hazardous. A comparison of FDI per capita during the late colonial period and today is extremely instructive but presupposes that we take the intervening inflation into account. This shall only be done sparingly. Current prices will generally be used when identifying patterns of FDI without comparisons across periods.

Our focus is on patterns of FDI, not on absolute volumes of FDI as such. Percentages referring to nationalities of investors, sectors of the host country economy or geographical locations obviously remain the same whether expressed in current or constant prices. This study also puts considerable emphasis on comparisons between host countries. Here the problem of current versus constant prices is largely alleviated. Most FDI volumes were originally given in local currencies and then converted into American dollars. Differences in the rate of inflation between host countries are likely to translate as differences between exchange rates with respect to the dollar. If prices rise exceptionally fast in a specific host country, then the exchange rate of this host country with the American dollar will fall more than elsewhere which means that FDI volumes will rise much less when expressed in dollars than in local currency. Stock data in a common key currency allow us to forget about that part of inflation which is unique to the individual host country.

The second aim of this book is to indicate the impact of FDI on the economy of the host country. FDI is not undertaken out of charity but in order to make profit. Similarly, the host country government tries to attract and regulate FDI so as to reap as much benefit as possible from it. In the ideal situation FDI will make both better off. In the situation depicted by the orthodox critics of FDI, only the multinational in question will gain whereas the host country might be even worse off than if there had been no FDI at all. The traditional literature was dominated by Western scholars. It stresses the supply side in the FDI equation and gives the recipient of capital a rather passive role. The more recent literature draws also on work by Japanese economists. The emphasis has shifted towards the demand side, i.e. active promotion of FDI by the host country. Today the attention is often called to the propitious juxtaposition of host countries wanting FDI precisely at the time when multinationals are looking for new investment outlets (Phongpaichit 1990: 100–107). It is important to keep both the supply and the demand sides of FDI in mind when assessing the final impact in the host country.

The first comprehensive study of the consequences of FDI for a host country was published as recently as the late 1950s. It concerned Great Britain. Since then a vast literature has emerged discussing 'linkages and leakages' and distinguishing between effects of FDI on capital formation, exports, employment, technology transfer, economic structure and even the socio-political climate in general (Hill 1990: 34–41). Effects range from being narrowly micro-economic to broad aggregative political or social categories. FDI thus affects industrial structure and performance, skills, wages and employment, choices of technology, savings, external positions, trade regimes and, most importantly, sustained rates of economic growth. The literature is voluminous enough but the systematic evidence is not abundant (Caves 1996: 224–38).

The best endowed host country in Southeast Asia in this regard is Malaysia. Two major studies have scrutinized the contribution of FDI in achieving the targets of Malaysia's New Economic Policy (NEP) during the 1970s and 1980s (Hoffman and Tan 1980; Ariff and Yokoyama 1992). For most host countries in the region, and certainly for the colonial period, evidence must be drawn from a variety of sources. Such evidence is often piecemeal and circumstantial.

There is a link between the rationale behind FDI and its effects on economic development in the host country. Dunning, who wrote the pioneering study on FDI in Britain, distinguishes between four types of FDI directed towards respectively natural resources (both physical and human), new markets, a higher efficiency in production and strategic assets in terms of technology and organization. Each type of FDI has its own contribution to the upgrading of the host country economy. The former two types (seeking resources and markets) may transfer new technology and stimulate future economic growth. The latter two types (seeking efficiency and strategic assets) may enable the host country to make better use of its comparative advantage through an improved international division of labour. The 1980s saw a shift away from the traditional types (seeking resources and markets) to the more modern types (seeking efficiency and strategic assets) (Dunning 1994: 36–9). General considerations of this kind aid us in tracing the impact of FDI in Southeast Asia from its very origins.

This book argues that there is an essential continuity in the importance of FDI in the economies of Southeast Asia during the twentieth century. FDI per capita is not widely different today than in the colonial period (when correcting for inflation). Yet both appearance and substance of FDI in the region look very different today as compared to the late colonial period. The face of capital, as it were, has changed both literally and figuratively speaking, and so has the contribution of FDI to economic growth in the region. The impact today is more profound and, above all, more favourable than under colonial rule. Moreover, the impact is more favourable precisely because the pattern of FDI has changed.

The argument is arranged in a globally chronological fashion. First, a long-run historical perspective is offered by way of a comparison between two points in time separated by about half a century, the late 1930s against the late 1980s (Chapter 2). This is followed up by more elaborate discussions of FDI in respectively the colonial period (Chapters 3 and 4) and during the contemporary era, i.e. since the 1960s (Chapters 6 and 7). The separate discussions of the two surges of FDI activity in the region are bridged by a brief digression on the turmoil of warfare and occupation, decolonization and national self-assertion in the 1940s, 1950s and part of the 1960s (Chapter 5). The chronological sequence highlights the continuity and discontinuity in the FDI experience of Southeast Asia during the twentieth century.

Several key themes are considered within the global chronological framework. One set of themes concerns the inception and further implementation of FDI in the context of the investing activity as such. The emphasis here is on individual pioneers in colonial times (Chapter 3) and foreign multinationals in the contemporary period (Chapter 6). A different set of themes refers to the wider context of economic and political development in which FDI takes place. FDI is positioned against the background of the predominant process of change in the colonial and contemporary periods respectively, or more specifically, colonial state formation in the former case (Chapter 4) and growth through industrialization in the latter case (Chapter 7). The narrow and wider contexts complement one another and allow us to more succinctly link patterns and impacts of FDI.

FDI can logically be approached from either one of two angles, the foreign investor and the host country. Both approaches are applied here but not always in the same way. It is believed that FDI activity in the narrow sense was shaped by local peculiarities in the colonial period, i.e. varying by host country, whereas today this activity depends above all on the nationality of the foreign investor. In the colonial period the nationality of the main foreign investor coincided with that of the metropolitan mother country that in turn exerted a decisive influence on the process of state formation in the colony. Today's process of rapid growth and industrialization, however, is above all coloured by the policies pursued by the individual host country. The host country approach is thus used for both the narrow context in the colonial period (Chapter 3) and the wider context in the contemporary period (Chapter 7). The investor-specific approach applies to both the wider context in the colonial period (Chapter 4) and the narrow context in the contemporary period (Chapter 6).

A brief note on terminology must be added. Geographical names are used in their present-day English version whenever the object in question has not changed, i.e. I speak of 'Thailand' with reference to the period (until 1930) when the country was called 'Siam'. Historical names are retained both when the object has indeed changed, e.g. '[British] Malaya' which is not the same as 'Malaysia', and in order to avoid overly anachronistic effects such as by referring to prewar Burma as 'Myanmar' or to preindependence Batavia as 'Jakarta'. The word 'dollar', finally, means 'American dollar' unless otherwise stated.

2 The Historical Perspective[1]

There is nothing new under the sun. This is a favoured expression among historians which certainly appears to hold true for the presence of foreign capital in Southeast Asia. Between the fifteenth and seventeenth centuries this region was integrated into the world trade system and came to play an increasingly central role in intra-Asian commerce (Reid 1992: 495–6). The foreign element was substantial, consisting not only of Europeans, but also, and probably more importantly, Chinese, Indians, Arabs and Malays. Substantial amounts of capital flowed into Southeast Asia in payment for agricultural produce and ample remittances emanated from sales in local Southeast Asian markets. Yet this was not the same as FDI, aimed at obtaining a lasting interest in the economy of the host country. Precolonial flows of capital served to control trade, not production.

It all changed in the late nineteenth and early twentieth centuries. Massive flows of capital from metropolitan sources dwarfed the preceding commercial credits. The aim was now to gain control over vital parts of the productive apparatus in the host country. That was the true novelty of FDI under the aegis of colonial rule. The historical perspective of today's vigorous FDI activity in Southeast Asia commences with the rise of FDI around the turn of the century. This chapter argues that the fundamental continuity with respect to FDI in Southeast Asia in the twentieth century does not preclude that patterns of FDI have changed dramatically.

The point of departure is a survey of FDI in Southeast Asia during the heyday of colonial rule (section 2.1). The description draws primarily on an authoritative contemporary account concerning the late 1930s (Callis 1942). FDI in Southeast Asia is observed as it had accumulated over decades of colonial rule and before being affected by the turmoil of the 1940s. The present-day pendant is formed by a comprehensive review of FDI in the region towards the end of the 1980s, half a century later (section 2.2). This survey relies on official statistics compiled by the United Nations. The choice for the late 1980s enables us to make use of comparatively recent data with a high degree of uniformity and to concentrate on long-run trends as they have evolved since the 1960s. A separate section gives an elaboration of the statistics underlying the comparison between the late colonial period and the recent past (section 2.3).

11

2.1   THE ZENITH OF COLONIALISM

Colonial rule came to Southeast Asia in stages. The Philippines, the Moluccas, Java and the Straits Settlements counted among the territories where European hegemony was established early. Elsewhere colonial authority was only effectively exercised towards the very end of the nineteenth century and even after 1900. Landmarks in the successive implementation of colonial rule include the Burma War in the mid-1880s, the surrender of Vietnamese sovereignty by the Imperial Court at Hue in 1885, the Dutch invasion of Lombok in 1894 which sparked off a series of annexations outside Java and, finally, the formation of the Federated Malay States in 1896. Thailand remained independent but under Rama V (Chulalongkorn, 1868–1910) it gradually merged into the orbit of British political and economic influence.

The thrust of colonial expansion in the late nineteenth century virtually coincided with a large-scale influx of private capital, especially from the metropolitan mother country. The debate has raged for a full century whether the 'modern imperialism' of the European powers (1870–1914) was driven by economic interests or political motivations. The original paradigm was formulated by Hobson and Lenin. It linked the urge of capitalists to invest overseas with the extension of territorial control. Later it was repeatedly demonstrated that the argumentation could not stand up against the empirical evidence. The second paradigm is associated with names such as Gallagher, Robinson and Fieldhouse. It gained ground after 1945 and stressed the primacy of political expediency and pragmatism, often at the periphery itself. The 1980s have seen the emergence of yet another paradigm, the non-Marxist economic explanation. This theory puts the main responsibility with financial as opposed to industrial interests, at any rate in Great Britain. This is the 'gentlemanly capitalism' that united City and Whitehall against Manchester in securing sources of invisible income on Britain's balance of payments. The pursuit of profit on overseas investment was the true driving force of imperialist expansion even though the final return was below expectations (Davis and Huttenback 1986: 301–18; cf. Cain and Hopkins 1993: II, 93–107).

In reality there was a continuous interplay between initiatives taken by private investors on the one hand and colonial administrators on the other. This process can only be studied properly on the regional or even local level by following individual actions and reactions by private pioneers and colonial administrators. Elsewhere I have examined the empirical evidence for a number of local case studies outside Java. Action by the presumptive investor was indeed often decisive. Examples include the administrative upgrading of Siak in eastern Sumatra in the 1870s in response to plans for investment, the explorations into Flores in 1890 undertaken because of unfounded rumours about a wealth of tin in the interior and, finally, the establishment of effective Dutch colonial rule in Jambi (southern Sumatra) in 1904–1907 only after oil had been discovered (Lindblad 1989a: 9–13; Locher-Scholten 1994: 230–55).

The examples from Sumatra in particular also demonstrate that colonial expansion could, at times, assume the form of implementing existing authority rather than venturing into virgin territories as in the stereotype version of 'modern imperialism'. Effective colonial rule offered the political stability and order considered essential by both investors and administrators. The realization of new projects was on occasion delayed for years at a stretch because the colonial authorities felt unable to guarantee the security of men and property on the proposed site of production. This happened regularly in remote corners of both Kalimantan and Sumatra during the concluding decades of the nineteenth century.

Effective colonial rule was a necessary but not sufficient precondition for FDI. The link between colonial expansion and more FDI was less than straightforward in the sense that a gestation period was needed for FDI to materialize on an appreciable scale. FDI in (French) Indochina before 1900 appears to have been utterly insignificant. In all of Burma in 1906 there were no more than 55 registered foreign companies with very little capital between them (Hlaing 1964: 98; Murray 1980: 105). Colonial Indonesia had already been opened up for FDI in 1870 when the dismantling of the Cultivation System in Java started. Even here accumulated FDI remained unimpressive until the turn of the century (Creutzberg 1977: 17–18). FDI in Southeast Asia was, to all intents and purposes, a feature of the twentieth century.

The pace of change quickened during the decade immediately preceding the First World War. World trade perspectives improved for major raw materials that could be procured from this part of the world in ever larger quantities. Examples include sugar and petroleum from colonial Indonesia and tin and rubber from Malaya. By 1914 these two colonies had emerged as the leading recipients of FDI in Southeast Asia. Aggregate FDI in the region was then estimated at $1.1 billion. Colonial Indonesia and Malaya accounted for three-quarters of the total. Colonial Indonesia claimed no less than $675 million (61%) whereas Malaya got $150 million (14%). Among the other major colonies in the region, the Philippines ranked highest with $100 million followed by Indochina and Burma at approximately $75 million each. The FDI estimate for Thailand was improbably low at $25 million (Table 2.1; Callis 1942: 23, 36, 56, 63, 70, 77, 85, 95, 106; Svedberg 1978: 770).

Table 2.1   FDI in Southeast Asia, 1914 and 1937

Total FDI (million $ and %)

	1914		1937	
Indonesia	675	61	1261	52
Malaya	150	14	372	14
The Philippines	100	9	315	12
Indochina	75	7	302	11
Burma	75	7	228	8
Thailand	25	2	90	3
Total	1100	100	2568	100

Note: Another estimate for Thailand cites total FDI at 144 million baht or $54 million (Manarungsan 1989:184). Chinese investment excluded. This was estimated at $150 million in colonial Indonesia, $200 million in Malaya, $100 million in the Philippines, $80 million in Indochina, $10–15 million in Burma and $100 million in Thailand. Conversion into US$ at the following rates: $1 = *f*2.50 = £0.21 = 2.00 pesos = 25 French francs.

By investor in 1937 (%)

	Britain	USA	Neth.	France	Other
Indonesia	16	7	71	3	3
Malaya	70	6	5	0	0
The Philippines	11	52	0	0	38
Indochina	0	1	0	97	2
Burma	90	0	0	0	10
Thailand	76	4	0	4	15

By sector in 1937 (%)

	Agriculture	Mining	Services	Other
Indonesia	56	19	13	12
Malaya	70	18	6	6
The Philippines	29	23	39	9
Indochina	32	16	36	16
Burma	6	66	24	4

Note: The composition by sector refers to Dutch investment in colonial Indonesia in 1937, British investment in Malaya in 1936, American investment in the Philippines in 1935, French investment in Indochina as accumulated over the years 1924–1938 and British investment in Burma c. 1937.
Source: Callis 1942: 17, 22–3, 29, 36, 39, 57–8, 62–3, 77, 85–7, 91, 95, 105–6.

An unprecedented economic expansion took place in Southeast Asia during the First World War and its immediate aftermath and throughout the 1920s. Export values soared, not only due to exceptionally high prices as in 1919 and 1920, but also in real terms. Foreign capital was instrumental in enlarging productive capacity which enabled output and export volumes to rise more quickly. This was the climax of FDI in colonial Southeast Asia. Between 1914 and 1930 FDI rose rapidly in most host countries (Callis 1942: 23, 95). Export-led economic expansion turned Southeast Asia into an exceptionally attractive investment outlet for private capital from the metropolitan world. This region was probably more favoured among investors than were Africa or Latin America. Then came the worldwide depression. The extreme deterioration in terms of trade for primary products meant both curtailed production and more pessimism among potential investors. Major exporters of primary products such as colonial Indonesia and Malaya were severely hit. Colonial Indonesia was hit more severely than Malaya since the Netherlands-Indian guilder was tied to the Dutch guilder which was depreciated only in 1936. FDI even appears to have declined somewhat in colonial Indonesia and Malaya, i.e. some disinvestment occurred. Elsewhere, however, FDI continued to increase, albeit at a slower rate.

Around 1937, when the world economy was recovering from its deep plunge into recession, a seemingly stable FDI position had been reached which formed the final outcome of several decades of capital accumulation. The regional total of FDI, excluding Chinese investment, now exceeded $2.5 billion or two and a half times as much as in 1914. We distinguish between three tiers of host countries. Colonial Indonesia was still in the first rank but it had to relinquish some of its originally very high share, and yet still accounted for almost one-half of the total or more than $1.2 billion's worth of FDI. In the second tier we encounter the other three major colonies of the region, Malaya, the Philippines and Indochina, each hosting between $300 million and $400 million of FDI which corresponded to 12–15% of the regional total. The third tier consisted of Burma and Thailand with proportions in the total at respectively 9% and 3.5%. It is worth noting that the ranking of the host countries by volume of FDI was exactly the same in the late 1930s as in 1914 (Figure 2.1; Callis 1942: 23, 36, 63, 77, 95, 106). This suggests a high degree of consistency over time in the late colonial pattern of FDI.

Absolute volumes of FDI give an incomplete picture when considered in isolation from the general characteristics of the host country economy. It is also necessary to review accumulated FDI in relationship to the size and strength of the host country economy. Three macro-economic

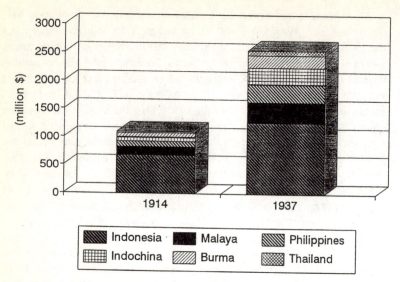

Figure 2.1   FDI stock, 1914 and c. 1937: ranking by host country

variables are selected here to express the dimensions of the host country economy: total population, GDP and export revenue. It should be noted that concepts such as GDP and total exports refer to annual flows, not to stock as is the case with accumulated FDI. Comparisons of the FDI stock with GDP and export revenues therefore only give a crude indication of the position of FDI in the total of economic activity.

Colonial Indonesia was by far the largest host country in the region. Its population, an estimated 65 million on the eve of the Second World War, was almost three times that of Indochina (23 million) and more than four times as large as that of either the Philippines, Burma or Thailand. Each of these countries numbered about 15 million inhabitants. Malaya was the smallest host country with a population of only 5.5 million (ECAFE 1949: 20–5; cf. Boomgaard & Gooszen 1991: 121, 224). In a ranking by FDI per capita Malaya, therefore, emerges far ahead of the rest. Indonesia and the Philippines share the second rank with Burma and Indochina following at some distance (Table 2.2). Colonial Indonesia got the largest slice of accumulated FDI in the region simply because it was so large. Malaya ranked second on account of a relatively high intensity of FDI.

Before the Second World War the Philippines counted as one of the wealthier countries in the region whereas colonial Indonesia was probably the poorest. GDP per capita in 1938 amounted to $43 in the Philippines against $32 in Burma or Thailand and $23 in colonial Indonesia (Booth

Table 2.2   Estimated FDI per capita and as a share of GDP and exports, 1937
and 1989.

	FDI per capita (current $)		FDI as share of GDP (%)		FDI as share of exports (%)	
	1937	1989	1937	1989	1937	1989
Malaysia	69	480	*	21	70	30
The Philippines	20	25	46	4	200	20
Indonesia	19	200	84	37	230	160
Burma	14	*	46	*	120	*
Vietnam	13	10	*	*	400	*
Thailand	6	100	19	8	125	30
Singapore	**	9600	**	90	**	60

Note: * = insufficient data; ** = not applicable.
Sources: ASEAN 1990; Callis 1942; ECAFE 1949; ESCAP 1991: 156–70,
216–31, 320–36, 408–20, 448–54; United Nations 1992: 141–72, 217–32, 261–74,
313–32, 339–48.

1991: 21). The ratio between FDI and GDP was therefore higher in colonial Indonesia than in the Philippines or Burma, let alone Thailand (Table
2.2). The difference was a lot smaller than when expressed as absolute
volumes of FDI alone. Regrettably, no comparable estimates are available
for GDP in Malaya in the late 1930s. Evidence from earlier and later
years, however, makes clear that Malaya had a higher per capita GDP than
all other countries in Southeast Asia (van der Eng 1994: 102). By implication the ratio of FDI to GDP is likely to have reached a higher level in
Malaya than in any of the region's other host countries.

Colonial Indonesia and Malaya were the major exporters in Southeast
Asia. In 1937 these two countries together accounted for more than two-
thirds of all the region's export revenue, roughly $1 billion out of a total
for Southeast Asia of $1.6 billion. Burma and the Philippines formed an
intermediate group of exporters, each pocketing $150–200 million.
Indochina and Thailand both earned less than $100 million from exports
(ECAFE 1949: 212). Linking FDI and export revenue enables us to identify two categories of host countries in Southeast Asia (Table 2.2). The
first group consists of colonial Indonesia, the Philippines and Indochina.
Here accumulated FDI was very high compared to annual export revenues,
twice as much or more. The second group comprises Malaya, Burma and
Thailand, host countries where accumulated FDI and annual export revenues were of about the same size. This in turn may be ascribed to either
very large export volumes (Malaya) or relatively small stocks of accumulated FDI (Burma and Thailand).

The confrontation of FDI figures with these three macro-economic variables produces some valuable insights into the late colonial pattern of FDI in Southeast Asia. The volume of FDI was only partially related to size and wealth considering the substantial stock built up in the largest but poorest host country (colonial Indonesia) as well as in the richest but smallest one (Malaya). The link was stronger with export performance since the two largest recipients of FDI, colonial Indonesia and Malaya, also earned the most in foreign markets. The connection between FDI and the size of the host country economy was also ambiguous in the cases of Indochina and Burma. Indochina received far less than the size of the economy would suggest. Burma might have been capable of absorbing more FDI on account of its vigorous export production. There was a higher degree of consistency in the cases of the Philippines and Thailand. The Philippines under American colonial rule occupied an intermediate rank on most accounts. In Thailand an unimpressive stock of FDI was accompanied by an unimpressive export performance.

The single most characteristic feature of FDI in the colonial context was the special position enjoyed by investors from the metropolitan country. Yet Southeast Asia displayed a whole spectrum of variation in this respect (Figure 2.2; Callis 1942: 22, 36, 58, 61–2, 91–2, 105). At the one end we encounter Indochina and Burma where virtually the entire FDI stock

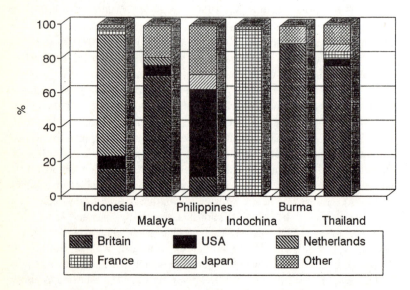

Figure 2.2   Total FDI stock c. 1937: composition by nationality

consisted of French and British capital respectively. The Philippines were at the opposite end with American firms accounting for scarcely more than one-half of all FDI. Colonial Indonesia and Malaya formed the middle of the spectrum with about 70% of FDI originating in the Netherlands and Britain respectively. It is instructive to calculate a so-called investment enforcement ratio expressing the extent to which the FDI of the mother country in its colony exceeded the share of this metropolitan country in the region's incoming FDI. This ratio was especially high for French and Dutch capital and significantly lower for British or American capital (Svedberg 1981: 24–6).

The variations in the share of the colonial mother country in FDI can be explained by looking at history, economic policy and structural change in the colonial economy. Historical tradition explains why this share was conspicuously low in the Philippines: Spanish heritage still made itself felt. Even in the 1930s the onetime colonial power in Europe accounted for about 30% of accumulated FDI. Thailand was a special case. Although formally not a colony, it did resemble one in the sense that a single European metropolitan country was responsible for most of FDI. Close commercial ties had been developed with Britain during Rama V and in the 1930s British firms were said to control 70–80% of the accumulated total (Callis 1942: 77).

Economic policy stayed liberal in most colonies throughout the late nineteenth and early twentieth centuries. A major exception to the rule was Indochina where French colonial policy in Indochina virtually barred entry of non-French capital. Currency regulations, high tariffs for third parties and direct constraints all contributed to a near-monopoly for investment capital from France (Murray 1980: 198–200). In Burma, where there was an equally extreme predominance of capital from the mother country, the situation was different. British colonial policy did generally not discriminate against non-British capital. Yet various restrictions did apply specifically to the oil industry. But this was precisely the sector attracting most FDI in Burma at the time (Callis 1942: 105).

The structure of the colonial economy changed as the colonies became integrated with the world market. This was especially pronounced in the region's two prime export earners, colonial Indonesia and Malaya. New lines of export production developed, e.g. tin and rubber in Malaya and rubber and oil in colonial Indonesia. Such a diversification of the economic structure stimulated the entry of firms from third countries, i.e. overseas sources of investment capital other than the mother country. The only precondition was that the investment climate remained liberal which was indeed the case in both of these two colonies. As a consequence, the Dutch share in FDI was very high in traditional agriculture such as sugar in Java but far lower in, for instance, the estate agriculture in East Sumatra (Keller 1940; Robequain 1954: 324). The overall Dutch share in FDI may, therefore, be considered as a statistical abstraction averaging two very different situations within the same colony. In Malaya, however, it was more a matter of a generally competitive policy also allowing non-British investors to seize the opportunities emerging in export production.

There was an unmistakeable symmetry in rankings of the mother country and third countries as far as several nationalities were represented among the investors in the first place. Britain ranked second in colonial Indonesia and immediately after the two colonial powers (USA and Spain) in the Philippines, whereas Dutch capital competed with American capital for the second position in Malaya. This was not coincidental. Conditions of FDI resembled one another in the entire region and experiences acquired in one colony could easily be put to use in another. Geographical proximity played its role as well. British rubber planters in East Sumatra, for instance, maintained close contacts with Dutch-owned rubber estates in Malaya across the waters of the Straits of Malacca.

FDI entered only certain parts of the colonial economy. There were two tendencies at work: one of concentrating capital in industries at the vanguard of economic expansion and another towards diversification across several walks of economic life (Figure 2.3; Callis 1942: 17, 29, 57, 87–8, 105). Burma was the prime example of the former tendency, with oil and other mining claiming two-thirds of all FDI. Indochina and the Philippines were at the other extreme. They attained a fairly even distribution of FDI over the sectors, with services alone covering at least one-third of the total. Colonial Indonesia and Malaya were, again, found in the middle. Large-scale export agriculture accounted for 55–70% of the total in these colonies but, significantly, this was seconded by substantial commitments of capital in mining amounting to about one-fifth of total FDI. In Thailand FDI successively shifted into trade, teak logging and tin mining, in that order, but the information does not allow a sensible breakdown by sector for the late 1930s (Falkus 1989).

The variation in composition of FDI within this region reflects differences in both resource endowment and economic policy. Oil had been discovered in Kalimantan, Sumatra and Burma around 1900 and modern tin mining rose to prominence in the Federated Malay States from the first decade of the twentieth century. The soils of Java and Luzon were particularly suited for sugar cane. The rubber plant flourished not only in Malaya but also in the Indonesian Outer Islands and parts of Indochina as well. These were raw materials and tropical primary products for which world demand kept

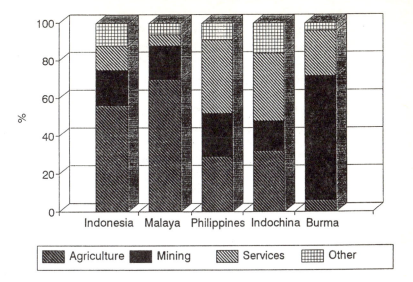

Figure 2.3   Total FDI stock c. 1937: composition by sector

increasing throughout the first three decades of the twentieth century. With the exception of rubber, such products were scarcely, if at all, produced for export purposes by indigenous entrepreneurs. FDI thus served here to open up new lines of export production.

Economic policy also had a part to play. The French colonial authorities in Indochina directed much investment capital into services, e.g. public utilities and banking, and into manufacturing or other miscellaneous industries (Murray 1980: 109–10, 123–8). In the Philippines joint ventures between American industrial firms and indigenous partners were especially favoured. The implementation of such a policy of fostering industrialization was greatly aided by the presence of a relatively large middle class in the Philippines, providing both needed skills and a domestic market (Yoshihara 1985: 31). Elsewhere, notably in colonial Indonesia and Malaya, liberal policies prevailed which automatically meant that FDI primarily entered export industries possessing a comparative advantage rather than venturing into production aiming at import substitution.

Chinese investment has so far been left out of the discussion. It does, however, add another dimension to the picture of FDI in Southeast Asia, regardless of whether it is considered as foreign or domestic investment or as something in between. According to a Japanese language survey published in 1939, total overseas investment by the Chinese amounted to more than 4 billion yen or $1 billion. This was distributed over the host countries as follows: $320 million in colonial Indonesia, $250 million in Malaya, $240 million in Thailand, $120 million in Indochina and $100 million in the Philippines (Hicks 1993: 199). Such estimates are considerably higher than those cited in Western sources. The error margin is especially wide for colonial Indonesia and Thailand (100%) and sizeable also for Malaya and Indochina (50%). Japanese and Western figures on Chinese invest-ment only coincide for the Philippines. For Burma the only available data are trifling and improbably low (Callis 1942: 20–21, 37, 64–5, 76–7, 95, 106; Andrus 1948: 184). The gross underestimation of Chinese investment in conventional Western sources, in particular with respect to colonial Indonesia and Thailand, is corroborated by a comparison with yet another Japanese language source published during the Second World War (Brown 1993: 87).

Investment by overseas Chinese constituted a very substantial comple-ment to FDI in Southeast Asia as it corresponded to 40% of accumulated FDI in the region. The impact of including Chinese investment would differ considerably by host country. It would raise FDI by 25–40% in colonial Indonesia, the Philippines and Indochina, whereas in Malaya the total would be 68% higher. Thailand is an extreme case since Chinese investment here was two and a half times the total FDI. The real question, however, is the extent to which Chinese investors merged into the local business élite thus becoming less eligible for the classification 'foreign'. Evidence from Thailand suggests that overseas Chinese, in fact, constituted most of the domestic class of investors so that it would be highly mislead-ing to group them with foreign investors (Suehiro 1989: 8–9).

Chinese investment did not only differ from FDI in the degree of what one, for lack of a better term, could call local entrenchment. Chinese investment had a very different composition from FDI as it was strongly geared towards services, in particular trading. Commerce alone accounted for 45% of total Chinese investment in Southeast Asia in the 1930s. Finance at 17% was almost as important as total agriculture (22%). Mining and manufacturing were largely insignificant (Hicks 1993: 199). Chinese investment was important but its position and impact probably differed fundamentally from FDI. This warrants separate treatment.

Such was the situation when the Pacific War broke out. FDI had grown rapidly but the relative positions of the host countries in Southeast Asia stayed the same. There was a general tendency towards a high concentra-tion of capital from the colonial mother country but the degree of predom-inance differed considerably. There was a general tendency towards resource-oriented investment but again there was much variation between host countries. Chinese investment played a supplementary role but its impact was not felt in the same way everywhere. Each country in Southeast Asia possessed a unique prewar heritage with respect to FDI. This heritage will be discussed in greater detail later (Chapters 3 and 4).

2.2 THE FORCE OF RESURGENCE

Japanese armies swept through the region in the early months of 1942. Foreign-held assets were confiscated and severely damaged, both during the Japanese occupation itself and at its conclusion in 1945. Decolonization followed and the break with the tranquil and stable climate for FDI under colonial rule became final. Sovereignty was relinquished either early and peacefully, e.g. in the Philippines (1946) and Burma (1948), or after much bloodshed and increasing international pressure, e.g. in Indonesia (1949) and Vietnam (1954). Peninsular Malaysia became independent in 1957, with Singapore following suit in 1959, but here the 1950s were clouded by the confusion and violence of the 'Emergency'. The newly independent states felt the urge to liberate themselves from the alleged yoke of Western capital. Policies towards FDI were at best ambivalent and often hostile. Burma was effectively sealed off for FDI by its Socialist regime. In Indonesia, under Sukarno, waves of nationalization struck first Dutch-owned, later also British or American assets. Elsewhere resentment against FDI mounted. With the possible exception of the Philippines, Southeast Asia was simply not an attractive place for foreign investors during the immediate post-war decades.

Change came in the 1960s as the climate gradually grew more conducive to incoming FDI. In three countries, namely Thailand, the Philippines and Indonesia, this improvement was directly linked to a change of government. Already, in 1957, the Sarit coup had paved the way for more liberal policies in Thailand. From 1962 the Board of Investment granted the privileges of 'promotion status' to joint ventures with multinationals (Wong 1979: 179). In the Philippines the newly established Marcos regime legislated new investment incentives for foreign capital from 1966. This was partly done in anticipation of the expiration of the Laurel-Langley agreement, which until 1974 guaranteed preferential treatment for American firms (Allen 1974: 16). In Indonesia the new Suharto government was quick to reverse the policies of Sukarno. In 1967 a more liberal law on foreign investment, 'Law no. 1', was issued and from 1973 new FDI projects were submitted for approval to the Capital Investment Coordination Board (BKPM after its Indonesian name Badan Koordinasi Penanaman Modal) (Gurney 1983: 529; Hill 1988: 28–30).

Very much in line with conventional wisdom in the 1960s, economic policy of the young nation states became increasingly directed towards attaining economic growth. Industrialization was furthered, first through import substitution, later by means of enlarging export-oriented production. Such a shift of emphasis occurred also in the absence of a radical change of government. This was the case in Malaysia and Singapore. In Malaysia 'pioneer status' was granted from 1965 to joint ventures with foreign multinationals in manufacturing and, in 1972, the first Free Export Zone (FTZ) opened its doors in Penang (Hoffman and Tan 1980: 36). Singapore forms, perhaps, the most extreme case where multinationals were invited almost unconditionally to aid in the process of rapid economic growth. The immediate cause to action was the withdrawal of British troops from the island in 1968 but the liberal legislation had already been laid down in the earlier Economic Expansion Incentives Act (Yoshihara 1976: 25–7).

The improvement in the investment climate was not sufficient and did not reach far enough. Actual inflows of FDI remained unimpressive for some time. In 1975, the accumulated total FDI amounted to no more than $11 billion for the entire region. This total was about four times the total that had prevailed in 1937 but prices had risen by more than that since the late 1930s. The 1937 total of FDI would correspond to almost $12 billion when expressed in the prices of 1975 which can be ascertained by applying a general American producer price index relevant to the world market at large (Booth 1991: 21). The initial resurgence of FDI in Southeast Asia in the late 1960s and early 1970s was barely enough to compensate for the disinvestment during the decades of turmoil.

The 1975 total corresponded to an average of about 20% of GDP. This was significantly less than in virtually all host countries during the late colonial period (ASEAN 1990: 107). FDI was lagging behind income growth. The mid-1970s also saw the shift towards more restrictive policies in the direction of FDI in both Indonesia and Malaysia. Indonesia was in the midst of exploring the outer boundaries of its bargaining power as a possessor of rich natural resources, oil and liquid natural gas (LNG) in particular. Malaysia had just started implementing the NEP. This policy gave a higher priority to *bumiputra* ownership of means of production than to attracting fresh capital from abroad.

Rapid growth has been a major feature of overall economic performance in most of Southeast Asia since the 1960s. Real annual growth rates averaged 4.2–4.5% in Indonesia, Malaysia and Thailand when viewed over the entire period 1960–1982. Singapore was ahead with an average above 7% and the Philippines lagged behind at less than 3% (Ariff and

Hill 1985: 8). An acceleration of the pace of growth followed in the late 1980s. Long-run growth rates in the ASEAN varied between 3.1% in the Philippines at one extreme and 8.9% in Thailand at the other (IMF 1991: 289, 352, 434, 472, 520; Yamashita 1991: 5). Since then, the leading economies of Southeast Asia are monitoring a process of structural change and industrialization. Singapore counts among the Asian NICs, Malaysia and Thailand already claim 'near-NIC' status. Indonesia is touched by 'dragonization' as well.

Policies with respect to FDI have undergone a continuous liberalization since the mid-1980s. This has happened in response to both the greater need for foreign capital and technology and the increased competition among potential host countries. Lower priority was attached to the once popular huge joint ventures between host country governments and foreign multinationals. Examples include the Krakatau steelworks near Java, the Asahan aluminium smelter in northern Sumatra and various cooperative schemes of President Marcos in the Philippines. Deregulation and privatization became the slogans for successful FDI in the region. The interplay between policies affecting the investment climate and macro-economic developments since the 1960s demonstrates that the improvement of the investment climate was a necessary but not a sufficient precondition for a large-scale resurgence of FDI to materialize.

There was a spectacular enlargement in the volume of FDI during the 1970s and 1980s leading to an accumulated regional total of some $77 billion by 1989 (Table 2.3). Some of the increase was undoubtedly due to inflation. The aggregate for 1975, for instance, $11 billion at current prices, corresponds to $20 billion when expressed in 1989 prices. There was an almost fourfold increase in real terms of accumulated FDI stock in Southeast Asia between the mid-1970s and the late 1980s, from $20 billion in 1975 to almost $80 billion in 1989 in constant prices.

Indonesia was indisputably ahead by about 1989 with 46% of the regional total, corresponding to $35 billion's worth of accumulated FDI. Singapore was in the second rank, holding one-third of the Southeast Asian aggregate. Malaysia and Thailand followed, in that order, with about one-tenth each, whereas the Philippines and Vietnam were at the very bottom of the scale (Figure 2.4; United Nations 1992: 146, 162, 222, 265, 319, 340). The hierarchy of host countries in the late 1980s resembled that in the colonial period to the extent that one very large recipient predominated. For the rest the differences were more conspicuous. The Malayan peninsula, excluding Singapore, was of lesser significance than before. Thailand had moved up while the Philippines had moved down. In the late 1980s Burma was still closed for foreign firms, whereas Vietnam had just

Table 2.3   FDI in Southeast Asia, c. 1989

Total FDI (million $ and %)

Indonesia	35 125	46
Singapore	26 016	34
Malaysia	8 314	11
Thailand	5 534	7
The Philippines	1 619	2
Vietnam	498	1
Total	77 106	100

Note: Total FDI stock given for 1990 in Indonesia and 1988 in Malaysia. Conversion into US$: $1 = S$1.95 = M$2.62 = 21.74 pesos = 25.70 baht.

By investor (%)

	USA	Japan	EC	NIC	Other
Indonesia	40	18	12	11	19
Singapore	33	31	29	0	7
Malaysia	6	20	24	35	15
Thailand	24	37	12	20	7
The Philippines	56	14	11	9	9
Vietnam	0	14	57	8	21

Note: The distribution refers to 1988 for Indonesia and Malaysia and to manufacturing only in Singapore. The Indonesian total contains a large portion ($11.1 billion) corresponding to the difference between aggregations with and without oil included. 'Other' includes an unallocated component reflecting investment from more than one country.

By sector (%)

	Agriculture	Mining	Manufacturing	Services
Indonesia	2	78	17	3
Singapore	0	0	42	57
Malaysia	13	15	41	30
Thailand	1	8	43	48
The Philippines	2	28	49	22
Vietnam	6	61	13	20

Note: The distribution refers to 1988 for Indonesia and Malaysia.
Source: United Nations 1992: 146, 149, 162, 165, 222, 225, 265, 267, 319, 322–3, 343, 345.

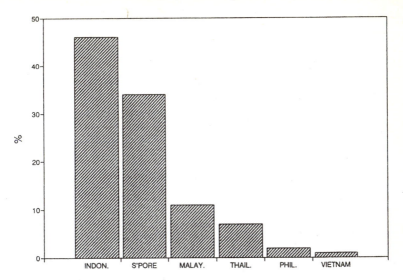

Figure 2.4   Ranking by FDI stock c. 1989: share in regional total

been opened up and obviously accounted for much less of the total than French Indochina had done in the colonial period. FDI has returned to Southeast Asia but not in the same fashion as before.

FDI per capita was exceptionally high in Singapore at little short of $10,000. This reflects the combination of a sizeable stock of FDI with the tiny population of the city state. Malaysia was in the second rank, primarily by virtue of its relatively small population. Indonesia followed in the third rank, above all because of its very sizeable stock of accumulated FDI. The low figures for FDI per capita in Thailand, the Philippines and Vietnam follow logically from the juxtaposition of a relatively large population and an accumulation of FDI that still had to gather momentum (Table 2.2).

It is highly instructive to compare the order of magnitude of FDI per capita with the situation in the late colonial period. The average for the whole region was $200 against $20 in 1938. Almost 80% of the increase can be ascribed to half a century of inflation. Nominal money values had changed beyond recognition and the ranking of host countries had been modified. Expressed in constant per capita terms, however, FDI in Southeast Asia was of almost the same significance in the late 1980s as in the late 1930s. This is an important observation that can only be inferred from a systematic comparison of statistics from the 1930s and today.

FDI volumes need to be compared again with national income and export data. Regional differences in the ratio of FDI to GDP have become more pronounced as compared to the late colonial period (Table 2.2). The very high share of FDI in Singapore's GDP gives an unambiguous testimony to the close link between foreign capital inflows and rapid economic growth in the city state. Indonesia now occupies an intermediate position whereas the ratio between FDI and GDP is particularly low for both Thailand and the Philippines. The ratios in the late 1980s were generally lower than those inferred for the late 1930s. This difference cannot be ascribed to inflation since price rises would affect FDI and GDP equally. There is, however, a real possibility that national incomes estimates for the colonial period are too low. This automatically raises the proportion of FDI in GDP.

The ratio between FDI and foreign exports has also declined significantly since the late colonial period. Considering the generally high quality of foreign trade statistics as compiled by the colonial administrations, this trend cannot be ascribed to an underestimation of total export revenues in the host country. The only possible explanation is that the expansion of exports has been faster in virtually all host countries than has the accumulation of FDI. The most extreme differences with respect to the late colonial period may be noted for Thailand and the Philippines. The ratios for Indonesia and Malaysia, however, were at least of a comparable order of magnitude.

The connection between FDI and GDP or foreign exports suggests a very considerable variation in the position assumed by FDI in the host country economy. This implies that the impact of FDI is likely to differ as well. The accumulation of FDI has clearly not kept pace with the enlargement of foreign trade and overall income growth. The salient question, however, is the extent to which the rapid growth of exports and income was conditioned by FDI in the first place.

A conspicuous difference with the colonial past concerns the nationality of the investor with the USA, Japan and, more recently, the Asian NICs appearing as the leading sources of investment capital (Figure 2.5; United Nations 1992: 149, 165, 225, 267, 323, 345). Around 1989 the USA ranked first among foreign investors in Indonesia and the Philippines. In Thailand, however, Japanese firms predominated whereas in Malaysia the first rank was claimed by NICs, in particular Singapore. In Singapore itself the pattern was very even with the USA, Japan and countries of the European Community (EC) responsible for one-third each. Japan was in the second rank in Indonesia, Singapore and the Philippines and ranked before Britain but after the EC at large in Malaysia. American investment in the region has focused on selected spearheads. Japanese commitments, however, have spread throughout the region. NIC capital is making rapid headway whereas EC investors have been effectively squeezed aside. It is also likely that FDI in the 1980s or 1990s has gained a more speculative character as compared to the colonial period.

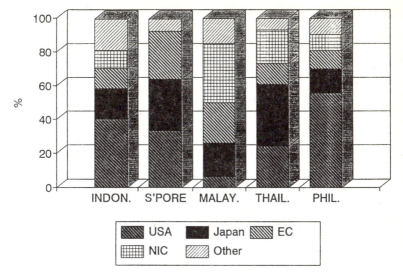

Figure 2.5 Total FDI stock c. 1989: composition by nationality

Tradition and heritage play a much less important role now than before the Pacific War. The colonial link is the weakest for Indonesia where Dutch capital accounted for only 4% of the total in 1989. It is the strongest for the Philippines with at least one-half of cumulative FDI still in American hands. Malaysia at the time occupied an intermediary position as Britain still supplied about one-sixth of its accumulated total. In Singapore, however, Britain vied with the Netherlands as the foremost supplier of FDI from Europe. In Thailand strikingly little had been retained of the traditional relationship: Britain now ranked behind both Singapore and Taiwan as a source of FDI entering Thailand.

The modern multinational is interested above all in utilizing comparative advantages in production. This implies that foreign subsidiaries fit into integrated systems or networks of production and marketing facilities. Production is relocated to the place where cost/benefit ratios are the most favourable at that particular time. This is altered again as comparative advantages change. This type of FDI stresses host country positions in general strategies of investors rather than old 'special ties' between overseas and metropolitan countries. It is often referred to as a 'flying geese' pattern of development in stages. The original idea of the flying geese, *ganko keitai*, was formulated by the Japanese economist Akamatsu in the 1930s and then applied to successive shifts in the development of manufacturing from imports to import substitution and from there to export-oriented production. Akamatsu's model was subsequently combined with the product cycle theory of Raymond Vernon which postulates that comparative advantage in production will shift according to the consecutive phases in the lifecycle of the individual product, i.e. introduction, growth and standardization (Vernon 1966: 199; Chia 1990: 37–8). It is argued here that Japanese and NIC investment in particular have emerged in this region because the host countries of Southeast Asia gained a comparative advantage in manufacturing production as wages at home rose and domestic currencies appreciated.

But shifting geographical constellations according to flying geese patterns provide only explanations of choices of host countries in strict economic terms. Bilateral links also arise, for instance, on the basis of geographical proximity, language and cultural affinity or personal visions of statesmen. A few examples may suffice. Of all NIC investment in Malaysia in the late 1980s more than 80% came from neighbouring Singapore. For Singapore Johor is indeed seen as the immediate hinterland. Widespread proficiency in English makes investment in the Philippines, Singapore and Malaysia a great deal easier but is still likely to be considered of secondary significance. Shared religious beliefs may contribute much to the enthusiasm with which Japanese firms jump on the bandwagon of rapid economic growth in Thailand. Mahathir's early admiration of everything Japanese is well publicized and has certainly enhanced Japanese FDI in Malaysia (Holloway 1991: 119–53).

The stress on comparative advantage, as opposed to unlimited access to raw materials, implies a very different structure of FDI in terms of economic activity as compared to the situation in the colonial period. In the late 1980s manufacturing and services reigned supreme in all host countries except Indonesia (Figure 2.6; United Nations 1992: 147, 163, 223, 266, 323, 343). Export agriculture had virtually vanished as a major destination of foreign capital and even mining, primarily oil and LNG, was only of importance in some host countries such as Indonesia, the Philippines and Vietnam. Manufacturing ranked first in Malaysia and the Philippines and second to oil and LNG in Indonesia. In Thailand a balance had been achieved between manufacturing and services. The tertiary sector loomed especially large in Singapore.

A few words of caution are warranted concerning the demarcations between sectors and the actual content of each sector. Distinctions by sector are not always consistent. Much heterogeneity hides beneath the broad umbrella of any particular sector. The example of petroleum is illustrative. Even if Indonesia has been investing heavily in refining facilities, the emphasis in the oil sector still seems to be more on extraction than was the case in the colonial period (Lindblad 1989b: 66–70). Most of the oil and LNG production, therefore, falls under the primary sector. In Singapore,

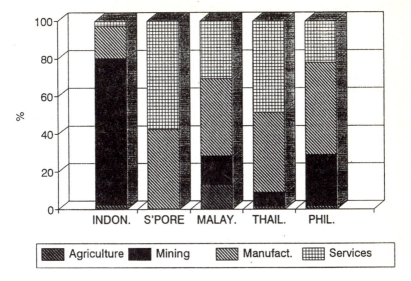

Figure 2.6　Total FDI stock c. 1989: composition by sector

however, the entire oil sector obviously consists of refining. In the 'Houston of Asia' petroleum thus counts as a manufacturing activity. In Thailand and the Philippines, oil accounts for most of mining. Yet here the main emphasis is on exploration rather than actual production, let alone refining.

Manufacturing can mean many things. The largest industry in foreign-controlled manufacturing is chemicals in the Philippines, basic metals and metal products in Indonesia but electrical equipment and electronics in Singapore, Thailand and Malaysia (Ariff 1992: 8; United Nations 1992: 147, 223, 266, 320). The contrast in manufacturing FDI between chemicals and basic metals on the one hand and electronics on the other mirrors the basic transition from traditional manufacturing to technologically sophisticated lines of production in the process of industrialization in Southeast Asia. FDI in manufacturing is geared towards the current stage of industrial development in each host country. It is likely to change as the host country moves up the technological ladder.

Services also look very different in each host country. In the late 1980s trading was the foremost foreign-controlled tertiary activity in Indonesia and Thailand. Finance and insurance occupied a similar position in Malaysia and the Philippines. Financial services, e.g. holding companies, accounted for as much as 35% of the sizeable FDI in the service sector in Singapore (United Nations 1992: 147, 163, 223, 320; Foreign Equity

1992: 4). This again suggests a dichotomy between traditional and modern types of activity within the same sector of the host country economy. Yet it is hazardous to infer too much from this with respect to the level of economic development in the host country. Banking and insurance are excluded altogether from FDI data from Indonesia whereas financial conglomerates in Thailand are not inclined to mix with foreign capital (United Nations 1992: 147; Suehiro 1989: 261–2).

Such was the situation in FDI in Southeast Asia at the end of the 1980s. The resurgence of FDI came to maturity as successive waves of foreign capital seeking outlets swept through the region. A hierarchy of host countries has evolved with sharp differences between those in the lead and those lagging hopelessly behind. American multinationals moved in where the European ones left but were in turn increasingly replaced by Japanese firms with those from the Asian NICs waiting for the next stage. FDI has shifted permanently into manufacturing, followed by services, thus becoming intimately linked to the quest for industrialization and economic development in each host country. The shift to new investors and the impact in terms of industrial achievement will be discussed in greater detail later (Chapters 6 and 7).

Investment capital in Southeast Asia today has become international to an extraordinary degree, moving at ease between markets in Bangkok, Jakarta, Kuala Lumpur, Manila and Singapore. Overseas Chinese play a key part in such transaction networks, often operating from the three predominantly Chinese of the four Asian NICs (Hong Kong, Singapore and Taiwan). The best known example is probably the business empire of Liem Sioe Liong, Jakarta-based but reaching throughout the region through subsidiaries and affiliations. The extreme mobility of investment capital has made it more difficult than ever to disentangle FDI from portfolio investment or short-run lending. The very distinction between foreign and domestic investment is becoming blurred. This should be kept in mind when assessing the most recent FDI curves that everywhere tend to shoot upwards sharply.

The boom is continuing unabatedly. FDI increases in this region are unrivalled by any other part of the world. The share of Southeast Asia, taken together with South and East Asia, in world FDI flows rose from 9% in the early 1980s to 19% in the mid-1990s (UNCTAD 1995: 52). The cumulative total in Singapore exceeded $39 billion by 1992 or 50% more than in 1989. This represents a substantial increase even after correction for inflation. Total approvals surged to an unprecedented $12 billion in Thailand in 1993 and neared a staggering $40 billion in Indonesia in 1995. In the latter year planned FDI in Malaysia exceeded $3.7 billion, whereas in the Philippines an aggregate of $2.1 billion was cited (*FEER* 24/2 1994,

12/10 1995; Indikator 1996: August: 71). Accumulated stock as of the late 1980s will be dwarfed by new incoming FDI even if we allow for inflation and those approved projects that fail to be realized.

The most publicized new feature of FDI in Southeast Asia has been the opening-up of the socialist regimes. It started with the new legislation on foreign investment in Vietnam in 1987. Despite uncertainties about its implementation, it had already caused a substantial inflow of capital by 1988. In Myanmar the first law on foreign investment in decades was passed shortly after the military coup in September 1988. The investors remained apprehensive because of political sensitivities until 1995 when FDI worth no less than $3 billion was approved in the course of only eight months (*FEER* 14/12 1989, 12/10 1995; Than 1990: 203–4). Even the borders of Cambodia no longer form absolute barriers to entry for FDI. In 1992 a handful of Western oil companies expressed interest in starting explorations. Approvals of Thai projects in transport, tourism, banking and logging elicited fears of a 'Baht imperialism' (*FEER* 25/6, 9/7 1992).

Vietnam highlights four major trends in current FDI in Southeast Asia. First, expansion has been very fast. The aim was set in 1991 to double cumulative stock of foreign investment by 1995, from $2.7 billion to $5.5 billion. By 1993 actual results, at $7.5 billion, had already exceeded the final target. Approvals in 1994 alone exceeded $3.6 billion (*FEER* 27/1, 3/2 1994, 12/10 1995). Second, the host country has adopted liberal policies designed to create an attractive climate for FDI. Joint ventures with a 99% foreign ownership are allowed in Vietnam and two Export Processing Zones (EPZs) were quickly opened near Ho Chi Minh City (*CTC Reporter* 1989: 25). Third, most FDI has been flowing into a relatively small number of key industries. In Vietnam these key industries were offshore oil exploration, light manufacturing, fishing and tourism (Vietnam Opportunities 1992: 368–72; Reinhardt 1993: 86–7; Gates 1995). Finally, a substantial proportion of the incoming total has been provided by Asian NICs. In 1994 this proportion amounted to one-half of total approvals (*FEER* 12/10 1995). The experience of Vietnam possibly points to the future, at any rate for those parts of the region where FDI is now unfolding.

The preceding two sections have offered a systematic comparison between FDI in Southeast Asia in the late 1930s and the late 1980s. This comparison has underscored a basic continuity in the attractiveness of the region for investors. Real FDI per capita was of the same order of magnitude on both occasions. The continuity also applies to the investment climate as shaped by respectively colonial state formation and more liberal policies, both in combination with a general economic expansion. In addition, there is much continuity in the high degree of variation between host countries when it comes to prospects for further economic development. At the same time, the identity of investors has changed and so have destinations of FDI. It is this juxtaposition of continuity and change that forms the topic of subsequent chapters.

2.3   ON STATISTICS

A major paradox in the study of FDI concerns the statistics, both with respect to the colonial period and today. For the colonial period statistical data are scarce but the information is clear cut and presents few problems of interpretation. For the contemporary period there is a superabundance of statistics on the size and composition of FDI in each country. The series display distressingly little coherence or compatibility. This has been demonstrated for instance for FDI in Indonesia during the period 1967–1985 using annual figures from four independent sources. Each displays a different pattern (Hill 1988: 158). This section outlines the best available statistics on FDI in Southeast Asia, i.e. the data that form the foundation for the comparison between the late 1930s and the late 1980s discussed in the preceding sections.

FDI statistics are compiled by national institutions and are, therefore, likely to differ considerably in terms of definition or coverage. For our purposes it is essential that the data, their national idiosyncrasies notwithstanding, have been filtered through a common assessment so that they are at least mutually compatible. This is the case with the two main statistical sources used here, the book-length account by Helmut Callis on FDI in the late 1930s and the authoritative compilation by the United Nations of FDI data for the late 1980s (Callis 1942; United Nations 1992). Both sources make liberal use of national figures of varying quality. The ultimate aim is to offer a coherent impression pertaining to a wider region, respectively Southeast Asia and Asia with the Pacific. Both books will be critically examined in brief.

Callis's book has attracted considerable attention among scholars since it is virtually the only comprehensive survey of FDI in Southeast Asia based on original data from before the Second World War. Most of the data refer to 1937 and only on occasion to 1938 (Indochina and Thailand). The tables give global aggregates by country with supplementary details added on the nationality of investors and sectors receiving much capital. The global aggregates have a tendency to creep into the literature on the most diverse occasions (Allen and Donnithorne 1957: appendix II-III;

Tate 1979: II, 28; Brown 1993: 86). Sometimes, such presentations overlook the important distinction between entrepreneur and rentier or portfolio investment, which Callis consistently applies (Sarkar 1976: 11). It sometimes occurs that the Callis totals are rendered only as graphic representations without any statistics attached at all (Dixon 1991: 113).

Readers of the Callis book tend to think that the total FDI figures should be considered conservative estimates that probably underrate the true volume of FDI (Allen and Donnithorne 1957: 288). This certainly appears to be the case for instance with Burma and Thailand for which Callis cites strikingly low totals. An independent estimate gives a figure three times the Callis total for Burma at about the same time, £155 million ($750 million) against £47 million ($228 million). The former estimate also includes assets held by Indian Chettyars, which may be considered domestic or semi-domestic investment, but the difference remains uncomfortably large (Callis 1942: 106; Walinsky 1962: 53–4). In the Thai case Chinese investment is, as said, hopelessly underestimated by Callis and his informants.

In other cases the Callis aggregates agree very well with totals given elsewhere. For Malaya total FDI in 1936 has been estimated at £79 million ($381 million). This is almost the same as the $372 million given by Callis for 1937 (Hauser 1937; Callis 1942: 63). For colonial Indonesia in 1940, my own reconstruction of total equity in Western-type enterprises, i.e. almost exclusively owned by foreign nationals or Chinese, produces a total of accumulated FDI which virtually coincides with the total given by Callis for 1937, ƒ3567 million ($1426 million) against $1411 million, a figure which also includes Chinese investment (Lindblad 1991: 193; Callis 1942: 36). Such comparisons increase our confidence that Callis at least provides the right order of magnitude of FDI volume. The quality of the data varies also within the source itself. Sectoral breakdowns often cover only FDI from the colonial mother country, i.e. the largest single investor. Such breakdowns are not always given for the same year as the aggregate. On occasion, notably for Thailand, no sectoral breakdown at all is available. Aggregates and compositions by investor and sector are presented in Table 2.1.

The United Nations account, published in 1992, is not the only or even the most recent statistical survey of current FDI in Southeast Asia. New statistics are continuously issued by both the agencies for the coordination and promotion of FDI and the central banks in each host country. The national agencies have the disadvantage that their figures are often provisional and refer only to approvals rather than FDI actually implemented. It is very hazardous to infer realized FDI from approval data as the example of Indonesia shows. Here, estimates of the rate of implementation range from 25% for the whole period 1967–1989 to 38% for the years up to 1983 or from 28% for Japanese firms to 46% for American investors during the early years of the Suharto regime (Kebschull and Mayer 1974: 23; Dunning and Cantwell 1987: 526; Thee 1991: 68–72). Figures from the central bank authorities are more easy to handle, although they will obviously not include FDI in the form of reinvested earnings. This holds equally true for the special register of incoming FDI maintained by the Bank of Thailand and the list of transfers of assets provided by the Securities and Exchange Commission of the Central Bank of the Philippines. In short, data from the boards of investment are by definition too high whereas figures from the central banks are likely to be too low.

The United Nations volume was prepared by the former Centre on Transnational Corporations at ESCAP in Bangkok. This Centre adopted a pragmatic approach, relying on data from what were believed to be the most accurate sources in each country. The United Nations data, therefore, count among experts as the most authoritative body of evidence for the contemporary period. Regrettably, the most recent trends, i.e. those taking shape in the first half of the 1990s, are not incorporated. The emphasis is on stock figures and implemented investment. A common format has been applied, proceeding from the aggregate of accumulated FDI to annual flows and distributions by investor and industry, followed by some inform-ation on the position of foreign affiliates in the host country economy. Most recent aggregates concern 1989. The series runs from 1975 for all countries except Vietnam. Local currencies are used except in the case of Indonesia where FDI is given in American dollars. Conversions were done at current exchange rates. Aggregates and distributions by investor and sector drawn from this source are presented in Table 2.3. Calculations of FDI per capita and FDI expressed as a percentage of both GDP and foreign exports make use of available information on population, GDP and export volumes in the literature. The resulting figures need to be consid-ered as rough indications rather than exact facts. The results are contrasted with corresponding figures for the late colonial period in Table 2.2.

3 Pioneers and Profits[1]

Many an enterprising young European man, who went to seek his luck in Southeast Asia in the late nineteenth century, would probably recognize the mixture of pride and disillusionment expressed by Joseph Conrad's hero, Almayer, as he overlooked the Berau river in East Kalimantan and remembered his arrival in the Outer Islands of Indonesia decades earlier: 'a young and slim Almayer, clad all in white and modest-looking, landing from the Dutch mail-boat on the dusty jetty of Macassar, coming to woo fortune ... ready to conquer the world, never doubting that he would' (Conrad 1947: 5).[2] This is the romantic view of pioneering that has proved strong-lived in popular mentality and literature. The Western entrepreneur opened up virgin lands on remote and desolate locations in the tropics. He took exceptional risks but also counted on extraordinary rewards were he to succeed. This chapter considers FDI as it actually took place in Southeast Asia in the late colonial period. It argues that pioneering at the time was characterized by an essential dualism between the outward orientation of the overseas profit-seeking entrepreneur and the interests of long-run local entrenchment in the colony.

Our tale oscillates around a number of case studies. The cases have been chosen so as to form a representative image of the situation prevailing in several major host countries in Southeast Asia during the late colonial period. The emphasis is first on banking and manufacturing in the Philippines and teak logging and trading in Burma and Thailand (sections 3.1 and 3.2). The experiences of leading managing agencies and a sample of Dutch firms in export production then serve to highlight the conditions of pioneering in Malaya and colonial Indonesia respectively (sections 3.3 and 3.4). Indochina is left out of the present discussion. FDI there was so closely bound up with the implementation of French colonial policy that it ought to be reviewed against the background of the process of colonial state formation in Indochina (section 4.1).

3.1 FROM BANKING TO INDUSTRY

The Hongkong and Shanghai Bank often counted as the doyen among foreign banks in Southeast Asian capitals. Its Manila branch opened as early as 1865, only a year after the British-owned bank had been established.

Saigon followed in 1870, Singapore in 1877, Batavia in 1884, Bangkok in 1888 and Rangoon in 1891. It financed sugar plantations in Luzon and Java and railways in Thailand. In Manila and Batavia it catered specifically to British and local Chinese businessmen. The loans in Thailand were urged by the Foreign Office and backed by the Bank of England. Its network extended throughout Southeast Asia and eventually came to include also numerous local branch offices outside the capitals, e.g. Iloilo from 1883, Penang from 1884, Surabaya from 1896. At a far later stage, local branches in Jesselton, Sandakan and Kuching were to play a crucial role in the initial economic development of British North Borneo (King 1987–1991: II, 133–5; III, 113–16; IV: 22, 463–81).

Actual operations of the branch office in Southeast Asia may be described in brief as follows. Local sugar exporters received credits in return for bills of exchange which were in turn used by the branch office of the bank as a collateral in obtaining a loan from the central bank of the colony, e.g. the Java Bank at Batavia, so that it could extend such credits. The colonial central bank in turn offered the bills of exchange for repayment at the London office of the Hongkong and Shanghai Bank. At the time when the sugar had been harvested and sold the exporters could pay back the advances that they had received from the local branch office in the first place (King 1987–1991: III, 18–19).

The Manila office specialized in sugar and was invariably affected by fluctuations in the world market. The vulnerability of these operations became particularly evident during the sugar crisis of 1884. Annual profits increased from 200,000 Hong Kong dollars ($182,000) in the 1880s to 500,000 Hong Kong dollars ($250,000) in the late 1890s, a figure that should be compared with total equity of the corporation at establishment in 1864, 5 million Hong Kong dollars ($5.75 million). In 1897 the Manila office of the bank gained some publicity. The insurgent General Emilio Aguinaldo obtained a deposit of 400,000 Hong Kong dollars ($207,000) with the bank as a first instalment of indemnities granted by the Spanish authorities in an effort to terminate the revolution. Yet this involvement in Philippine politics was considered to be an entirely commercial matter (King 1987–1991: II, 102–22).

The early arrival and active marketing of an institution such as the Hongkong and Shanghai Bank did much to smooth the path for European-controlled trading throughout Southeast Asia. Other examples of European banks include the Chartered Bank, established in London in 1853 and active above all in Malaya, and the Nederlandsche Handel–Maatschappij (NHM), established in Amsterdam in 1824 (Yoshihara 1988: 15–16, 138, 146). Before switching to banking in the 1880s, the NHM was vested with the monopoly rights of exporting the produce of the forced cultivations in Java (1830–1870) to the international staple market for tropical goods in Amsterdam.

Banking associated with trading was not, in the first instance, directed towards enlarging productive capacity in the economy of the host country. The banks remained somewhat aloof, preferring to support risk-taking by others. The latter in turn became more entrenched in the host country economy. In the long run, there was a fundamental shift in European commitment of capital to this region from financial facilities to actual production. One of the rare instances where this process was accomplished within one and the same firm is provided by the Ayala concern, the oldest commercial house of Spanish origin in the Philippines.

Antonio de Ayala was the nephew of a Spanish archbishop and arrived in Manila in the 1830s where he set up a partnership in commerce with the two Roxas brothers. He also married their sister, Margarita, an exceptional woman who supervised palm lands in Panay and coal mines in Cebu. The couple became the sole proprietors of a vast tract of land, today the Makati business district in downtown Manila. In 1868 the activities of the Ayala family firm were extended into banking and insurance as well. Upon Antonio de Ayala's death in 1876, the Ayala y Compania was formally established under joint ownership of the two sons-in-law of the founding father, Pedro Pablo Roxas and Jacobo Zobel Zangroniz. Roxas set up an oil factory and assumed control over the newly founded San Miguel breweries that later was to become the largest private business firm in the Philippines, the San Miguel Corporation (SMC). Zangroniz became known for having organized the tram services in Manila (Lachica 1984: 35–48, 63–82).

The turning-point for the Ayala concern came in 1914. The firm was then reorganized into two branches, one concentrating on manufacturing, starting with beer, and the other continuing with finance, real estate and insurance. The two branches were headed by two sons-in-law of Pedro Pablo Roxas, Eduardo Soriano and Enrique Zobel de Ayala. The latter had married his first cousin, Consuelo, herself the daughter of two first cousins. This underscores how close family ties served business interests. The grandsons of Enrique Zobel de Ayala and Consuelo Roxas count among the captains of industry in the Philippines of the 1990s.

Diversification progressed rather slowly during the interwar decades and gained momentum only after Independence. Joseph McMicking, yet another illustrious in-law, was the one who began exploiting the Makati property and investing profits in all walks of economic life, especially manufacturing. Today, more revenues in the Ayala concern accrue from industrial production, e.g. food processing, than from real estate (Lachica 1984: 153, 159; Yoshihara 1988: 164, 199).

The Ayala experience is unique on account of the very high degree of indigenization and local entrenchment. Even by the wildest stretch of the imagination, we cannot at any stage regard the Ayala concern as FDI. Yet it did start out as such, achieving success and consolidation only through relying on personal contacts with the local élite and a cautious strategy towards diversification. In the Philippines of the late colonial period Western banking paved the way. Yet FDI in manufacturing possessed the best chances of being encapsulated into the host country economy.

3.2   TEAK AND TRADING

The Bombay–Burmah Trading Corporation was registered at Bombay in 1864 with an initial equity of 2.5 million rupees ($1.3 million). Its prime asset was a teak concession that the Englishman William Wallace had obtained from King Mindon at Mandalay some years earlier. Other assets included a sawmill in Moulmein in Upper Burma, an office at Rangoon and even 89 elephants. William Wallace's younger brother, Alexander, became chairman of the ostensibly British-Indian firm which was in fact run from its London office. Exports of teak expanded steadily, from 85,000 tons per year in the 1860s to 275,000 tons per year in the 1880s. New teak concessions were acquired after King Theebaw had assumed office in Upper Burma in 1878. Annual dividends rose from 10% prior to 1880 to an average of 18% in the 1880s and 22% in the 1890s (Macaulay 1934: 8, 21, 26; Pointon 1964: 5–12). This was one British enterprise of which it was later said that it initiated modern export production in Burma but thwarted indigenous entrepreneurship to such a degree that the colony was still underdeveloped at Independence (Khin 1970: 36).

Just as Ayala during the Philippine revolution, the Bombay–Burmah Trading Corporation became quickly involved in regional politics. In 1885 a conflict arose. Bombay–Burmah Trading refused to lend money to King Theebaw who retaliated with heavy duties and fines. Bombay–Burmah turned to the Chief Commander at Rangoon. Randolph Churchill subsequently authorized the annexation of Upper Burma which in turn forced King Theebaw into exile. Even if the dispute about the refused loan was probably an occasion rather than a cause for going to war, there are few cases in the history of modern imperialism where political and economic expansion were as intimately connected as in Upper Burma in the mid-1880s (Pointon 1964: 20).

Effective colonial rule guaranteed the new long-term leases. From the 1890s these leases offered the continuity needed for large-scale capital outlays. Bombay–Burmah Trading was joined by four other major British firms: Steel Brothers & Co., MacGregor & Co., Foucar & Co. and T.D. Findlay & Son. By 1914 these five firms had reportedly invested 100 million rupees ($33 million) in teak logging in Burma. Between them, they controlled three-quarters of the colony's teak output and employed 55,000 persons (Hlaing 1964: 101). Bombay–Burmah remained the largest one. Since 1911 it was permanently managed by a newly created agency, Wallace Brothers & Co. at London. The Steel Brothers ranked second and was known for exceptionally high profitability levels. In 1923, 1924 and 1929 the shareholders pocketed dividend payments at 40% or more (Andrus 1948: 186).

Initially, most of the profits in Bombay–Burmah Trading originated in logging alone. From about 1910 the emphasis shifted towards simple processing in the sawmills. In addition, some diversification did take place but primarily outside Burma. Already, from the 1880s, teak concessions at Chiang Mai were exploited in cooperation with a local British pioneer, Louis T. Leonowens. A sawmill near Surabaya was purchased in 1906 and a rubber estate in Java followed in 1907 but neither grew to much significance. The company left Burma in 1949 and shifted logging operations to Sabah (Pointon 1964: 71, 108).

A high degree of oligopolization characterized the teak industry in colonial Burma. The considerable profits realized by both Bombay–Burmah Trading and other firms should be associated with the small number of companies controlling most of output. High profits were characteristic for British enterprise in Burma at large, reaffirmed by the scarce information available on the results of the Burmah Oil Company. In the 1930s dividends on ordinary Burmah Oil shares averaged 15%, even when the calculation includes years during which no dividend at all was paid out (Andrus 1948: 120, 186).

The British-owned Borneo Company was the very first to obtain a lease on teak from Chulalongkorn (Rama V), in 1888. It was soon joined by both Bombay–Burmah Trading, Louis T. Leonowens, the Anglo-Siam Corporation and the Danish and French East Asiatic companies. In the 1890s these six foreign firms controlled more than one-half of total output in the Thai teak industry. One of them, the French East Asiatic, was said to be owned by Chinese merchants. In 1899 total capital invested by the six market leaders was estimated at £2.5 million ($12.1 million). It was a situation resembling that prevailing in Burma at the time (Ingram 1971: 107; Brown 1988: 111–19; Manarungsan 1989: 127).

The story of the Østasiatiske Kompagni, the (Danish) East Asiatic Company, is one of the most extraordinary in the history of Western pioneering in Southeast Asia. The company's founder, Hans Niels Andersen (1852–1937), grew up in the small port of Nakskov in Denmark, became a sailor and went ashore in Bangkok at the age of twenty-five. He got in touch with Chulalongkorn via a high-ranking Danish-French official in the Thai civil service, Count Armand du Plessis de Richelieu, and was commissioned to ship teak to Europe with the king's vessel *Thoon Kramom*. Upon his return to Bangkok in 1884, Andersen purchased the Oriental Hotel and adjacent warehouses to set up a trading firm. He renovated the hotel, sold it at a profit and expanded into both shipping and sawmilling. A second trip to Europe was required to raise funds for further expansion. The Danish banks only agreed to support Andersen after lengthy negotiations. In 1897 the East Asiatic was incorporated in Copenhagen with an equity of 3.5 million Danish kroner ($930,000) of which 2 million kroner were used for immediate investment in Thailand. Andersen became the company's first executive director and remained in the post for another four decades. He settled permanently in Copenhagen where he became a most colourful and influential public figure. He displayed an exceptional capability for moving in royal circles in his native country as well, and soon relatives of the new Danish king, Christian X (1912–1947), took an active part in his business operations (Ernst 1937; Heinberg 1943).[3]

The East Asiatic engaged in scores of activities. Sawn logs were transported along the rivers from Muang Prae in the north to Bangkok and shipped abroad. Imports included materials for the railways under construction in Thailand. Wharves and its own shipping line contributed to its reputation as the major Western business corporation in Bangkok. Subsidiaries were set up for operations outside Thailand, e.g. shipping along the coast of Malacca, to Singapore and the rubber estates in Johor. In later years expansion spread far beyond Southeast Asia and came to include factories in Scandinavia, trading in South Africa and shipping in the West Indies. At the death of Andersen in 1937, aggregate turnover exceeded 233 million Danish kroner ($51 million). Total assets at that time amounted to almost 80 million Danish kroner ($18 million) (Macmillan 1923: 139–40; Heinberg 1943: 109–11, 205–6; Skougaard 1943: 18–28).

Teak logging in the hilly uplands was only the starting-point for the Western pioneers entering Burma and Thailand in the late nineteenth century. Profits and contacts were used to extend into commercial activities. This implied the emergence of small networks of foreign oligopolists. In both Burma and Thailand the foreign subsidiaries remained entirely oriented towards the overseas parent corporation where the gains were pocketed.

3.3 RUBBER AND MANAGEMENT

The object of Guthrie & Co., as stated at consolidation in Singapore in 1903, left little to be desired in terms of scope for future expansion. Guthrie was to function as 'general merchants, exporters and importers, general storekeepers, wholesale and retail traders, shippers, bankers, agents for bankers, shipowners, shipping agents, carriers, insurers against losses of all kinds, commission and insurance agents, estate and property agents, warehousemen, lightermen, ships agents, contractors, builders, guarantors, wharf and dock owners or lessees, owners of lessees of railways and tramways, owners of mining, planting and other properties wherever situated, owners or lessees of craft plant and appliances for pearl shell seeking by diving, planters, miners, dealers in shares and stocks, brokers, general or special agents or managers'.[4] The new firm formed the continuation of a partnership between the London-based Scott & Co. and Singapore-based Guthrie. Total equity amounted to 1 million Straits dollars ($429,000), one-half for John Anderson, who also received a life-time appointment as the firm's governing director, and one-half for the estates of the late Thomas Scott and James Guthrie. This constellation developed into one of the foremost managing agencies in Malaya.

The consolidation of Guthrie & Co. was very timely, occuring as it did during one of the sudden spurts of activity. This gave the emergence of FDI in Malaya its typically skewed pattern. Rubber was responsible for the boom. The first successful shipment had just taken place, prices were soaring and applications for rubber land in Perak, Selangor and Negeri Sembilan mushroomed. The colonial government actively encouraged FDI, offering tax incentives, allocating estate land near existing roads and railways and acting as an intermediary in importing coolie labourers from British India (Kato 1991: 124; Drabble 1972). It was in this environment of high expectations that Guthrie consolidated its business operations in the Straits Settlements.

The Guthrie family was of ancient ancestry already occupying a castle in the Scottish Highlands in 1066. One descendant, Alexander Guthrie, went with Raffles to Singapore in 1819 and set up a trading business in the newly founded Southeast Asian metropolis. His possessions included a nutmeg and clove estate at the far end of Orchard Road. He was succeeded by his nephew, James, who retired in 1856 leaving the firm to a brother-in-law, Thomas Scott. The firm maintained an entrepot in Singapore for coffee, sago and forest products. It financed Chinese trading and construction in downtown Singapore. An extremely profitable investment was the establishment of the Tanjung Pagar docks in the Singapore harbour. The last scion of the Guthrie family was Alexander, only son of James Guthrie. He took charge at twenty-three in 1873 but died unexpectedly at twenty-eight. The reins of power now passed into the hands of the merchant John Anderson, later Sir John (1852–1924), one of the leading personalities in the business community at Singapore in the early twentieth century (Cunyngham-Brown 1971).

John Anderson was very good at acquiring agencies. He participated in the coffee boom in Johor in the 1880s and took a vivid interest in the upsurge of rubber estates in the late 1890s. He was one of the first to switch to dredging in tin mining in 1907. At the time of reorganization, in 1903, Guthrie boasted 23 general agencies in the most diverse walks of economic life: tin and gold mining, tobacco, tapioca, sugar, tea, coffee and rubber estates, manufacturing, a beer brewery and a cement factory. The pace of expansion quickened after the consolidation in 1903. Assistance at the flotation of new rubber companies resulted in numerous agencies during the rubber booms of 1903–1905 and 1908–1910. In 1913 a branch office was opened up at Medan to coordinate management contracts in Sumatra rubber. At a later stage, in the 1920s, activities were extended to include palm oil estates in Malaya and Sumatra (Cunyngham-Brown 1971: 173, 192–8; Allen and Donnithorne 1957: 53–7).

The financial results booked by Guthrie were most satisfactory. Annual average profits climbed from 163,000 Straits dollars ($80,000) in 1903/07 to 443,000 Straits dollars ($252,000) in 1911/13 and further to no less than 2.3 million Straits dollars ($1.3 million) in 1916/19 only to stabilize at 546,000 Straits dollars ($307,000) in 1924/27. Since total equity remained constant at one million Straits dollars, these results represent profit rates of 16%, 44%, 226% and 55% respectively and compare favourably with the average rate of 8.1% which has been calculated for a large number of British firms investing in the Empire in the late nineteenth and early twentieth centuries (Davis and Huttenback 1986: 107).

Profitability levels at Guthrie were high but uneven. Between the peaks mentioned in the preceding paragraph, there were several years with rather disappointing results, in particular during the early 1920s when the immediate post-war boom faded away. In addition, the firm's total equity up to 1927 was kept artificially low so as to minimize dividend obligations. This by definition implies a higher profit rate than would otherwise have been the case. John Anderson and the other shareholders found it more important to create a solid base for expansion in the long run rather than to secure maximal short-run benefits for themselves.

The use of profits at Guthrie reveals how the management altered its policies in the course of time. Immediately after the consolidation in 1903, reserves or dividend payments assumed roughly equal proportions, 35–40% each, of total profits. Shortly before the First World War, the emphasis shifted towards accelerated depreciations, especially on property and newly purchased business interests, although one-third was still devoted to reserves alone. Profits were large enough to allow statutory dividend payments at 8% as well. Windfall profits during the years 1916–1919 brought yet another distribution with reserves increasing each year by 1.6 million Straits dollars ($890,000). This exceeded total equity by 60%. The remainder was spent on continued additional depreciations on property and increasingly on bonuses to European staff. Handouts of the latter type at that time averaged 375,000 Straits dollars ($208,000) per year. But these practices were discontinued in the 1920s and as soon as profits were realized again, in the first place from 1923, reserves and dividends were given highest priority. Dividend payments now exceeded the statutory amount by a large amount and this anticipated the enlargement of equity in 1927, from one million to 12 million Straits dollars ($6.7 million) at one stroke.

Much of the profits were retained in the firm, not only because of the disproportionately low dividend obligations but also by accumulating named and hidden reserves. Such reserves were urgently needed when the immediate post-war boom collapsed in 1920 and prices fell generally in world markets. Business in that year was described as 'very unsatisfactory' and there was talk of a 'severe financial stringency' and a need for a conservative revaluation of all stock 'at cost or market value whichever is the lower'. Losses in 1920 alone exceeded 5 million Straits dollars ($2.1 million) but the reserves were sufficiently large to absorb them. A major objective in designating use of profits later on in the 1920s was to replenish general reserves.

Management policy at Guthrie combined a zeal for expansion with conservatism in financing. Openness towards auditors was, at times, less than exemplary and on one occasion, in 1912, it even appears that one of the directors had made a rather liberal use of his position. The auditors stated that 'the withdrawal of large amounts from the Company's funds by a director of the Company for his personal ventures as is disclosed by the Company's accounts is most irregular'.[5] To make matters worse, the company paid interest on these funds but the director in question did not. Guthrie & Co. was a tightly-knit enterprise which operated very much like a family firm.

Harrisons & Crosfield appeared in Malaya much later but was soon to rival Guthrie among the British managing agencies operating out of Singapore or Kuala Lumpur. The firm was originally founded in Liverpool in 1844 but soon moved to London and developed a specialization in tea imports. The breakthrough in Malaya came with the floating of the Pataling Rubber Estate Syndicate in 1903. The subsequent rapid expansion was monitored by Arthur Lampard, one of the leading figures in the history of Malayan rubber. In 1905 Harrisons & Crosfield amalgamated eight rubber estates in Negeri Sembilan into the Anglo-Malay Rubber Company. In 1907, when the office in Kuala Lumpur was opened, six major estates in Malacca, Selangor and Perak were brought under the umbrella of the Asiatic Rubber & Produce Company. This firm was in turn managed by Harrisons & Crosfield. A long list of appointments as agents or secretaries for newly established rubber companies followed during the boom years of 1909–1912 (Pugh *et al.* 1990: 28–49).

In 1908 total equity at Harrisons & Crosfield amounted to £307,500 ($1.49 million). This corresponded to slightly more than one-half of the total book value of assets. Ten years later equity was increased to £2.5 million ($12.1 million). This was still less than the book value of assets. The intervening decade had seen a continuous expansion of activities, not only in Malaya, but also in Sumatra, British North Borneo, Java, Ceylon and even Australia and Canada. The estate of United Serdang (Sumatra) Rubber Plantations in Deli was eventually to become one of the largest estates in the world, measuring more than 100,000 acres. The partnership with the managing agency Darby and the British North Borneo Company was formed for the development of the timber industry in Sabah. In 1921 Harrisons & Crosfield was the agent for 42 European firms in Malaya, Sumatra, Java and Sabah. One of the directors was Eric Macfadyen, later Sir Eric, who was to become the brain behind the international rubber restriction schemes in the 1920s and 1930s (Pugh *et al.* 1990).

Stated profits at Harrisons & Crosfield rose from an annual average of £56,000 ($271,000) during the years 1902–1907 to £105,000 ($508,000) around 1910 and £223,500 ($1,082,000) in the early 1920s. The profit rate rose quickly as long as equity remained low, namely from 9.5% on average in 1902–1907 to 34% by 1910. Yet after the issues of new shares in 1917 and 1918 the rate fell below 9%. The peak, as far as absolute profits are concerned, was in 1929 when net proceeds approached £390,000 ($1.9 million) which corresponded to 15% of equity (Harrisons & Crosfield 1943: 32–5, 54, 59, 61, 66). A remarkable difference with Guthrie was the quicker adjustment of equity in Harrisons & Crosfield to the actual scale of operations. The available data do not permit any further observations as to the trade-offs between dividend payments and accumulation of reserves.[6]

The rubber booms in Malaya were vehicles of expansion for both Guthrie and Harrisons & Crosfield. The story of how the *Hevea* was brought from Brazil to Kew and from there to Malaya has been often been told in the literature and need not be repeated here. The first sterling capital rubber company was Selangor Rubber, founded in 1899 with £20,000 ($96,800) of equity and the Klang estate of the pioneering planter W.W. Bailey as its main asset. A true proliferation of companies followed with 48 new firms being established by 1909 and another 75 following suit during the subsequent three boom years. As the experiences of both Guthrie and Harrisons & Crosfield demonstrate, the erection of a whole new branch of industry in Malaya in the course of just a decade was the accomplishment of a number of capital-rich British managing agencies (Drabble 1973: 21–2, 49–51, 78–86).

Handsome profits could be made in rubber in Malaya. A few examples may suffice. Guthrie-controlled Linggi Plantations in Negeri Sembilan saw dividend percentages at 60% in 1908, 238% in 1910 and 131% in 1911. The Pataling Rubber Estate Syndicate in the Harrisons & Crosfield group offered dividends at 250% in 1911. The Selangor Rubber Co. went up to 275% (Jackson 1968: 247; Cunyngham-Brown 1971: 185). Average dividend rates of rubber companies established prior to 1909 exceeded 70% in 1911 and 1912 and varied between 34% and 67% during the years 1913–1929 (Drabble 1973: 228).

There has been some controversy in the literature about how to assess the participation of the managing agencies in the rapid growth of rubber in Malaya. One line of argument goes that, even if the managing agencies did improve access to the capital market in London, they also made excessive profits and ended up enjoying a virtual monopoly over the entire sector (Puthucheary 1960: 37). A final verdict on the role of the managing agencies would have to be founded upon a systematic comparison of the costs and benefits of the rubber industry for the host country economy.

The rubber export boom and institutionalized management of British capital interests in the colony laid the basis for the impressive expansion of FDI in Malaya before the Second World War. Strong links with the capital market in the colonial mother country were maintained. In the colony, however, long-run strategies in terms of extending the scope of activities applied. This dualism in terms of management perspective was the single most important characteristic of FDI in Malaya. It presupposed a perpetual trade-off between the interests of finance far away and those of production on the spot, between City and Selangor.

3.4 TWO TYPES OF EXPANSION

The abolition of the Cultivation System in Java, from 1870, meant a switch to private corporate investment in export production in colonial

Indonesia, in Java and eventually also in the Outer Islands. The accumulation of FDI in colonial Indonesia in the late nineteenth and early twentieth centuries gained momentum hesitantly and proceeded only in a gradual fashion. Different from in Malaya, this development was not marked by sudden and short-lived outbursts of floating new companies on the capital market at home. Nevertheless, the accumulated stock of FDI had already reached a value of ƒ750 million ($300 million) before the First World War (Furnivall 1944: 312). Much FDI was clearly undertaken by way of retained profits and it has later been estimated that retained earnings made up 25–35% of total profits (Korthals Altes 1987: 41). The successive integration of colonial Indonesia into the world market in the late nineteenth century provided much of the capital needed to build up foreign-controlled lines of export production.

The practice of pioneering in colonial Indonesia can only be adequately described in terms of individual enterprises. For this purpose a small sample of four firms may serve as a collective case study. Such an approach ensures that justice is made to the variegation of FDI experience in colonial Indonesia. The four firms in the sample are: the multicrop plantations of Michiels-Arnold in West Java, the sugar estates of Wonolangan in East Java, the Deli tobacco company (Deli Maatschappij) in East Sumatra and the Billiton tin company on the island of Belitung. The analysis of our sample will focus on three topics: different types of FDI in the colonial context, management strategies and links with the surrounding local economy. First, however, a brief description must be given of each of the four firms.

Billiton was the oldest of the four. The company was founded in 1860, partly on the initiative of Prince Henry, a younger brother of King William III. It was based on a forty-year concession for tin mining on the island of Belitung. Initial equity amounted to ƒ5 million ($2.25 million). An attempt to accelerate the prolongation of the tin concession as early as 1882, under very favourable conditions, caused a scandal in Dutch politics. The Dutch state demanded a larger slice of profits than the proposed 10%. Only in 1892 was the concession renewed for another term of forty-five years.

History appeared to repeat itself in the early 1920s when the company again tried for an accelerated renewal. Again there was resistance from the States-General at The Hague and a new construction was created in 1923, with a holding company and several subsidiaries for purposes of exploration and mining throughout the Indonesian archipelago. Henceforth, the Dutch state received 62.5% of profits but shared also in the risks. At long last, the second concession was finally renewed in 1927, but then the drive towards diversification had already begun to bear fruit. Eventually, Billiton became involved not only in tin mining but also in nickel mining in Sulawesi (Kamp 1960: 54; Broersma 1985: 27–48; Gruythuysen and Kramer 1990: 20–4).

Deli was the first to set up business on a large scale in the tobacco belt of East Sumatra. It was incorporated in 1869 with an equity capital of ƒ300,000 ($133,000) and substantial backing from the NHM. Its long-time director, Jan Theodoor Cremer, moved at ease between Dutch political and business circles. He even doubled for a while as Minister of Colonial Affairs. Deli took the lead among the proliferation of tobacco estates that were established in East Sumatra between the 1870s and the 1890s. Significantly, its administrator as a rule held the office of chairman of the employers' organization in East Sumatra, the Deli Planters Vereniging (DPV).

Nominal equity at Deli was raised successively, to ƒ8 million ($3.2 million) at the turn of the century and ƒ30 million ($12 million) in 1920 and later to ƒ40 million ($16 million). Much new capital was spent on takeovers of other estates. A tendency of concentration of control and ownership into fewer hands, in fact, signified the development of the whole tobacco industry in Deli in the early years of the twentieth century. Eventually, Deli came to play first fiddle in an oligopolistic structure of four major concerns, next to Deli-Batavia, Senembah and Arendsburg, which controlled virtually all tobacco production in East Sumatra. Deli did make an attempt at diversifying activities. Yet this was largely confined to rubber. Such efforts remained secondary to the high quality tobacco for which it was renowned among cigar smokers all over the world (Deli Maatschappij 1919, 1929).

Michiels-Arnold was a family firm based on the possession of a vast tract of land purchased from the Dutch East India Company, the Verenigde Oost-Indische Compagnie (VOC), in the eighteenth century. The land was located between Bogor and Bandung in Priangan in West Java and measured about 115,000 hectares. The firm was incorporated in 1887 with an equity capital of ƒ4 million ($1.6 million) distributed among the seven daughters and one son of the proprietor of the land, J.W. Arnold, who had died in 1885. Initially, all the land was leased to Chinese rice farmers but in the 1890s the company's administrator took to exploiting some parcels himself while also experimenting with other crops such as coffee and cinchona. From 1905 onwards all parcels were exploited directly by the company and the emphasis now shifted from rice to tea. After 1910 the coffee and cinchona were replaced by *Hevea*.

The twin basis of exporting rubber and tea proved rewarding in the 1920s but made the whole enterprise all the more vulnerable in the 1930s. Among the numerous estates in West Java, Michiels-Arnold was unique on account of the size of its land and also because of some legal prerogatives inherited with the land. In its dependency on world market prices, however, its fate resembled that of many other agricultural enterprises in the Dutch colony (Godée Molsbergen 1937: 7, 27, 32–42).

Wonolangan emerged in 1895 as the amalgamation of three sugar estates in East Java, Umbul and Wonolangan near Probolinggo and Wringin Anom not far from Bondowoso further east. Just as earlier with Deli, the NHM was instrumental in providing access to market outlets and capital and retained a special link with the Wonolangan estates.

An arrangement with a major financial institution or large trading firm (which the NHM had been before) often provided the financial means for investment in new productive capacity in the large sugar industry in Java. Other Dutch firms involved in financing the sugar estates included the Koloniale Bank and the Nederlandsch-Indische Handelsbank, as well as Internatio and the Handels Vereeniging Amsterdam (HVA), both large trading firms. Both the NHM and the HVA also operated fully-owned sugar estates in Java (Knight 1996: 157). British-type managing agencies were not found in colonial Indonesia, nor indeed in French Indochina. It is tempting to seek an explanation for this in the smaller size of the Dutch (or French) capital market at home. Financial commitments of managing agencies in colonial production were, in the late nineteenth century, under-taken by the so-called colonial banks (*cultuurbanken*) in Java. In the course of the twentieth century this function was increasingly fulfilled by leading trading corporations operating throughout the archipelago, the so-called 'Big Five', i.e. Lindeteves, Jacobson Van den Bergh, Internatio, Borsumij and Geo. Wehry.

At Wonolangan initial equity capital amounted to ƒ1.8 million ($720,000). It was only adjusted upwards, to ƒ3.5 million ($1.4 million), in 1919. The area under cultivation stayed virtually constant until the early 1930s at 2,500 hectares. Total output doubled between 1914 and 1928. The increase in productivity of the land may be ascribed to both intensified cropping and higher yield cane variety. The depression brought not only declining prices and losses but also the necessity to curtail output. The successive implementation in Java of the international sugar restriction as stipulated in the Chadbourne Agreement caused the termination of pro-duction at one of the three estates, Oemboel. On this occasion in 1937, the equity capital was reduced by one-half. The history of Wonolangan does not seem to include many other dramatic events. Wonolangan was proba-bly a sugar company in Java of a rather conventional type.

The four firms in the sample shared several common features. They all dated from the second half of the nineteenth century. They were all run under the tacit assumption that Dutch presence was to remain a permanent feature in the Indonesian archipelago. All four were Dutch-owned and exclusively oriented towards producing for exports which made them all highly dependent on the ups and downs in the world market. They all had their main operations in rural areas of the colony where they formed self-contained settlements. Such common characteristics assure that the sample possesses an appreciable degree of representativeness for FDI in colonial Indonesia in general.

The four firms also represented two fundamentally different types of FDI in the colony, one still focusing on Java and the other contributing to the opening-up of the Outer Islands for Western business and the world market. These two types could coexist because the economy of colonial Indonesia was still a far cry from an integrated cohesive whole. In a very tangible way the contrast between these two types mirrored the dichotomy between the centre of Dutch colonial rule, Java, and a vast periphery that was traditionally more oriented towards mainland Southeast Asia than to Java (cf. Dick 1996: 33–4). The differences concerned lines of production and financial performance in particular.

The economic expansion of colonial Indonesia rested on an extension of the range of export products rather than old staple commodities simply being replaced by new ones. The traditionally strong products in the export agriculture of Java, in particular sugar, continued to expand and was supplemented by newer commodities from the Outer Islands, e.g. tobacco, rubber and oil. The latter lines of export production grew faster and by the 1920s the Outer Islands accounted for a larger share in the total export revenues of colonial Indonesia (Lindblad 1996b). In our sample of four firms, the Java pattern is represented by Wonolangan as far as sugar goes and by Michiels-Arnold with respect to other commercial crops. Deli typifies export agriculture in the Outer Islands whereas Billiton with its tin mining underscores the importance of non-agricultural lines of production outside Java. FDI in the Outer Islands was by definition more geared towards the newest additions to the range of exports from colonial Indonesia.

Financial results at all four firms were highly conditioned by the vicissitudes of fortune in the world market. This was most pronounced during the times of rapid expansion in the 1920s followed by an equally rapid contraction in the 1930s (Figure 3.1).[7] Measured by dividend rates, all firms did well in the 1920s and less well in the 1930s. Billiton and Deli continuously ranked above Michiels-Arnold or Wonolangan. The sole exception was at the time of the extreme inflation of sugar prices in 1920. The depression of the 1930s hit all four severely. Yet only Deli and Wonolangan were forced to discontinue paying out dividends during some of those years. The recovery in the late 1930s brought Billiton and Deli to the forefront of financial performance again. This reinforces the higher level of returns to be reaped from investing in the Outer Islands as opposed to in Java.

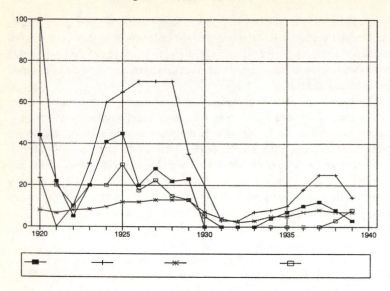

Figure 3.1   Financial results in Indonesia: selected dividend rates, 1920–1939

The results at the selected four firms may be offset against the level of returns that an investor in the Dutch capital market in the interwar period could expect. The customary dividend rate on ordinary shares in Dutch corporations at the time was 6%. Interest rates on loans scarcely ever climbed above 5% (de Vries 1989: 381). Profitability levels, as crudely indicated here by dividend rates, in the colony probably compared favourably with the most ready alternatives at home.

There were also striking differences within the two pairs of firms representing foreign-run export production in Java and the Outer Islands respectively. Michiels-Arnold first ranked below, then above Wonolangan whereas Billiton almost always paid out more generously than Deli. The former difference was occasioned by the type of commodity produced. Sugar never recovered after the depression of the 1930s but tea and rubber did. For Michiels-Arnold the originally good prospects deteriorated but then improved again. For Wonolangan it was only a downward trend, from bad to worse. The latter difference in dividend rates, between Billiton and Deli, probably testifies to the higher level returns on the oligopolistic tin market as compared to the more competitive market for high quality tobacco.

Management strategy is in particular revealed by the allocation of profits reflecting the choice between quick gains for shareholders and accumulation of reserves to safeguard the investment in the long run. This part of the discussion considers the priorities set at Billiton, Michiels-Arnold and Deli.[8] Good profits were made by Billiton which, as we saw, did not escape the attention of the Dutch government in 1882. The ratio between profits and equity was substantially higher than in Michiels-Arnold, at any rate up to 1928 (Figure 3.2). On occasion, notably in 1920, 1923 and 1925, profits at Billiton actually exceeded equity. At Michiels-Arnold profits, at the very most in the early 1920s, corresponded to one-quarter of equity. This can be explained in two ways: either profits were indeed higher at Billiton or equity was kept artificially low. Both explanations hold true for the better part of the 1920s but only the former applies to the late 1930s when the profit/equity ratio at Billiton again climbed above that of Michiels-Arnold.

Equity at Billiton had initially amounted to ƒ5 million ($2.25 million) but was later reduced to ƒ1 million ($400,000) in order to accelerate depreciations on the tin mining concession. This was done out of precaution. It bore testimony to the obsession with the risk that the concession on the island of Belitung would not be renewed. In 1917 unexpectedly large profits allowed for dividend payments at 439%, as such possibly unprecedented among owners of FDI in Southeast Asia. Most of this, 400% or ƒ4 million ($1.6 million), was used to restore the original equity level of ƒ5 million ($2 million) (Kamp 1960: 278). In 1928 equity was adjusted

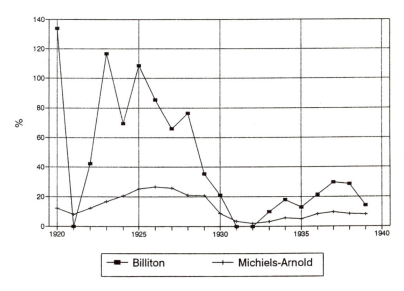

Figure 3.2   Financial results in Indonesia: profit/equity ratios, 1920–1939

upwards again, to ƒ10.5 million ($4.2 million). The profit/equity ratio was so high during much of the 1920s because actual assets were grossly undervalued.

A low equity by definition means less obligation to pay out dividends. During several decades Billiton in fact paid out such low dividends and accumulated such large reserves that the firm would have been capable of restoring the original equity already by 1914, i.e. even in the absence of the later windfall gains. The policy of building up reserves continued unabatedly and in 1921 some ƒ3.2 million ($1,280,000) were needed to cover the heavy losses incurred as the world market for tin temporarily collapsed. Later in the 1920s this was followed by a change of priorities that favoured paying out dividends above replenishing reserves. The new policy remained in force even at the nadir of the depression, in 1931 and 1932, when a small dividend was paid out despite actual losses.

The emphasis on lavish dividends at Billiton can be interpreted in two ways: either reserves were deemed sufficiently large already, or the owners considered Billiton a source of revenue in the first place rather than as a long-term investment in productive capacity. Budgetary interests of the colonial government, which was entitled to a fair proportion, five-eighths, of total dividends, may have played a role. At any rate, the long-term strategy of the management of the tin enterprise was certainly not one geared towards continuous expansion as with for instance Guthrie or Harrisons & Crosfield in Malaya. Public greed was instilled by the budgetary pressures of an ambitious colonial policy (cf. section 4.2). It was reflected in, among other things, relatively high corporate tax rates.

At Michiels-Arnold equity was held constant at ƒ4 million ($1.6 million). The profit/equity ratio improved successively between 1922 and 1927. The downward trend in world markets was felt from 1930 although no losses were registered even at the nadir of the depression. The average profit/equity ratio increased from 14% in the early 1920s to 24% during the later part of the decade but fell below 5% in the early 1930s and recovered to little short of 8% in the late 1930s. This cyclical pattern of variation over time in profitability levels was probably reiterated in a great many Western firms in colonial Indonesia during the interwar years.

Michiels-Arnold remained essentially a family firm even if shares, without voting-power, increasingly passed into other hands. Several of the shareholders were not actively involved in the daily business of the firm. This may explain the outspoken preference for dividend payments above creating more reserves. In the 1910s at least 80% of profits were paid out as dividends which implied that even the statutory reserve was built up at a very slow pace. Only the rising profit rate during the 1920s enabled continued dividend payments to coexist with an accumulation of reserves. The statutory reserve reached its legally prescribed magnitude at one-tenth of equity in 1925 and additional reserves touched ƒ1 million ($400,000) by 1927. The depression occasioned a return to the policy of using most of profits for dividend purposes. The average share of dividends in profits was 96% in the early 1930s and 88% towards the end of the decade. Just as with Billiton, the dividend policy adopted by Michiels-Arnold betrayed the fact that reserves had reached a sufficient level whereas the owners were getting impatient to see their gains realized.

Deli was perhaps the most famous prototype of a Western pioneer operating outside Java. The enterprise was set up early, expanded quickly and set an example for others. It relied heavily on personal contacts, not only with sultan Mahmud at Medan when the concession was granted in 1863 but also with the NHM in Amsterdam and the Bataafsche Petroleum–Maatschappij (BPM), joint subsidiary of Royal Dutch and Shell, in The Hague (Deli Maatschappij 1929: 13). It catered exclusively to the international staple for tobacco at Amsterdam and strived deliberately to establish an oligopoly among suppliers in East Sumatra. It gained a certain notoriety by its vehement opposition to the abolishment of the ill-reputed penal clause in coolie labour relations, a standpoint which could conveniently be voiced via the planters' association DPV (Langeveld 1978: 300–302; van Kommer 1989: 100–102). Its management policy was self-assertive and expansive but also conservative and cautious.

The financial position at Deli was sound. Solvability was high by any standard only rarely falling below 2.5 whereas liquidity was satisfactory at an average of 1.35.[9] Total capital, i.e. equity and debts, grew at an annual rate of 15% in the years 1922–1925. Profitability, here related to total capital instead of equity alone, climbed to 25% in 1924 and exceeded 9% on average at the end of the 1920s. Actual losses were only registered during the severe depression years of 1931–1933 and the recovery from 1935 pushed the average profit rate for the latter half of the decade above 5%. Deli managed to tide over the depression of the 1930s on account of its financial strength and sizeable reserves but also by rigorously cutting costs and massive layoffs (Gevers 1991). Ironically, the company was in a position to reduce the labour force fast when the depression set in precisely because the penal clause was gradually being abolished from 1931.

All four firms in our sample were managed from their headquarters in the Netherlands: Deli in Amsterdam, Billiton and Michiels-Arnold and (from 1918) Wonolangan in The Hague. Business strategies were obviously defined to suit the interests of the Dutch owners and there were frequent differences of opinion and outlook between directors in the mother country and administrators on the production site in the colony. Priorities shifted in favour of generous dividends as soon as the accumulated reserves had reached an acceptable level. In this comfortable position it was possible to satisfy both the short-run interests of the foreign capital owners and the long-run interests of continuity and consolidation of the investment itself.

Links with the local economy are examined against the background of substantial investments in lasting enlargements of productive capacity on location in the colony. Deli bought up neighbouring estates, Billiton erected mine establishments, Michiels-Arnold cleared new lands and Wonolangan set up sugar factories. Such outlays had repercussions that reached further than the process of production itself. In reviewing the links with the local economy it is convenient to distinguish between forward and backward linkages, and this is indeed often done in the literature. The former term refers to further processing of the product in question whereas the latter denotes activities supporting or preceding actual production (Hirschman 1977; Salleh 1992: 88–93).

Cane planting and harvesting and mechanized refining were fully integrated into the production process at Wonolangan. Demand for labour varied by the season and much additional employment was created during the campaigns, drawing workers from as far afield as Madura. Virtually all capital equipment was imported from abroad, especially from the Netherlands. Improvements of local infrastructure included the construction of a small railway to Probolinggo and the maintenance of *desa* roads between the sugar factories and the railway. Hand carts were rented from local residents for the transport over the *desa* roads. This last activity constituted a backward linkage in the most genuine sense of the word but it is difficult to ascertain whether this augmentation of local income was more than marginal. Between 1914 and 1940, Wonolangan invested about ƒ500,000 ($200,000) on average per year in production facilities and infrastructure, an amount corresponding to one-seventh of equity.

An exceptional feature on some of the lands of Michiels-Arnold was the persistence of corvée labour, the right of the landowner to dispose over one day, or one night, of unpaid labour per man and week. It was an anomaly dating from the nineteenth century, highly unusual on privately owned estates and bought off by the local dwellers whenever they were in a position to do so. On the Cileungsi land alone, southeast of Lemah Abang, revenues from such compensatory payments rose to almost ƒ80,000 ($32,000) in 1930 which corresponded to more than one-half of total profits from that part of the Michiels-Arnold estate. In addition, tax (*cukai*) had to be paid at one-fifth of the value of the *padi* harvest on these lands. Such burdens certainly contributed to the positive results of

Michiels-Arnold and formed, as it were, a kind of negative backward linkage between the Dutch-controlled export production and local agriculture. This arrangement was, however, atypical of estate agriculture in colonial Indonesia.

Backward linkages of a different kind materialized in the form of brick yards and tile works serving the construction of housing and factories on the Cileungsi and Cibarusa lands. In 1938 a separate subsidiary, a firm called 'Bomema', was established for construction and measurement purposes. Infrastructural provisions included a hydro-electric plant delivering to the tea factories at Selawangi and Tinggarjaya. The company constructed a tramway connecting the *sawah* with the rice peeling mill at Lemah Abang. The tramway was used, against payment, by both the government and the BPM. All these facilities were necessary to make production possible in the first place. Other facilities were auxiliary, and did not involve any further processing, e.g. the subsidy to the *desa* school, the small polyclinic at Cibarusa and the football field at Selawangi. There was even an attempt at some simple technological transfer by organizing demonstration planting of tea on spots that local residents allegedly were in the habit of passing by (Godée Molsbergen 1937: 45, 52).

Billiton around 1920 was a large enterprise employing more than 20,000 labourers, primarily Chinese coolies. The labour force was supervised by a small group of Europeans, some 200 persons. Labour conditions were reported to be considerably better than those at Bangka (Mollema 1922: 151, appendix 3; Somers Heidhues 1992: 125–6). Backward linkages abounded, especially in infrastructure, since no large-scale mining using modern technology had been carried out on the island before. A network of roads and tramways extending all over the island was constructed in close cooperation with the colonial authorities from the 1860s. The years 1898–1904 saw the erection of waterworks, telecommunications and electricity stations. Until 1904 the company itself maintained steamship lines with Singapore and Batavia. All these facilities obviously benefited the local economy, the company even asserting that the free tram rides in Manggar furthered social intercourse among the indigenous population.

Rails for wheelbarrows connected the various mines with Tanjung Pandan and Manggar but smelting was increasingly done at the Straits Trading Co. in Singapore which, incidentally, implied that the Billiton product was marketed as 'Straits tin'. Only one brief experiment was done with smelting on the island of Belitung itself. The smelter at Lipat-Kajan near Manggar started functioning in 1910 but was closed again in 1921. The supply of coal needed in the smelt ovens was erratic and it proved difficult to recruit qualified Dutch engineers to supervise production. This experiment could, if not so soon discontinued, have developed into a major forward linkage at Billiton. Subsequent plans for one central tin smelter in Java, serving both Billiton and Bangka, never got off the ground and eventually, in the late 1930s, facilities for further processing of tin were erected at Arnhem in the Netherlands (Kamp 1960: 175–80).

Production at Deli was considerably more labour intensive than at Billiton and in 1920 the labour force at Deli neared 40,000 coolies. More than one-half consisted of Javanese men where Chinese coolies accounted for only one-quarter of the total. Just as at Billiton, but unlike Wonolangan and Michiels-Arnold, virtually the entire regular labour force had been imported and inevitably formed an alien element in the local economy. Again an inaccessible region with scarcely any infrastructure had to be opened up for the operations of foreign capital. Local infrastructure was improved fast during the concluding decades of the nineteenth century, sometimes with and sometimes without financial support from the colonial government. When, in 1883, the authorities showed little interest in constructing a railway connection with the port at Belawan, a separate company was established for this very purpose, the Deli Spoorweg Maatschappij, with Deli as largest shareholder and Cremer as its first director. The railway network was successively enlarged, extending over more than 400 km by 1920 and about 550 km at the end of the colonial period (Weisfelt 1972: 13). Local brickyards formed another tangible backward linkage at Deli.

Miniature societies arose on the Deli estates in East Sumatra, comprising coolie barracks, schools for indigenous children, hospitals and shops, tennis courts for the European staff, even occasions for dancing and gambling. Yet it is difficult to consider such facilities and activities as linkages of the foreign firm. It was all largely confined to the site and process of production, as such, therefore, exerting a minimal influence on the surrounding economy. No processing of Deli tobacco took place in East Sumatra. The estates housed only one small latex factory for rubber that was of only secondary importance to the company. More generally, i.e. with respect not only to Deli but to all of East Sumatra, it has been convincingly argued that FDI enclaves contributed preciously little to the economic development of the region (Thee 1977: 43–5, 80–3).

Our sample of four Dutch firms illustrates what Western pioneering looked like in the Indonesian archipelago in colonial times. We may discern three pairs of contrasting characteristics. There were two types of FDI with the one in the Outer Islands more geared towards innovation in export production and also more profitable compared to the one in Java. There were two perspectives in the management of FDI, one biased towards the capital owners in the Netherlands and the other linked to the vested interests built up on the production site in the colony. Two kinds of linkages could emanate from the FDI enterprise but, in reality, the backward linkage resulted in considerable improvements of the local infrastructure whereas the forward one scarcely materialized.

This Chapter has presented several case studies of FDI in Southeast Asia during the colonial or prewar era, two in the Philippines, one in Burma, one in Thailand, two in Malaya and four in colonial Indonesia. It has identified a number of common traits in FDI at the time. Investors were quick to seize the opportunities offered by the latest boom in exports and eager to seek the protection of exclusive personal contacts on location. Profitability was high by any comparison and management policies were geared to combine a solid financial backing with rapid expansion. There was a tendency towards local entrenchment which reached its most conspicuous shape in the transformation of FDI into domestic investment in the Philippines. There was also a tendency towards FDI almost exclusively serving to maximize profits for the metropolitan capital owners which was especially pronounced in FDI in Burma and Thailand. In both Malaya and colonial Indonesia, the two major destinations of FDI in the region, both these tendencies existed alongside one another and grew to maturity simultaneously. In Malaya this was associated with the institutionalization of the management of British capital, whereas in colonial Indonesia it formed the common denominator uniting diverse types of FDI. In both of these major host countries dualism in terms of orientation, the alien with the local, remained the most salient characteristic of FDI. Such was the art of pioneering in Southeast Asia in colonial days.

4 Inside the Colonial State

In April 1921 the French colonial minister, Albert Sarraut, submitted a comprehensive plan for the development of the country's overseas possessions, a 'programme générale de mise en valeur des colonies françaises'. It aimed at more than just providing an adequate infrastructure in the colonial economy. Sarraut envisioned improvements in political and social, even intellectual and moral respects that were intimately tied to material advancement, a process that could only take place within the decentralized environment of colonial states or, as he paternalistically put it, 'états en devenir' (Sarraut 1923: 23, 83, 107). Sarraut's ambitious plan was not immediately executed but he had coined an expression, *mise en valeur*. The deeper connotation of this expression is not properly rendered by a literal translation of the two nouns involved ('investment' and 'value'). *Mise en valeur* became synonymous with the highly interventionist colonial policy in French Indochina, a policy aiming at colonial state formation in its most supreme form. This chapter considers FDI in Southeast Asia before the Second World War in its appropriate wider context, that of the colonial state.

The term 'colonial state' underscores that what gradually emerged in the colony was more than just a mirror image or dependency of the metropolitan mother country. It was a system in its own right, based on permanent settlement and vested interests. The system had been built up over time. It possessed its own identity and ideology, institutions and networks (Cribb 1994: 2–3). Our main concern here is not with colonial state formation as such but rather with the position of FDI with respect to that process. This chapter argues that the shape and long-run impact of FDI depended highly on the peculiarities of the colonial state in the host country.

Colonial states come in various forms. We may differentiate between four distinct types in Southeast Asia, each betraying some basic traits of political culture and heritage from the metropolitan mother country. The French version was steeped in mercantilist tradition and culminated in the *mise en valeur* of the interwar period (section 4.1). The Dutch brand blended extreme liberalism with ethical aspiration. This guaranteed both freedom and stability for the private investor (section 4.2). British aspirations were less lofty and it was probably even more committed to classical liberalism (section 4.3). American liberalism and idealism provided the most far-reaching form of colonial self-government in the Philippines.

Filipinos were regarded as junior partners on the road to independence (section 4.4). Thailand is omitted as it was not a formal colony. There is a concluding section on the statistical evidence about investment patterns in the colony (section 4.5).

4.1 *MISE EN VALEUR*

Chaos reigned throughout Indochina in the 1880s. French colonial rule was in the process of being forcefully implemented and rapidly changing local colonial administrators had inadequate means to improve the deficient infrastructure. The decisive changes came in the 1890s, especially when Paul Doumer was Governor-General (1897–1902). The last remnants of indigenous opposition against foreign rule were crushed and the colonial administration ventured on an ambitious programme of railway and road construction. This included both the trans-Indochina line from Saigon to Hanoi and the Yunnan railway further north, ill-reputed because of the many casualties during construction, as well as hundreds of miles of highway running through largely uninhabited forest. About 2000 km of railway were built between 1898 and 1910 by private firms working under state contracts and eventually Indochina came to possess one of the best road networks of the Far East (Murray 1980: 169–77).

State and private interests were entangled from the very beginning of French colonial rule in Indochina. The state-owned Banque de l'Indochine, for instance, frequently acted as an intermediary between the colonial administration and private investors. This bank had been set up in 1875 with an equity of 8 million francs ($1.5 million). It was authorized to issue currency, as a state bank, but it made much profit from extending commercial credits and discounting private bills of exchange on a large scale, both in Indochina and in China. Equity rose to 72 million francs ($14 million) in 1920 and 150 million francs ($29 million) in 1942 (Murray 1980: 114–6, 134). A great many private firms followed in the wake of its expansion.

The juxtaposition of the interests of colonial rule with those of private capital may be examined from three complementary angles: the successive accumulation of private capital, public investment in the colony as opposed to private investment and, finally, colonial economic policy as it was actually executed. In this context it is important to recall both that FDI in this colony almost coincided with French investment and that the composition of FDI by sector differed markedly from the pattern in most other host countries in Southeast Asia.

Between 1888 and 1918 some 490 million francs ($98 million) of French private capital were invested in Indochina. Significantly, about one-half of this aggregate went into mining (here combined with manufacturing) whereas transport accounted for one-quarter. Both percentages are high by any comparison among colonial recipients of investment capital. Trading absorbed only 15% of the total whereas export agriculture received less than 10%. This made for a highly unusual composition of foreign investment by type of production (Robequain 1944: 161). The strong emphasis on infrastructure reflects the priorities of territorial expansion and consolidation of areas under colonial authority. The preference for mining above agriculture may be associated with the need for self-sufficiency in energy supplies. Just as elsewhere in Southeast Asia, this was considered urgent by the colonial government.

Coal mining in Upper Tonkin was the first focus for concentration of French private investment in the colony. It was succeeded by some tin mining in the same area. Total employment in mining increased fast, from 5000 in 1904 to almost 50,000 in 1938. The largest coal mining company, Société des Charbonnages du Tonkin, alone was responsible for one-half of all employment in mining while the mines at Dong Trieu ranked second (Shepherd 1941: 14–17). These were large enterprises of an enclave character on remote locations. The literature makes scarcely any mention of forward linkages on the site of production. Backward linkages, however, were likely to materialize as local equipment was needed and local transport facilities had to be provided.

The early wave of French investment in Indochina was characterized by a concentration to a relatively small number of individual firms. This can be illustrated by looking at a sample of 32 major firms, 31 French and one Chinese, which were all set up in Indochina between 1888 and 1913. Total equity at incorporation amounted to 85 million francs ($16 million) or 17% of all French investment in Indochina during the period 1888–1918 (Nørlund 1991: 87). Equity in most of these firms was raised substantially during the late colonial period and by 1942 the combined total amounted to no less than 1.1 billion francs ($212 million). This is an impressive enlargement of capital committed to private enterprise in the colony even if we account for the continuous deflation of the French currency since the turn of the century.

Agriculture initially attracted scant attention from capital owners and banks in Paris. Outlays by the colonial government in this sector were primarily geared towards improving irrigation in rice cultivation. The rubber boom reached Indochina at a later stage than Malaya or colonial Indonesia. By 1913 only 125,000 hectares had been planted. Seven rubber firms had just started up but they were still relatively small with an average equity amounting to a mere 2 million francs ($400,000). Nevertheless, this group of seven did include one of the later giants in Indochina rubber, Société des Plantations des Terres Rouges. This firm had been established in 1910 with an initial equity of 2.3 million francs ($460,000) (Nørlund 1991: 87). By 1940 Terres Rouges possessed an equity of 110 million francs ($21 million), an almost fiftyfold increase since its incorporation. Terres Rouges alone held one-fourth of the total land in Indochina planted with rubber, 33,000 hectares out of 132,000 hectares. Together with two other large firms, Michelin and Indochinoise des Plantations de Heveas, the Terres Rouges concern developed into a true oligopoly in the supply of estate rubber from Indochina (Murray 1980: 570).

The shift from mining and infrastructure to agriculture and services came in the 1920s. Between 1924 and 1928 almost 1.9 billion francs ($365 million) of shares were issued by French firms operating in Indochina. Agriculture accounted for 788 million francs ($152 million) or 42% of the total with rubber taking the largest share, 700 million francs ($135 million) or 37% of the grand total. Significantly, mining and banking shared the second rank at some 310 million francs ($60 million) or 16% each. The influx of capital continued in 1929 and 1930 at a volume of possibly half a billion francs ($100 million) per year. From 1931 FDI tapered off, eventually falling below an annual level of 50 million francs ($9.6 million) as the depression deepened (Robequain 1944: 161–7; Murray 1980: 125, 130; Nørlund 1991: 85; Elson 1992: 159).

According to a contemporary Japanese source, accumulated private FDI in Indochina by 1932 amounted to more than 7 billion francs ($1.3 billion). This composition by sector was as follows (Hicks 1993: 206):

(1) mining and manufacturing with 2.6 billion francs ($500 million) or 36%;
(2) banking and finance with 1.7 billion francs ($327 million) or 23%;
(3) agriculture with 1.3 billion francs ($250 million) or 18%;
(4) trading with 870 million francs ($167 million) or 12%;
(5) transport with 790 million francs ($152 million) or 11%.

Such a structure of FDI is a far cry from the stereotype focus on monocultures and exploitation of natural riches in overseas territories. An unmistakeable diversification has been attained and both services and transport received more attention than was usually the case with colonial investment in Southeast Asia.

There are few indications in the literature about the profitability of French private investment in Indochina. According to one rare contemporary estimate, annual profits of French private firms in the colony amounted to some 70 million piasters ($27.3 million) which would correspond to 9% of the accumulated investment of about 1935. Out of total profits, 57% (40 million piasters), was remitted to France whereas 43% (30 million piasters) was retained in the colony and supposedly reinvested in the firm in question (Thompson 1937).

Public investment lay at the core of the policy of *mise en valeur*. Rather than forming a mere corollary to FDI in the more narrow sense of the word, public investment set the pace. Annual flows of public investment, as estimated from colonial budgets and foreign trade balances, almost always exceeded the simultaneous flows of private French capital entering Indochina during the four first decades of the twentieth century (Figure 4.1; Table 4.4). The difference between the two was somewhat marginal until the First World War, when public investment started to ascend steeply and private commitments even declined for a while. Annual flows of both increased substantially during the 1920s. This can be ascribed partly to the depreciation of the French currency. The gap narrowed in the late 1920s as private investment rose and public investment fell. The depression of the 1930s reduced private flows more than public flows so that the original gap between the two was restored.

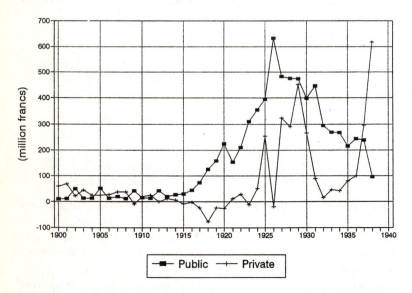

Figure 4.1   French capital in Indochina: public and private flows, 1900–1938

Table 4.4   Estimates of French capital investment in Indochina, 1900–1938

(thousand French francs)

	Capital goods imports	Interior investment	Loans	Investment Public	Private
1900	72 300	11 100	0	11 100	61 200
1901	81 800	12 100	0	12 100	69 700
1902	73 400	15 700	70 000	50 700	22 700
1903	59 200	14 600	0	14 600	44 600
1904	41 300	14 900	0	14 900	26 400
1905	77 600	11 600	80 000	51 600	26 000
1906	41 900	13 900	0	13 900	28 000
1907	58 600	21 000	0	21 000	37 600
1908	51 900	12 900	0	12 900	39 000
1909	35 800	17 400	53 000	43 900	-8 100
1910	36 700	15 300	0	15 300	21 400
1911	40 600	14 400	0	14 400	26 200
1912	43 800	18 200	50 000	43 200	600
1913	33 300	21 200	0	21 200	12 100
1914	35 000	28 300	0	28 300	6 700
1915	24 400	32 000	0	32 000	−7 600
1916	43 100	44 900	0	44 900	−1 800
1917	51 400	74 600	0	74 600	−23 200
1918	48 900	126 100	0	126 100	−77 200
1919	133 900	157 800	0	157 800	−23 900
1920	197 700	223 500	0	223 500	−25 800
1921	166 200	153 900	0	153 900	12 300
1922	240 000	190 000	411 000	210 550	29 450
1923	298 200	310 000	0	310 000	−11 800
1924	404 800	353 700	0	353 700	51 100
1925	647 400	395 000	0	395 000	252 400
1926	613 100	631 700	0	631 700	−18 600
1927	806 100	482 700	0	482 700	323 400
1928	765 400	475 300	0	475 300	290 100
1929	926 800	475 000	0	475 000	451 800
1930	663 500	397 200	2 000	398 200	265 300
1931	536 100	346 600	200 800	447 000	89 100
1932	308 700	207 700	171 800	293 600	15 100
1933	314 600	152 500	232 200	268 600	46 000
1934	310 800	147 600	238 400	266 800	44 000

Table 4.4   (*Cont.*)

(thousand French francs)

	Capital goods imports	Interior investment	Loans	Investment Public	Private
1935	296 900	142 500	145 800	215 400	81 500
1936	341 400	185 800	111 700	241 650	99 750
1937	532 800	204 600	66 000	237 600	295 200
1938	714 300	0	193 700	96 850	617 450

Note: All values at current prices. Interior investment expenditures are recalculated here since the original computer program used at Université Paris VII mistakenly adds the Cochinchina figure twice while leaving out the Tonkin one.
Source: Computerized file on French colonial budgets and foreign trade balances, 1900–1938, kept at the Université Paris VII.

The paths of development of public and private investment were roughly parallel up to 1925 and again during much of the depression but not in the late 1920s or later on in the 1930s. The share of public capital in the total flows oscillated around 60% in both 1925 and the late 1920s but climbed above 80% in the first half of the 1930s. The greater downward rigidity of public capital flows as opposed to direct private investment during the 1930s testifies to both the higher sensitivity of private investment to adverse business cycles and the long awaited implementation of the policy of *mise en valeur*.

Financial predicaments in the early 1920s compelled the French state to effectively postpone the execution of Sarraut's ambitious scheme for *mise en valeur*. There was, instead, a greater emphasis on stimulating private investment. There was a shift in total investment from public to private capital flows in the 1920s. This was all the more ironic since the public debate at the time abounded with Sarraut's elevated rhetoric. The Sarraut plan was reintroduced in 1931 when the depression had brought the influx of private capital into Indochina to a virtual halt. The policy of *mise en valeur* now translated into a cardinal measure to counter the downward business cycle. In other words, its final implementation depended more on the changing external conditions than on the merits of the Sarraut plan itself.

The French authorities set two priorities in its new active colonial economic policy: infrastructural improvement and industrialization. The ambition of improving the physical infrastructure carried, whether deliberately or not, the Keynesian undertone of a government effort to bolster effective demand when private enterprise failed to do so. The aim of industrialization was considered the quickest road to modernization. Yet it should not interfere with the interests of industry in the mother country. This had been one of the tenets in Sarraut's original conception as well. *Mise en valeur* remained subordinated to the vested interests of the bourgeoisie at home.

Sarraut's plan was implemented at long last. In the first year of operations alone, 1931/32, no less than 1.6 billion francs ($70 million) were spent on infrastructure in Indochina, above all railroad and road construction. Direct subsidies were given to rubber plantations confronted with abysmally low world market prices (Murray 1980: 203–4). The effect was to increase state control over export production in Indochina and thus to reinforce the existing tendency towards interventionism in colonial economic life. The emphasis in public expenditure during most of the 1930s remained with infrastructure and export promotion.

The efforts at industrialization lagged behind. Only some haphazard support was given to existing light manufacturing, e.g. paper, tobacco, silk, cement, glass and wood industries. It took until late into the 1930s before private French enterprises fully accepted the idea of a state-led industrialization in Indochina. One of the chief proponents of such a policy was the banker and economist Paul Bernard who acted not only as managing director of the Société Financière Française et Coloniale (SFFC), a subsidiary of the Banque d'Indochine, but also as the president of firms such as 'Caoutchoucs d'Extrême-Orient', 'Phospates du Tonkin' and 'Papeteries de l'Indochine'. Bernard was especially attracted by Sarraut's view that colonization should explicitly aim at making profits for the bourgeoisie in the metropolitan mother country. This was not best accomplished by public investment in infrastructure or private ventures reaping short-run benefit from a boom in the world market as with estate rubber in the 1920s.

According to Bernard, fresh capital should be directed towards long-run enlargements of productive capacity in manufacturing. The new lines of production must not be oriented to sales in the world market, where the colonial produce would compete with goods from France, but rather towards domestic consumption. Vietnam possessed mineral resources and a potential for the generation of hydro-electric power. Cambodia in turn appeared well suited for handicrafts and cotton manufacturing (Hardy 1994).

A comprehensive survey in 1938 identified the possibilities and limitations of industrialization in Indochina. The governing principle, however, remained that there must be no competition with French industry. In practice this ruled out a number of new and possibly interesting alternatives for

Indochinese manufacturing, such as textiles and chemicals. Only two innovations ensued from this attempt at a comprehensive approach to industrialization in the colony: new state investment in jute cultivation and tyre manufacturing (Murray 1980: 208–9). Jute cultivation did not compete with French products and met a sizeable demand for package material from the rice trade. The manufacturing of tyres formed a rare and potentially interesting forward linkage in the foreign-controlled rubber industry.

In 1938 Bernard laid down his conception of the colonial economy:

> The point of an industrializing Indochina is to equip the colony once and for all such that it can, alone, constitute an independent economy entity, able to produce everything necessary for its population to live and improve its lot. In short, we aim to turn this country by means of its full industrial development, into a living body, having a harmonious equilibrium between the turns and limbs, a veritable second-metropolis, forming an economic unit more or less distinct from that of France.
>
> (Marseille 1984: 241)

Mise en valeur is a difficult term to translate. It conveys the ideology of unrestrained ambition and intervention in colonial economic policy. In Indochina the French state set the pace where private capital followed. This meant a heavy discrimination in favour of capital from France. It also implied a greater emphasis on infrastructure, manufacturing and services than elsewhere. The structure of FDI became diversified and potentially advantageous for economic development in the host country. Yet better roads, railways and bridges formed the sole lasting benefits whereas linkages in production were few and far between. An independent colonial economy was the aim but it should serve the interests of France only. Such was the vision of men like Albert Sarraut and Paul Bernard – a vision that perished under Japanese occupation and on the battlefields in the war for independence in Indochina.

4.2   A NETWORK ORANGE[1]

There was something special about the Netherlands Indies, the huge colony in Southeast Asia controlled by a tiny European power on the shores of the North Sea. The colony was important to the Netherlands because it made it the smallest of large metropolitan powers rather than the largest of small countries in Europe. Dutch prosperity was believed to depend on the colonial possession. There was widespread resistance in all quarters to the embryonic prewar strive for independence among Indonesian nationalists. Two economists, including the later Nobel Laureate Jan Tinbergen, estimated the colonial contribution to Dutch national income at 14% just before the Second World War, a percentage which is high by most standards (Derksen and Tinbergen 1945). In the late 1940s the slogan *Indië verloren, rampspoed geboren* ('Indies lost, calamity born') rallied massive popular support for two military interventions by the Netherlands in Indonesia that met with severe international criticism, and prolonged Dutch acceptance of Indonesian independence by half a decade. The emotional undertones of Dutch colonialism in the Indonesian archipelago can, in part, be explained by the peculiar circumstance which combined the largest colony in Southeast Asia with the smallest metropolitan power active in the region. It also meant that Dutch colonial rule in Indonesia did not remain superficial but developed into a heavy commitment bordering almost on an emotional attachment.

The economic importance of the colony to the Netherlands and Dutch responsibility for progress in the colony were two sides of the same coin. This was amply illustrated in 1903 when the then Minister of Colonial Affairs, A.W.F. Idenburg, defended the granting of a loan without interest of ƒ30 million ($12 million) for development projects in the colony by referring to the large Dutch share (one-third) in total imports of colonial Indonesia. Incidentally, this gave a rather misleading impression of the true importance of the Indonesian market for Dutch export production since only one-thirtieth of Dutch exports ended up in the colony (Lindblad 1996b). The Minister's plea for financial support of the colony fitted into the newly inaugurated Ethical Policy of the Dutch government. This policy was elevated in subsequent decades into the best known feature of Dutch colonial policy.

The Ethical Policy had been launched by Queen Wilhelmina of the House of Orange in 1901. It was conceived as a means of repaying a 'debt of honour' incurred by the Netherlands during the long years of profitable forced crop cultivation in Java (1830–1870). Now, after the Cultivation System had been dissolved and the flow of profits for the state had dried up, the colony needed funds for its development. The Ethical Policy aimed at the 'uplifting of the indigenous peoples', to use the terminology of the time, and the alleviation of poverty and population pressure in Java in particular. The slogan for the Ethical Policy became 'Irrigation, education and emigration'. Whatever the sincerity and effects of such lofty ambitions may have been, the Ethical Policy as a conception came to typify the Dutch brand of colonial rule in Southeast Asia during the first half of the twentieth century.

The Ethical Policy presupposed a far-reaching involvement on the part of the colonial administrators in local affairs, as well as an extension of effective colonial rule throughout the entire archipelago. It was based on a tacit partnership with private capital, primarily of Dutch origin, which was invited to invest in the colony after the system of forced cultivation had been abandoned in Java in 1870. The colonial government by and large refrained from engaging directly in production. Notable exceptions to this rule were found in mining, either when security issues were at stake or when there were extraordinary opportunities for enlarging state revenues. The safeguarding of coal provisions were, just as in Indochina, considered to be of such vital importance that state involvement only increased in the course of time. Eventually, the authorities not only operated the largest coal mine in colonial Indonesia, Ombilin in West Sumatra, but also two of the four mines in the second rank, Bukit Asam in South Sumatra and Pulu Laut off the Kalimantan coast (Lindblad 1988: 40–41, 92–3). In tin the initial profits pocketed by Billiton exerted an irresistible lure for the Dutch state whereas in oil the nice profits of the oil giant BPM (Bataafsche Petroleum Maatschappij) urged the government to insist on a joint venture with the Royal Dutch/Shell when the exploitation of the oil-fields of Jambi came up to discussion (section 4.4; Locher-Scholten 1994: 308–9).

The investment climate at the time of the Ethical Policy was very liberal. In principle, no barriers were erected against capital from other overseas sources than the Netherlands. In practice, entry for non-Dutch foreign investors was unrestricted in certain industries, notably rubber, but less so elsewhere. In oil, for instance, the colonial government did side with Royal Dutch/Shell in trying to keep Standard Oil out of colonial Indonesia for as long as possible (Lindblad 1989b: 54–5). The liberal approach had its counterpart in the trade regime. From the early 1870s to the early 1930s no tariffs or other trade restrictions applied in the Indonesian market, i.e. Dutch goods were not favoured against imports from third countries nor did indigenous products enjoy any protection. Economic liberalism formed the logical counterweight to the interventionism in the public domain in Dutch colonial policy in Indonesia in the early twentieth century.

A colonial state emerged in the Indonesian archipelago under the double aegis of the Ethical Policy and economic liberalism. The process of colonial state formation embraced the elaboration of the administrative apparatus, the extension of effective control to the most remote locations, a harmonization of standards and practices and an intensification of inter-island communications. It is symbolized by the monetary unification of the colony which was achieved through successive purges of foreign currencies from circulation in the Outer Islands, in particular the expulsion of Straits dollars as means of payment from the planters' society in East

Sumatra about 1907 (Potting 1987: 132–4). Thus a cohesive entity emerged that had not existed before and that was more clearly demarcated from adjacent countries than in previous times.

The new creation is best understood in terms of networks. It has been demonstrated that the process of state formation in colonial Indonesia entailed the erection of three parallel networks: an administrative one accommodating the colonial bureaucracy, a maritime one set up by the leading shipping concern, the KPM (Koninklijke Paketvaart Maatschappij) and, finally, an economic one based on trade links. The three networks reinforced and supplemented one another. The development began around the turn of the century. Between 1892 and 1910, the number of ports included in the maritime network of the KPM almost doubled, rising from 115 to 223, whereas numbers of ports included with an administrative or trading function increased by respectively 85%, from 82 to 151, and 70%, from 54 to 92 (à Campo 1992: 528–32, 569–78, 613–6, 624–7, 658). The current literature does not bring the account of these three networks further than to the eve of the First World War but we may safely assume that this process continued unabatedly throughout the rest of the late colonial period. Our concern here is with the corporate structure evolving amidst the political and maritime networks. We will look at its emergence, consolidation and economic impact.

The *Gründerzeit* in corporate business in colonial Indonesia may be dated to the final quarter of the nineteenth century (à Campo 1996: 72–5). Numbers of corporations increased from 133 in 1883 to 1075 in 1898 and further to 2779 in 1914. Incorporation into limited companies was the mechanism by which the corporate network extended and the initial flows of FDI entered the colony. Many of these young firms were short-lived as the prospects for quick returns proved overly optimistic. Others grew up to become permanent institutions in the economic organization of colonial Indonesia. The survival rate for corporations varied between less than one-quarter for firms founded in the 1890s to more than two-fifths for firms dating from before 1890 (à Campo 1995: 48). During pioneering times many had to try for some to succeed.

The relative youthfulness of corporations in colonial Indonesia is noticeable when we examine the 2800 odd firms in operation at the culmination of long-run economic expansion in the colony (Handboek 1930). These corporations can be divided into three categories of about equal size when it comes to age: one dating from before 1910, a second one founded in the 1910s and the final one that had been in business for less than ten years. The single most popular year of incorporation was 1920 when 170 firms were established which testifies to the widespread euphoria during the immediate aftermath of the First World War. Only 67 firms, or 2% of the total, had started out before 1870. The proportion of young enterprises was higher in the Outer Island where 80% had been established no earlier than in 1910. The very age structure of corporate business underscores that FDI materialized on an appreciable scale precisely at the time of colonial state formation and rapid export-led economic expansion.

Some diversification was present from the start. Export agriculture dominated throughout but new lines of production were added, e.g. rubber and copra, whereas mining (including oil) accounted for an increasingly large part (à Campo 1995: 67). There was as yet little emphasis on services or infrastructure, let alone manufacturing. Public investment lagged behind and still corresponded to one-third of private investment or less by 1913. It only increased substantially during the First World War and the early 1920s (Booth 1995: 11). A gestation period was needed before the Ethical Policy could be fully implemented and the heavy reliance on private capital as opposed to public funding linked the build-up of FDI more closely to the opportunities in foreign export markets than in, for instance, Indochina.

The consolidation of the corporate network followed as the export-led economic expansion gained momentum during the First World War and the 1920s. The total number of corporations rose to almost 3700 around 1920 but then started to decline again touching 3300 by 1925 and 2800 in 1930. The last-mentioned year is especially interesting since it represented the zenith of economic expansion in colonial Indonesia. The cyclical development in incorporating new business revealed swift responses to changing prospects in foreign markets. It affected ever larger parts of the archipelago. There was great optimism among foreign investors in colonial Indonesia in the years between 1914 and 1930. The colonial authorities did little more than try to offer the best possible conditions for new undertakings. When the tide turned in the 1930s, pessimism took over and numbers of corporations fell dramatically. About 1940 colonial Indonesia counted scarcely more than 2150 corporations, about 25% less than in 1914 or 1930.

The corporate network matured into a seemingly permanent structure that may be characterized in terms of both the nationality of the capital owners and its spatial elaboration. With respect to nationality it is recalled that the colonial context necessitates a differentiation by shades of alienness rather than a simple dichotomy between FDI and domestic investment (Chapter 1). We apply the following three categories of more or less 'foreign' investors:

(1) Netherlands-Indian firms, i.e. corporations operated by permanent Dutch residents in the colony who by definition were more locally entrenched than their compatriots giving instructions from overseas;

(2) Dutch firms, i.e. corporations operated from the Netherlands and guided by priorities that had more to do with the Dutch economy than with local conditions;

(3) Foreign firms, i.e. corporations run by investors from third countries for whom colonial Indonesia was intrinsically no different from any other host country.

The distinction between Netherlands-Indian and Dutch firms is primarily qualitative. The crudest cue is offered by the location of the firm's head office, in the colony or in the Netherlands respectively. In addition, it is also possible to isolate Chinese business as a separate category apart from both FDI and enterprises which were indigenous in every sense of the word.

The single most striking observation with respect to nationality in the corporate network refers to the substantial share occupied by so-called Netherlands-Indian firms: 51% in 1914 and 43–44% in 1930 or 1940. Even if many were small and some might even have been fully owned by foreign multinationals these business firms provide the living testimony to the existence of a comprehensive and sophisticated organization of economic life in the colonial state serving partly other interests than those of private capital in the metropolitan mother country.

The firms actually run from outside colonial Indonesia were generally larger and less susceptible to short-run movements of the business cycles. The Dutch firms ranked second after the Netherlands-Indian firms and proved more resistant at the time of the depression in the 1930s. Their numbers fell at a slower pace than those of Netherlands-Indian firms and their share in the total rose, from 23% in 1930 to 29% by 1940. British firms predominated among those here considered to be truly foreign. London, in fact, ranked only after Amsterdam and The Hague as the most popular location of headquarters outside colonial Indonesia itself (Table 4.5). Even so, the corporate network in the colony remained essentially a Dutch construction with portraits of Queen Wilhelmina on the wall in countless offices all over the archipelago. Paraphrasing Anthony Burgess, such was the 'network orange' in the Dutch colony.

Chinese business has for generations occupied a unique position in Indonesia, fully entrenched in the local economy, yet often perceived as possessing an alien character. Within the wider category of Chinese businessmen we may distinguish between China-born immigrants (*totok*) and those of Chinese descent who had lived all their life in colonial Indonesia (*peranakan*). Most Chinese firms were relatively small and most were in the services sector. Equity often remained suspiciously unchanged for decades at length. This suggests that profits were retained rather than handed out as dividends or used to augment equity. Total Chinese investment in colonial Indonesia was estimated at ƒ340 million ($136 million) in 1918. Batavia counted at least 15 Chinese millionaires, including Huang Yu-Kien from Fukien who had assets worth ƒ100 million ($40 million). Semarang was a

Table 4.5   Corporate enterprises in colonial Indonesia,1914–1940

	1914	1930	1940
Nationality			
Chinese	521	693	396
Netherlands-Indian	1422	1220	945
Dutch	641	656	627
British	162	170	138
Japanese	2	21	16
Other	31	49	33
Total	2779	2809	2155
Location			
West Java	1023	912	782
Central Java	377	412	261
East Java	685	759	535
East Sumatra	158	212	175
Other Outer Islands	271	404	255
Total	2514	2699	2008
Main locations of head office			
Batavia	654	378	388
Surabaya	393	329	267
Amsterdam	347	363	330
Semarang	198	179	310
The Hague	180	194	181
London	121	96	78
Bandung	111	168	124
Medan	35	96	85
Main locations of activities			
Batavia	509	300	344
Surabaya	331	306	268
Semarang	154	152	106
Bandung	115	186	144
Medan	43	95	86

Note: Distributions given by absolute numbers of firms. The nationality could be established for virtually all individual firms. Locations of operations in colonial Indonesia could be established for 2514 firms in 1914 (91% of the total), 2699 firms in 1930 (96%) and 2008 firms in 1940 (93%).

Source: Databases on corporate business in colonial Indonesia processed at the University of Leiden in 1988/89 and 1993/94. Original information in Handboek 1914, 1930, 1940.

well known centre for Chinese economic activity at this time housing more Chinese millionaires than Surabaya (Hicks 1993: 54–62).

Semarang was also the base of the most famous Chinese businessman in colonial Indonesia, Oei Tiong Ham. He was a *peranakan* Chinese who in the late nineteenth century used profits from his opium farms to buy up sugar factories all over Central Java, including one at Redjoagoeng which was said to be the largest sugar mill in colonial Indonesia at the time. Oei Tiong Ham eventually expanded into shipping and real estate development at Semarang. His initial company, Kian Gwan, named after his father's *kongsie* (a cooperative undertaking), was incorporated in 1893 with an equity of ƒ1.4 million ($560,000). The sugar concern that he left behind when he died in 1924 had an equity of ƒ40 million ($16 million) and rivalled the leading Dutch trading firms in the colony (Liem 1989; Dick 1993).

Chinese business fared well during the expansion and was badly hit by the depression as is evidenced by the cyclical development of its share in the total network: 19% in 1914, 25% in 1930 and 18% in 1940. The link between the establishment pattern and the ups and downs of economic life was stronger for the Chinese than for other firms. The majority of Chinese firms could not draw on the kind of reserves at Oei Tiong Ham's disposal. There was a strong emphasis on trading in the activities of many small Chinese enterprises. At first, many local Chinese traders depended on contacts with Chinese merchants in commercial centres such as Batavia, Semarang and Singapore. Later, many established direct trading links with major European or American merchant houses. One illustration of this may be found in the export trade of West Kalimantan that was of old dominated by local Chinese. In 1920 a Chinese bank, The Fak Tong, was established at Pontianak and shortly afterwards the Chinese exporters started bypassing intermediaries in delivering to foreign markets (Ranken 1989: 203).

The spatial dimension of the corporate network is also best understood in terms of numbers of firms rather than volumes of capital invested. The network extended to the remotest corners of the archipelago like the tentacles of a gigantic octopus and for the penetration of local economic activities sheer presence and diversity often counted more than size. Diversity was a key feature of the network. In 1930 there were as many as 167 locations with just one Western-type firm in operation, e.g. Kota Baru on Pulau Laut where only the Kotabaroesche Electriciteits Maatschappij (Kota Baru Electricity Co.) remained of the auxiliary service sector surrounding the local coal mine. The strength of the network derived to a large extent from its very elaboration.

Java remained the core, housing approximately four out of every five firms in the network (Figure 4.2; Table 4.5). Within Java, Greater Batavia and

Priangan continuously ranked above Surabaya and neighbouring sugar districts whereas Central Java lagged behind with its high dependency on subsistence agriculture. The three major parts of the island, today's provinces, underwent a slightly different development. West Java lost much of its lead when Surabaya and Semarang appeared as viable alternatives to Batavia in setting up business during the boom period between 1914 and 1930. In the 1930s, however, the pendulum swung back to Batavia where business was less adversely affected by the economic depression (Lindblad 1992: 22–4). The two single most popular locations were Batavia and Surabaya, followed at some distance by Semarang and Bandung.

East Sumatra was the cradle of Western expansion in the Outer Islands that, taken together, accounted for 17–23% of the grand total. Among individual residencies in the colony, East Sumatra ranked fourth in 1930, after Batavia, Surabaya and Priangan, but above Semarang. Meanwhile, Medan became the fifth most important single location immediately following Semarang in the ranking of cities. The second-ranking single location outside Java was Macassar (Ujung Pandang). Medan and Macassar represented the westernmost node of a vast network extending throughout the eastern part of the archipelago.

The network was consolidated by great numbers of relatively small corporations set up all over the colony with the focus primarily on local economic affairs. Average equity was moderate but increased over time, from ƒ680,000

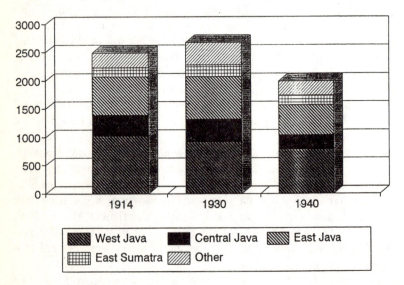

Figure 4.2   Firms in colonial Indonesia: numbers by region, 1914–1940

($272,000) in 1914 to ƒ1.3 million ($530,000) in 1930 and further to ƒ1.6 million ($640,000) in 1940 (Handboek 1914, 1930, 1940). Once consolidated the corporate network exerted a powerful impact on the economic development of the colony. We may distinguish between two types of effects, one referring to the gains to be had from FDI and the other to the type of economic activity promoted by FDI. The gains from FDI were in particular conditioned by who controlled which part of the corporate network. The type of activity promoted is decisive for the future path of economic development in the host country. In either case we must consider FDI in terms of equity and profits rather than reviewing only numbers of enterprises.

Dutch firms, as opposed to Netherlands-Indian ones, held by far the largest proportion of aggregate equity invested in colonial Indonesia (Figure 4.3; Table 4.6). The proportion held by genuinely Dutch firms rose from 63% in 1914 to 71% in 1930 but fell back slightly in the 1930s reaching 68% by 1940. This impressive share in aggregate equity reflects above all the larger size of Dutch corporations, more than ƒ4 million ($1.6 million) on average in 1930. The one at the top, the BPM, could draw on a paid-up equity of ƒ300 million ($120 million) whereas other leading concerns, the NHM and the KPM, were good for respectively ƒ80 million ($32 million) and ƒ30 million ($12 million). The many small firms stood in the shadow of a select group of very large corporations.

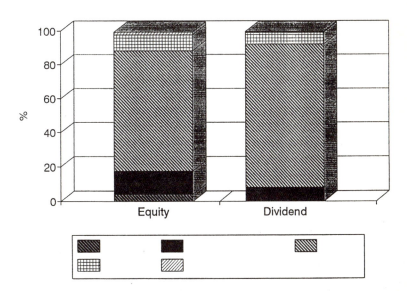

Figure 4.3   Firms in colonial Indonesia: capital by nationality c. 1930

Table 4.6   Equity and dividends in corporate investment in colonial Indonesia,
c. 1930

Distribution c. 1930

	Equity		Dividends	
	f million	%	*f* million	%
Nationality				
Chinese	150	4.0	0.3	0.1
Netherlands-Indian	515	13.8	32	8.2
Dutch	2650	70.8	329	84.1
British	358	9.6	27	6.9
Other	66	1.8	3	0.7
Total	3739	100	391	100
Selected sectors				
Sugar	473	16.5	37	11.6
Rubber	399	13.9	33	10.3
Other agriculture	624	21.8	60	18.7
Oil and mining	1026	35.9	160	50.0
Trade	340	11.9	30	9.4
Total	2862	100	320	100

Numbers of firms
by range of dividend rate (%)

	c. 1914	c. 1930	c. 1940
1 – <10	212	270	292
10 – <20	123	206	104
20 – <40	78	126	41
40 – <60	19	36	9
60 – <100	11	28	3
100 –	2	4	0
Total	445	670	449

Note: Equity refers to paid-up capital. Some American and Japanese firms failed to provide information on equity and dividends. A small part of equity in a few major companies may refer to activities outside colonial Indonesia. Dividend payments cited were actually made in1929, on occasion in1928.
Source: See *Table* 4.5.

The share of Netherlands-Indian firms in the total fell successively, from 16% in 1914 to 14% in 1930 and finally to 11% in 1940. There was a proliferation of small firms obviously geared towards performing functions in local economic life. Their average size, in terms of paid-up equity, scarcely exceeded ƒ400,000 ($160,000) even in 1930. Chinese firms were even smaller, ƒ220,000 in 1930, but it is recalled that much of the profits made in these firms were probably retained so that considerably more expansion might have taken place than shows in the equity figures alone.

Firms owned by investors from third countries, i.e. other than either colonial Indonesia or the Netherlands, occupied a middle position. They were generally larger than corporations with a head office in the colony but smaller than those with head offices in the Netherlands. Average equity amounted to ƒ1.8 million ($720,000) in 1930. The combined share of these truly foreign firms in the total rarely exceeded 12% which, however, underestimates the extent to which non-Dutch capital was invested in the colonial economy. Many third-country investors opted for setting up a subsidiary with headquarters inside colonial Indonesia. With the procedure of assigning nationalities adopted here, such subsidiaries count as Netherlands-Indian firms. Contemporary estimates using other methods of identifying the nationality of the firm suggest that the share in total equity held by capital owners in third countries was about twice as large as the 12% derived from the location of headquarters (Callis 1942: 36).

Examples of foreign-owned firms registered with headquarters in colonial Indonesia were especially numerous in mining since Dutch legislation prescribed that an explorer of mineral riches should be recognizably 'Dutch'. Shell, for instance, started out in Balikpapan in East Kalimantan in 1898 under the label of Nederlandsch-Indische Industrie- en Handel-Maatschappij (Netherlands-Indies Industry and Trade Co.) which sounded Dutch enough but was, in fact, a wholly-owned subsidiary of the London firm, as everybody in the colonial bureaucracy knew. In 1912 the main American rival, Standard Oil, at long last gained a foothold in colonial Indonesia with its subsidiary Nederlandsche Koloniale Petroleum Maatschappij (Netherlands Colonial Petroleum Co.), incorporated at The Hague with an equity of ƒ24.5 million ($9.8 million). It is a matter of interpretation whether the oil giant BPM, with 8% of all equity in the colony and headquarters in the Netherlands, should be treated as exclusively Dutch or as 40% British in accordance to the distribution of the five shares in the company between the Royal Dutch (three shares) and Shell (two).

Non-Dutch FDI was above all present in regions at the vanguard of the export-led expansion. In 1920 the Dutch share in capital investment in East Sumatra was reported at only 54%. British rubber estates accounted for the better part of 18% of the total. American rubber and Franco-Belgian interests in rubber and palm oil claimed another 11% each of total capital invested (Gruythuysen, Guleij and Tempelaars 1988: 18). Major American corporations entering East Sumatra rubber included Firestone, Goodyear and U.S. Rubber whereas the region's palm oil industry was developed by both Philippine Manufacturing, a subsidiary of Procter & Gamble, and the Société Financière (Socfin) group which was also active elsewhere in Southeast Asia, notably in Malaya and Indochina (van Zyll de Jong 1940; Gould 1961: 84–95).

Much equity obviously also means much profit and the traditional Dutch-language literature on the colonial past contains several references to the substantial gains accruing to the Netherlands from its colonial possession (Derksen and Tinbergen 1945; Baudet 1975: 439). The slice of total profits ending up with Dutch companies, as roughly indicated by dividend payments, was even larger than their already sizeable share in equity: 84% against 71% around 1930, i.e. at the culmination of the protracted export expansion. The very opposite held true for Netherlands-Indian firms: 8% of total dividends against 14% of total equity. The remainder of total dividends, 8%, was tiny and almost fully absorbed by British firms. The share of Chinese companies in dividend payments was unbelievably low, one-tenth of 1%, which only reinforces our impression of the practice of retaining earnings. Chinese firms apparently found Western-type organization, with incorporation and fixed equities, expedient when doing business, perhaps also to gain social acceptance. Yet they largely refrained from actually using the facilities offered by such a form of organization in terms of mobilizing capital for expansion and channelling returns.

The average dividend/equity ratio was 11% for the entire network. It was twice as high in Dutch firms as opposed to Netherlands-Indian ones, 12.4% against 6.2%. This difference may in part be explained by a higher propensity to retain profits in Netherlands-Indian firms which in turn follows logically from the higher degree of local entrenchment in the colonial economy. As may be inferred from various case studies in pioneering in colonial Indonesia (section 3.4), management strategies were geared towards building up reserves in large Dutch-controlled enterprises, yet rarely at the expense of dividend payments at the statutory level. This was probably quite different in Netherlands-Indian firms. There was an inverse relationship between the degree of local entrenchment and paid-out profits whereas the volume of profits increased more than proportionally as the size of the firm grew. The large Dutch firms earned relatively more on their investment and occasioned a larger outflow of funds than did their smaller compatriots on location in the colony.

Profitability did not only differ by the nationality of the invested capital but also by line of production. Oil and mining rendered more profits than did other economic activities, at any rate as judged from dividend payments. This sector of the colonial economy was responsible for a far larger share of profits (as measured by dividends) than what could be predicted from its share in aggregate equity (Figure 4.4; Table 4.6).[2] The average dividend percentage for this industry was 15.6% or 50% more than the average for the entire corporate network (11%). Other sectors reported a share in total dividends that was less than proportionate when compared to the distribution of equity. Average dividend/equity ratios in sugar, rubber and trading all oscillated around 8.5% whereas services with a rate at 10.7% stayed rather close to the average for the network as a whole.

Especially good perspectives for profit seekers were offered in industries such as cinchona in Priangan, tobacco in East Sumatra, tin in Billiton, oil refining in Palembang or Balikpapan and, finally, commercial services in Semarang, Batavia and Surabaya. Coffee appeared to be more profitable than tea and timber ranked below all major branches of export agriculture. Within the tertiary sector, finance and transport offered higher rewards to the investor than utilities and general trading.

There was a considerable variation among the individuals firms with some paying extraordinary dividends and others paying nothing. Only a

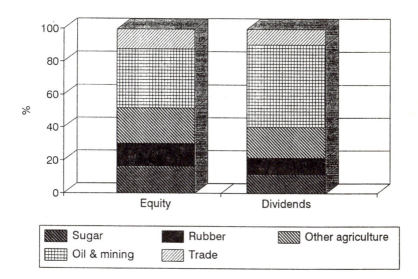

Figure 4.4   Firms in colonial Indonesia: capital by industry c. 1930

minority of firms paid out dividends in the first place. The relative size of this group of firms changed considerably over time, from 16% around 1914 to 24% around 1930 and 21% around 1940. Other firms made either no profits at all or chose to retain all earnings or did not disclose this information to outsiders. The variation in the size of this category does, however, reveal the influence of the ups and downs in economic life, i.e. initial expansion prior to the First World War, the boom of the late 1920s and the cautious recovery in the late 1930s.

Differences by range of dividend rates highlight changes in profitability levels, perhaps also in strategies between the years of observation covered by this analysis. Numbers of firms were the highest in all categories of dividend rates around 1930. There were even four small firms handing out more in the form of dividends than they possessed in equity. Such extreme generosity was displayed by the two tea estates of Santosa and Kertasarie in Priangan (200% and 198% respectively), the agricultural estate Soekaboemi near Surabaya (121%) and the Rotterdamsche Cultuur Maatschappij at Kendal near Semarang (106%).

The number of firms paying out dividends in the first place was virtually the same around 1914 and 1940, about 450, despite the fact that the entire corporate network had been reduced by almost one-quarter in the course of the depression. The least vulnerable firms survived the 1930s and these firms were, by their very viability, more likely to make profits. Interestingly, however, numbers of firms with very high dividend rates were larger around 1914 as compared to around 1940. In 1914 two firms, the BPM subsidiary Dordtsche Petroleum and the sugar factory Phaiton & Olean in Probolinggo, paid out more than 100%, whereas in 1940 Billiton with 75% offered the highest pay-out rate. In other words, profits were higher around 1914 than around 1940 but in the former year relatively more firms gave priority to building up reserves above satisfying the immediate demand for income from the overseas shareholders.

Dividend rates are likely to render the most conservative estimate of the level of actual profits since a firm will under exceptional circumstances only draw on reserves to pay shareholders. The actual profit rate was higher than the overall average rate of dividend payment which about 1930 came down to 11%. A rate of return in excess of 11% must be considered quite satisfactory from an investor's point of view, especially if we take alternatives in capital market in the metropolitan home country into account (de Vries 1989: 381). The majority of recipients of such dividend payments lived in the Netherlands or third countries.

The sizeable outflow of returns constituted a major effect of FDI in colonial Indonesia. The recent literature has witnessed a lively discussion about the outflow of profits from colonial Indonesia. This drain is often expressed as a large surplus on the current account of the balance of payments. It is the result of budgetary and exchange rate policy as well as an insufficient generation of demand for foreign imports at home. To the extent that it was excessive, by whatever measure, the drain is held responsible for the lack of economic advancement in Indonesia at the time of independence (Maddison 1989; Booth 1990: 289–94; van der Eng 1993; Lindblad 1994: 57–9). Suffice it to say here that substantial gains were indeed reaped from FDI in colonial Indonesia that could probably have been put to a more productive use in the host country economy.

The long-run impact on the economic development in the host country is highly conditioned by the sectoral composition of FDI. This determines which types of economic activity are effectively promoted by the influx of foreign capital and technology. As already noted, FDI in late colonial Indonesia possessed a twin basis combining export agriculture with mining, including oil (section 2.1). Export agriculture accounted for more than one-half of total equity as invested by 1930. Mining held more than one-third so that no more than 12% remained for trading, the sole other branch of importance. The virtual absence of manufacturing is striking and underscores the extreme dependency of Indonesia, both before and immediately after independence, on foreign markets for tropical crops and unprocessed raw materials.

Industrialization did not rank high among the priorities of economic policy in colonial Indonesia as it did for instance in Indochina. Up to 1933 the liberal trade regime failed to offer any protection against imports of goods that could possibly have been produced in the colony. The colonial government, for its part, only actively started supporting embryonic initiatives in manufacturing towards the very end of the colonial era, around 1940 (Segers 1988: 29–31).

The liberal and ethically inspired colonial state in Indonesia offered a climate conducive for massive commitments by foreign capital investors eager to seize the opportunities in foreign export markets. The accumulation of FDI gave birth to a corporate network of an overwhelmingly Dutch flavour that spread out through the entire archipelago from its base in Java. The network combined a small number of large foreign-controlled firms with a large number of small enterprises with a high degree of local entrenchment. By virtue of its size and elaboration, the corporate network itself became the most lasting impact of FDI on the economic development of Indonesia. Its strong local orientation and high profitability held promises for the future development of the host country economy but the two were not sufficiently linked. The network remained orange.

4.3   AGENCIES AT THE APEX

British imperialists carefully nurtured the myth of a worldwide empire being run in an almost amateurish fashion by a handful of leisured gentlemen dividing their time between clubs in Piccadilly and desolate corners of other continents. It was not all myth. The management of the vast imperial possessions was indeed entrusted to fewer than 6000 individuals, even in the 1890s when Britain's imperial effort reached its culmination. In India, for instance, a tiny group of administrators was said to cherish 'gentlemanly' ideals and exercise the rights of privilege while performing their nation building with a zeal born out of commitment and devotion (Davis and Huttenback 1986: 13–14; Cain and Hopkins 1993: II, 177–83). The salient point here is that the British approach to colonial administration by necessity meant advocating a far-reaching economic liberalism and keeping interventions into the social and economic fabric of overseas societies to a minimum. The British version of the colonial state differed from both its French and Dutch counterparts by its stubborn insistence on classical liberalism. This section discusses the key position played by the managing agencies in the economy of Malaya and Singapore, a position which could only materialize in an aloof colonial state.

In 1950, not long before the end of colonial rule, there were 958 foreign companies in Malaya, i.e. with owners outside the federation. It is not known how many dated from before 1942 nor the extent to which they were seconded by firms controlled from inside the federation (Annual Report 1951: 70). The corporate network was smaller than in colonial Indonesia but it was also more homogenous and to a far higher degree controlled by a small group of British managing agencies. The agency houses initially competed with each other but eventually came to strive for oligopoly control in the supply of major export commodities (Brown 1994: 252–3). The managing agencies were seen as spiders in complex webs of controlling and intertwined interests. They mobilized the capital needed to feed the export-led expansion in the early twentieth century and permanently shaped FDI in late colonial Malaya. We will briefly consider the evolution and wider implications of FDI as undertaken by managing agencies in the two leading export industries of Malaya, rubber and tin.

The rubber boom in Malaya around the turn of the century benefited strongly from the institutionalization of capital mobilization. The number of management contracts held by the six leading agency houses at Singapore doubled between 1885 and 1901 and again between 1901 and 1911. Eventually, a closely-knit group of managing agencies, including

Guthrie, Harrisons & Crosfield, Boustead and Barlow, assumed virtual responsibility for the very rapid expansion of acreage in European estate rubber in Malaya, an increase from less than 19,000 hectares in 1905 to almost 480,000 hectares by 1920 (Drabble 1972: 261; Drabble and Drake 1981: 307). A full-fledged, large-scale export industry could emerge so fast precisely because of the wide access to the London capital market.

By 1932 Malaya counted 2300 rubber estates of at least 40 hectares, of which 957, or about two in every five, were European-owned. Total planted area exceeded 750,000 hectares with Western estates accounting for 560,000 hectares or three-quarters. An overwhelming majority of the European estates, 793 out of 957, was owned by public companies with limited liability. Perak, Selangor and Negeri Sembilan, were, in that order, the most favoured locations (Grist 1933: 2–3, 5, 11, 19-22; Lim Chong-Yah 1967: 331–3). In 1938, although the total number of estates had been reduced to 2050, there were more European estates than in 1932, 996 as opposed to 957, now almost one out of every two. Numerous Chinese-owned estates had succumbed in the meantime. Significantly, only one Chinese estate measured more than 2000 hectares whereas there were 47 European estates of such large dimensions (Li 1982: 86). The capital injection from London provided for production units which were less vulnerable to downward business cycles than those of the local rivals.

Rubber in Malaya attracted much capital. By 1936 the cumulative value of new issues on the London market for this purpose was estimated at £38.8 million ($187.8 million) corresponding to one-half of all FDI in Malaya at the time (Gull 1943: 127). It is not known how much of this capital passed through managing agencies but eventually, towards the end of colonial rule, managing agencies were reported to hold at least 40% of the total equity in Malayan rubber, either directly through shareholdings or indirectly via other rubber firms. Almost all holdings by managing agencies may be classified as portfolio investment. Five agency houses alone, namely Harrisons & Crosfield, Boustead-Buttery, Guthrie, R.E.A.-Cumberbatch and Sime Darby, controlled 229 rubber firms and 324,000 hectares of estate land. Only three major conglomerates (Dunlop, Malayan American Plantations, Socfin) remaining outside their sphere of influence (Puthucheary 1960: 28–35, 44–6; Drabble 1973: 64–5). Such was the outcome of a protracted process of increasing oligopolistic control of the industry.

Control in rubber was exercised through supervision of estate management, marketing, imports and especially fulfilling secretarial functions for the newly established rubber firms. Fresh capital was provided and the managing agencies excelled in elaborating constructions of intercompany shareholdings and interlocking directorships. A group of 25 individuals sat on the board of 200 odd rubber companies and Sir Eric Macfadyean of Harrisons & Crosfield acted as the spokesman of an entire industry. The oligopolistic system smoothed a rapid enlargement of output and secured comfortable profit margins, as is evidenced in the experiences of Guthrie and Harrisons & Crosfield (section 3.3.). A rare estimate of total profits quotes a figure of $70 million in Malayan rubber for 1937 when world markets were recovering (Khor 1983: 58). Profits at that level would correspond to a rate of 37% which appears extremely high.

Tin used to be a Chinese prerogative in Malaya. This seemed to change only marginally at first, during the closing decades of the nineteenth century. There was a proliferation of small British firms entering the industry and coexisting with the Chinese producers. The boom started in Pahang in 1883. By 1895 no fewer than 28 companies had been floated in London to raise funds for investment in mining facilities. A second wave of establishing joint ventures with Chinese miners followed in the years 1895–1913 when 83 new mining corporations were floated (Wong Lin Ken 1965: 124–5, 214). Just as in the rubber industry, the British agency houses provided the channels for quick access to investment capital. However, the shareholdings in the newly created firms were, in fact, portfolio investment rather than FDI in the strict sense of the term.

The first decade of the twentieth century saw a worldwide reshuffling in the production of tin. Cornwall lost where Southeast Asia gained. The breakthrough for European tin in Malaya came with the introduction of large-scale dredging around 1907. This was a major technological innovation which put European firms at an immediate advantage above the Chinese competitors. The share of European mines in the total output of tin in Malaya reached 22% in 1910 and rose further to 36% in 1920 and 63% in 1930. There is some confusion in the literature whether the position of European mines grew stronger or weaker during the international tin restriction during the 1930s but the high share at 60–65% at the end of the 1940s is undisputed (Lim Chong-Yah 1967: 65–7; Li 1982: 66, 82). Tin in Malaya forms one of the most clear-cut illustrations of how foreign capital could gain control over an entire industry by virtue of a technological lead.

Several leading managing agencies in Malaya participated in the tin boom but their role in building up the subsequent industry remained far less pronounced than was the case in rubber. A possible explanation may lie in the larger scale of production units which favoured a consolidation of ownership rather than networks of control through management contracts. A small group of agency houses did, however, play a crucial role also at a later stage by setting up new mines thus gaining control over a sizeable part of the total tin output of the colony (Puthucheary 1960: 54–8). A prominent member of the group was Harrisons & Crosfield where the directors had taken an almost instinctive interest in tin as soon as the first dredges came into operation.

Oligopoly, or even monopoly, power soon held sway in the industry. In 1925 the London Tin Corporation (LTC) was established and gained an immediate hold on tin mining in Malaya. Its wholly-owned subsidiary, Anglo-Oriental (Malaya) Ltd., provided management services to 19 major tin firms with between them 40 dredges and an output of 18,000 tons or one-third of the total output from European mines. Anglo-Oriental worked not only for other firms in the LTC group but also for subsidiaries of the other leading parent company among tin firms, British Tin Investment. In addition, Anglo-Oriental was connected, via interlocking directorships, with agency houses such as Osborne & Chappel and Neill & Bell. These two firms rendered management services to subsidiaries of both British Tin Investment and General Tin Investments, yet a third major parent company among tin mines. To make matters even more complex, General Tin and LTC counted among the largest shareholders in British Tin (Allen and Donnithorne 1957: 157, 160; Puthucheary 1960: 85–94; Lim Chong-Yah 1967: 69–70; Yip 1969: 184; Burke 1990: 48–9). Ownership was concentrated in few hands to an extraordinary degree in the tin industry of Malaya.

Oligopolies are generally associated with wide profit margins and tin was no exception to the rule. In 1937 the tin mines of Malaya were said to generate almost as much revenue for their owners as the entire European rubber sector, $58 million or 45% of the profits in the rubber and tin industries taken together (Khor 1983: 58). Contemporary estimates asserted that less capital was invested in tin than in rubber. This would imply, then, that profit rates were even higher in tin than in rubber (Callis 1942: 57). The flow of profits to the international tin concerns abroad constituted the most immediate effect of FDI in mining in Malaya. Other effects of FDI pertain to the generation of employment, the use of modern technology and spill-overs to new lines of production.

Tin mining was, and still is, a relatively capital-intensive line of production but the rapid enlargement of output and initial low levels of productivity guaranteed that much new employment was generated. In Perak, the foremost tin region, a peak was reached in 1913 with no fewer than 126,000 workers, a figure that may be compared with the 57,000 tappers on the European rubber estates in Malaya a couple of years earlier. But mechanization set in and in 1929, at a peak output of 71,300 tons, total employment in the tin industry amounted to 100,000 workers. The depression and the simultaneous international restriction scheme forced down output to 37,000 tons in 1934 whereas employment was reduced to one-half, to 50,000 labourers. Substantial productivity gains only materialized in particular in the 1950s when employment fell further still whereas output levels remained largely constant (Lim Chong-Yah 1967: 68; Jackson 1968: 239; Loh 1988: 11). Just as on the European rubber estates, the employment effects emanating from the Western tin mines in Malaya were substantial precisely because mechanization lagged behind.

The most immediate forward linkage in the tin industry is smelting and this materialized in Malaya. The Straits Trading Company was founded by 1887 and it expanded quickly, taking over numerous local Chinese smelters. The two major plants of Straits Trading were located on Pulau Brani and in Butterworth. For some successive decades this company was the foremost smelter in the region also processing tin from Bangka and Belitung, at any rate up to the establishment of the Dutch smelter at Arnhem in 1937. Early expansionary efforts even included an attempt at acquiring a ten-year monopoly on the tin from Thailand. The request was declined but Straits Trading possessed such an advantage above competitors that it eventually received most of the supply from Thailand also without monopoly rights (Brown 1988: 102–3).

The sole rival of consequence in Malaya was the Eastern Smelting Company which was based on the takeover of a Chinese smelter at Penang in 1907. In 1929 Eastern Smelting merged into the newly established Consolidated Tin Smelters. The latter firm cooperated closely with LTC and also acquired shares in the Dutch smelter at Arnhem (Allen and Donnithorne 1957: 156–61). The forward linkage was an integral part of the oligopolistic structure in the Malaya tin industry. It contributed to the continuous outflow of profits and offered little incentive for still further processing or manufacturing using tin as an input.

The managing agencies in Malaya have been criticized for squeezing aside Chinese capital in mining and retarding industrialization altogether (Jomo 1986: 183–7, 271). Such an assertion suggests that Malaya, just like colonial Indonesia, possessed a real chance for experiencing a take-off into self-sustained economic growth at the time of the export-led expansion prior to the Second World War. It is tempting to associate the missed opportunity with the extreme liberalism and aloof nature of administration that characterized the British colonial state in Malaya. It was the type of colonial state that left a vacuum, in turn filled by managing agencies that remained by and large oriented towards the interests of the capital owners in Britain. The agencies were at the apex of the corporate structure that arose by means of FDI in Malaya. They enjoyed the powers and profits of oligopoly and left an inheritance with future potential.

4.4   UNDER *COMPADRE* COLONIALISM

The first Manila Carnival was organized in 1908 primarily by American businessmen who said they believed in 'Oriental' development and were not afraid 'to take a chance' (Gleeck 1975: 4). Adventure and a pioneering spirit formed the ideology of the first generation of American investors starting out in the early years of the twentieth century when it had become evident that the USA intended to retain its new colonial possession. Several of these businessmen had a background as army suppliers, arriving in Manila with the American troops in 1898 or shortly afterwards. They came to function in an environment of an outspoken economic liberalism with a legislation favouring exports to the USA, especially after the Underwood-Simmons Tariff Act had come into effect in 1913. There was an immediate link between business in the Philippines and the American market which, significantly, survived colonial rule itself and effectively remained in force until 1974 when the Laurel-Langley agreement expired.

As a young nation, which itself had felt the pangs of decolonization at its birth, the USA took a different approach to colonialism from the older metropolitan mother countries in Europe. There was a strong current of anti-imperialism underlying American colonial rule in the Philippines. The USA never assumed full power over the social and economic life in the Philippines. Perhaps more importantly, American colonial authorities did not intend to do so. A first step towards Filipinization of the administration had been taken by 1901 when the municipal government was entrusted to the indigenous population, a measure which would have been unthinkable in French Indochina, colonial Indonesia and British Malaya. The first Philippine legislature assumed its nation building tasks with great enthusiasm in 1907 and in 1935 Manuel Quezon became president of the newly formed Philippine Commonwealth. The path to full independence began early and combined the idealism of the American commissioners with the self-confident participation by the traditional Filipino élite (Jenista 1971: 78–9; Owen 1971: 3–9). The colonial administration developed into a kind to ritual parenthood in which American 'Godfathers' guided their younger Filipino partners towards self-assertion in both politics and economics. This was accompanied by substantial American investments in human capital through new institutions for secondary and tertiary education.

The *compadre* colonialism of the USA in the Philippines was characterized by openness and optimism. The investment climate was liberal with few restrictions to entry for investors from third countries. This resulted in an unusual diversity in the composition of FDI by nationality. The prospects for eventual independence and a greater Filipino autonomy also in economic matters seemed to inspire confidence rather than apprehension and conservatism. Joint ventures between American firms and Filipino businessmen flourished, especially in the 1920s and 1930s. The pattern of FDI as it evolved under the auspices of the American-style colonial state will be further explored here by linking a few key industries with main investors.

Abaca had found its way to the American market long before 1898. This strong fibre, used to make ropes, was a virtual Philippine monopoly. It accounted for two-thirds of total export revenues around 1900. British and American exporters had penetrated the Manila market already in the 1880s but the true breakthrough for American capital in this industry came in 1904 when International Harvester took over the Cebu offices and warehouses of the leading British merchant Macleod. Subsequent years saw a rapid expansion of the abaca estates which continued up through the 1930s. Japanese investment in this industry were so voluminous that the foremost supply region, the estates along the Gulf of Davao, acquired the name 'Davao-ku'. The local price in Davao was estimated at 60% of the export price, excluding costs of baling and freight, which hints at the sizeable profits that could be made (Hartendorp 1958: I, 32, 58; Gleeck 1975: 29–30; Owen 1984: 66, 107).

In 1923 Tubbs Cordage Co. of San Francisco set up at factory at Manila to benefit from the readily available supply of fibre and the lower wages of Filipino workers. This cordage factory, which still exists, is interesting in at least two respects. Tubbs Cordage was a rare example of a type of FDI that gained prominence in Southeast Asia only after the colonial period. It also represented a potentially important forward linkage of a kind that seldom materialized elsewhere in the region. Eventually, there were five cordage factories in operation but the scale remained modest. Combined assets were valued at only $3 million and employment did not exceed 1000 persons. The forward linkage in abaca was only of marginal importance compared to the primary line of production (Shepherd 1941: 98–9; Gleeck 1975: 84–5).

Sugar was much favoured by legislation. The peace treaty after the war of 1898 included an obligation to continue delivering sugar to Spain but this agreement expired in 1909 and was replaced by the Payne-Adrich Tariff Act which opened up the American domestic market for Philippine sugar. A wave of construction of American-financed sugar factories ensued, including San José in Mindoro, San Carlos in Negros and Calamba in Laguna, all in operation by 1912. A major participant in this boom was the Atlantic, Gulf and Pacific Corporation, established in 1900 and known for draining the moats of downtown Manila in the first couple of years of its existence. Total investment in sugar factories was estimated at 185 million pesos ($92.5 million) in 1935. A sizeable proportion of this capital was owned by Filipino *hacenderos* who borrowed money from the Philippine National Bank and eventually became the first indigenous millionaires in the Philippines (Hartendorp 1958: I, 30–31; Gleeck 1975: 12–14; Yoshihara 1985: 32–3).

The foreign interest focused on processing in other lines of export agriculture. Copra, for instance, became an industry with almost as much capital invested in sugar but, again, with a very large share held by indigenous residents. Foreign participation was concentrated in processing that in turn accommodated only 5% of total investment done in this industry. Seven of the eight large coconut plants set up in the 1920s were foreign. Only two of them were American. Rubber, however, never caught on as a major export crop, possibly because of American legislation limiting landholdings by corporations to a maximum of 1000 hectares. Tobacco was far smaller than both rubber and copra but here the old Spanish dominance remained in force (Hartendorp 1958: I, 30–32). In fact, the country's largest corporation, SMC, retained its 'Spanish' character as late as the 1960s when board meetings were still being conducted in Spanish.

There was an unmistakeable tendency towards manufacturing in American investment flowing into the colony. This was reflected in the high American share in processing industries as compared to the proportions held by Filipino, Chinese or third country investors. In the 1930s the share of American firms amounted to one-half in both cordage manufacturing and sawmilling, one-third in sugar refining and three-quarters of the embroidery industry (Porter 1938). In 1914 the colonial government started to encourage embroideries in rural Luzon. American entrepreneurs moved in and succeeded in altering a top quality production for high society in Manila and Cebu into low cost production for mass consumption in the United States. Some European rivals, even including French and Belgian nuns who had arrived earlier, were instantly squeezed out of the market. In 1935 about 30 export firms procured the rural product and sold it abroad, almost exclusively in the USA. American businesswomen played a conspicuous part in the boom which as such was highly unusual in FDI in general in Southeast Asia at this time. Embroideries run by women included the firms of Louise Brown, Elaine Elser and Daisy Embroidery Co. (Hartendorp 1958: I, 33–4; Gleeck 1975: 58, 69–73).

American investment in the Philippines continued to increase. The precise volume of accumulated American capital in the Philippines is difficult to ascertain for several reasons. One is a question of definition referring to the extent to which assets held by permanent American residents in the

Philippines should be considered 'foreign' in the first place, a matter akin to the distinction between 'Dutch' and 'Netherlands-Indian' capital in colonial Indonesia. Another ambiguity concerns whether or not to include the very sizeable American holdings of real estate in the Philippines. Suffice it to say here, i.e. without resolving these two matters conclusively, that estimated aggregates range between $100 million (in 1923 and 1935) and $260 million (in about 1930). It is likely that there was a peak around 1930, in excess of $200 million, a decline during the depression towards some $165 million and a rather quick recovery to at least $200 million during the late 1930s and early 1940s (Facts 1924: 52; Lockwood 1936; Callis 1942: 22; Chapman 1946; Robequain 1954: 325; Hartendorp 1958: I, 54–5; Subido 1975: 54–66; Valdepenas and Bautista 1977: 137; Tsuda *et al.* 1978: III, 52–3; Golay 1983: 135; Hicks 1993: 204–5). Prospects remained bright for American investors in the face of pending decolonization.

American 'permissiveness' was held responsible for the massive entry of non-American capital, especially towards the end of the colonial period (Goodman 1983: 45, 58). Japanese British and firms moved in whereas Spanish and Chinese enterprises remained strongholds in the shadow of the American multinationals. But not all investors were interested in the same types of economic activity. By the end of the colonial period a segmented pattern of capital investment had emerged in which specializations developed by the nationality of the investor (Figure 4.5; Subido 1975: 54–66; Tsuda *et al.* 1978: III, 2–6). American firms were well represented in several industries, in particular export agriculture (sugar), mining (gold) and services (utilities). The Chinese focused on trading, with rice milling as a line of secondary importance. The Spanish firms stayed with the old sugar and tobacco estates. British capital was particularly active in financing the Manila railroad, with the remainder dispersed over several industries. The Japanese investors favoured abaca which absorbed as much as one-half of the Japanese total whereas trading followed in the second rank. Such patterns of specialization or division of labour along lines of the investor's nationality remind us of the situation in, for instance, colonial Indonesia where sugar and tin were virtually monopolized by Dutch capital whereas the Anglo-Saxon share was conspicuous in rubber.

Openness and optimism about incoming FDI and its post-colonial role are two sides of the same coin. Both indicate a relatively weak link between FDI and the colonial state. In this respect the Philippines formed the very antithesis of Indochina. The American colonial authorities probably spent significantly less on improving the physical infrastructure than did the zealous executioners of Sarraut's *mise en valeur* policy in Indochina. There was more competition, more indigenous participation

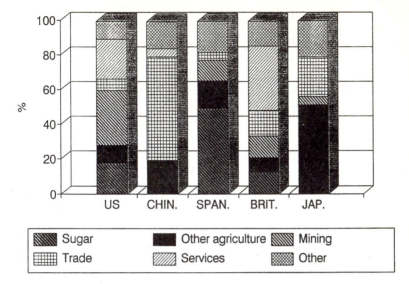

Figure 4.5   FDI in the Philippines: composition by investor, 1940

and more diversification in the Philippine pattern of FDI. The creation of a class of Filipino entrepreneurs was actively promoted through joint ventures. There was a shift, however modest, away from primary production to manufacturing and some forward linkages did materialize that anticipated the industrialization efforts elsewhere in the region by decades.

We have come full circle. American liberalism formed the other extreme on the scale of colonial policy measured by the degree of interventionism. French exploitation of the natural resources of Indochina explicitly served the interests of the French bourgeoisie. Such a statement of purpose was necessary in order to safeguard a massive flow of public funds to the colony. The explicit ambition of 'uplifting' the indigenous people fulfilled exactly the same purpose in colonial Indonesia. This colony represents an intermediate case on the scale ranging from French Indochina to the Philippines under American rule. Yet the rhetoric, in whichever direction, must not lead us astray. The rationale behind FDI in the colony was to develop the host country's economic potential by making use of its natural riches. Whether this development was 'exploitive' or not is primarily a matter of standards and criteria. This is most clearly demonstrated by the discussion on the colonial drain. The outflow of profits was substantial. It takes some twisting of arguments to make plausible that such outflows represented no more than a warranted return of invested capital.

The impact of FDI on the host country is in part, though not completely, determined by the rationale behind FDI. This chapter has shown that both the character and impact of FDI were shaped by the peculiarities of the colonial state in each host country. A line of demarcation runs between Indochina with its highly interventionist *mise en valeur* and the other colonies where *laissez faire* ruled. In Indochina the influence of the colonial administration became manifest in the form of an improved infrastructure and belated targets for new industrial production. In colonial Indonesia the elaboration of a vast local network proved compatible with a large drain of profits. In Malaya oligopoly power prevailed which limited production to the exploitation of the country's rich natural endowment. In the Philippines American tolerance facilitated diversification and indigenous participation without jeopardizing the interests of American business at home. Good roads in Indochina, integrated economies with an external drain in Indonesia, a hierarchy of powerful agencies in Malaysia, optimistic Americans in Philippines: such was the heritage of foreign investment inside the colonial states of Southeast Asia.

4.5   ON MEASURING COLONIAL INVESTMENT

The statistics on FDI in the colonial period leave much to be desired. The published estimates provide neither continuity over time nor sufficient detail. There are two ways of alleviating these shortcomings. One is to extrapolate time series on FDI from related macro-economic variables. The other implies constructing a database on FDI from data on the micro level, i.e. about individual firms. These two methods are applied to French Indochina and colonial Indonesia respectively.

The French method assumes that investment volumes can be inferred from the colonial budget and the foreign trade statistics. The equation works as follows. Public investment consists of two parts: the sum of grants for interior investment projects, registered by province, and a sizeable proportion of loans incurred to finance further expenditures in Indochina. This proportion is assumed to be 50%. Public investment, thus calculated, is subsequently subtracted from total imports of capital goods. Private investment of French capital then appears as the residual.

Private investment = capital goods imports − public investment
Public investment = interior investment + 50% of loans

This method was designed by Professor Cathérine Coquery-Vidrovitch at Université Paris VII in 1981. The method and resulting estimates have

since then gained acceptance in the literature (Marseille 1984: 117–18).
The data were kindly put at my disposal in 1993. My results are presented
in Table 4.4.

The Dutch database draws on a directory listing all formally incorporated business firms operating in colonial Indonesia. The directory was
published each year between 1888 and 1940 and offers a very complete
picture of Western-owned corporations and a less than complete coverage
of Chinese firms in particular. The directory gives the following information for each individual enterprise: name of the firm, year of incorporation
or change of statutes, nominal and paid-up equity, latest dividend percentage paid, type of activities, locations of headquarters, branch offices and
production sites, names of trustees, directors and local administrators. The
extreme degree of disaggregation is a source of both strength and weakness
in the directory. It enables the researcher to explore fully the nuances and
variations in the corporate network but it also makes processing extremely
labour-intensive and time-consuming. The information in this source has
been fully extracted for the period 1888–1913 and complete samples have
been built up for the years 1914, 1930 and 1940 (Lindblad 1991; Handboek
1914, 1930, 1940; à Campo 1995; 1996). Results based on these three
samples are brought together in Tables 4.5 and 4.6.

5 Low Tide and High Hopes

The chairman of United Temiang (FMS) Rubber Estates, B. Russell, probably exaggerated slightly when he formulated the board's conclusion: 'We may be wealthy but there is no point in throwing money down the drain'.[1] The occasion was an extraordinary general meeting of shareholders of this rubber firm within the Guthrie group held on Tuesday, 29 December 1959. Annual profits at the time neared £49,000 or 20% of issued equity in United Temiang, but there was no room for extravagant investment plans. The imminent dangers and the many casualties of the Emergency in Malaya had produced a policy of extreme caution among British managing agencies symptomatic for foreign investors in general in Southeast Asia between the 1940s and the 1960s when uncertainties abounded even with respect to the very near future. Few could imagine how dramatically this was all going to change again in the 1960s.

This chapter is about the times of transition at mid-century when the climate for FDI in Southeast Asia underwent exceptionally rapid change. It argues that a decisive break with the past was necessary for a return to the favourable climate for FDI in much of the region. First two widely divergent patterns of transition are illustrated by reviewing some experiences of two neighbouring host countries, Thailand and Burma (section 5.1). Then our attention shifts to the strategies of accommodation which were required in the face of decolonization in host countries such as the Philippines, Indonesia and Malaysia (section 5.2). The final topic here concerns the gradual improvement of the FDI climate from the 1960s in most host countries (section 5.3.). This improvement was a process possessing both common traits and features specific for the individual host country.

It should be stressed that this chapter does not provide an exhaustive survey of the economic development in Southeast Asia between 1942 and the mid-1960s. That is a topic in its own right which is too broad for our scope of analysis. The countries of Indochina, i.e. Vietnam, Laos and Cambodia, are left out of the discussion since this again would require a separate treatment of the links between colonial warfare, the exodus of French capital, the influx of American capital and eventual Communist victories. These topics are interesting in their own right but a full treatment would take us too far afield from the main concern of this book, which, after all, is primarily the impact of private FDI on economic development in host countries.

5.1 SEEDS OF REVOLUTION

It did not all begin with the Japanese occupation and the subsequent acceleration of decolonization. The first step towards a radical alteration in the FDI climate of Southeast Asia was taken outside the colonial territories, in Thailand in 1932. The bloodless coup d'état in Bangkok in June 1932 not only ended the absolutism of the Rama kings but it also meant the gradual introduction of more nationalist economic policies that, by definition, discriminated against Chinese and foreign capital. The revolution of 1932 caused much nervousness among foreign firms and the final outcome was the emergence of a bureaucrat class of indigenous capitalists that eventually was to predominate in private capital accumulation in Thailand (Thompson 1938; Suehiro 1989: 106–34).

The nervousness among foreign investors in Thailand in 1932 was not without reason. Foreign control over the export-oriented part of the Thai economy had grown considerably since the pioneering days of the East Asiatic Company and logging around Chiang Mai at the end of the nineteenth century. The pendulum swung from trading to teak and tin. Bucket dredging was introduced in Phuket in 1907 by Tongkah Harbour Tin which had been set up with British funds only the year before. The newly founded foreign dredging companies pocketed profits cited at five times initial outlays. Total FDI in tin mining in Thailand increased to 234 million baht ($104 million) by the late 1920s. Almost all tin mines using advanced technology were in foreign hands. Most of them had British owners (Ingram 1971: 99–100; Manarungsan 1989: 150–2; Suehiro 1989: 66–8).

A network of foreign business firms grew up at Bangkok in the early decades of the twentieth century. The East Asiatic was still the undisputed doyen of the foreign business community but it was joined by enterprises such as the Borneo Company, Bombay-Burmah Trading, British-American Tobacco, Mitsui Bussan Kaisha and the Swiss merchant Diethelm & Co., to name but a few. Some relied on special ties with the Thai royal family. The teak logger Leonowens was founded in the 1890s by Louis T. Leonowens who had, as the son of Chulalongkorn's English governess, in fact been brought up with the king in the 1860s. The premises of the merchant house John Sampson & Co. counted among the most elegant in Bangkok and the firm had delivered Chulalongkorn's riding boots already when the king visited London. British influence was enhanced during the First World War when the Hongkong and Shanghai Bank assumed control over the Siam Commercial Bank which had previously been managed by German bankers.

There was an exceptionally strong Danish component in foreign business in Thailand which may be attributed to the leading part played by the East Asiatic. Siam Electricity was incorporated at Copenhagen in 1898 with the purpose of acquiring concessions for tramways and electrification in Bangkok. The first manager was Aage Westenholz from Denmark who, like Hans Niels Andersen at the East Asiatic, benefited from close contacts with the du Plessis de Richelieu clan. Siam Cement was founded in 1912 with the royal family as principal shareholder and Danish engineers as managers. One of the very few manufacturing industries at the time was launched around 1920 by Siam Industries Syndicate which imported Danish flints to make soap under supervision of engineers from Copenhagen (Macmillan 1923: 141–81).

The strong position of foreign capital in Thai economic life may be illustrated by a survey of those 166 companies that gained official recognition during the three decades leading up to the 1932 revolution (Figure 5.1; Suehiro 1989: 12–13, 101–2).[2] Companies with a majority of Europeans on the board constituted less than one-third of the total, 51 out of 166 firms, but commanded more than one-half of total equity as stated at registration, 39.5 million baht out of 75 million baht. This included the Siam Electricity Company which had an equity of 22.5 million baht.

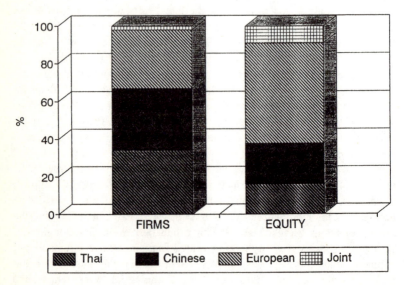

Figure 5.1   Corporations in Thailand: distribution by nationality, 1901–1932

The share of Chinese firms, again as designated by ethnic origin of board members, was also about one-third but their proportion of total equity was scarcely more than one-fifth whereas genuinely Thai companies were about as numerous but smaller still on average. At a slightly later stage, towards the end of the 1930s, Chinese assets were estimated at nearly 1.2 billion yen ($300 million) which was almost as much as all assets held by foreign corporations between them (Hicks 1993: 207).

The fears among foreign businessmen in Bangkok in 1932 were exaggerated in the sense that no nationalizations ever occurred and few overt discriminatory measures were taken in the short run. Still the investment climate was undeniably changing and this became all the more apparent when the foreign managers returned to reopen businesses after the conclusion of the Japanese occupation. Political instability was rampant and the new leaders from 1947, Phin and Phibun Songkhram, launched the slogan 'Thai economy for the Thai people' which scarcely encouraged new FDI.

In 1954 European capital in Thailand suffered a severe blow when the old teak concessions around Chiang Mai were not renewed. Foreign firms adapted by shifting into other types of economic activity such as light manufacturing where virtually only the Siam Industries Syndicate, Unilever and the Swedish Match Co. had been active before the Pacific War. The East Asiatic started producing pharmaceutical goods and foods, Leonowens turned to auto parts and the Borneo Company took an interest in cosmetics and machinery. It is ironic, viewed with the benefit of the historian's hindsight, to observe how foreign investors became pioneers in precisely those fields that held the future but only because they were being squeezed out of their traditional strongholds (Intarathai 1974: 40–45; Suehiro 1989: 173–7). In the meantime little new FDI arrived (Yoder 1957).

In neighbouring Burma the initial situation looked very similar but events there took an entirely different turn. British capital traditionally predominated in vital lines of export production such as timber, oil, rubber and tin. In 1938 logging in Upper Burma employed 53,000 labourers and produced 7% of the colony's total export revenue. Most of the long-term leases in teak logging were with European firms and Bombay-Burmah Trading ranked first. Burmah Oil was responsible for three-quarters of the total crude output. Dividend payments at this company averaged 22% during the years 1922–1938. The European share in manufacturing in the 1920s was 25% overall but 90% when it came to enterprises with at least 200 employees (Walinsky 1962: 43–5; U Khin 1970: 45).

Burma became the prototype for the kind of FDI that met with contempt and disgust among nationalists throughout Southeast Asia. FDI under the protection of the colonial state was not only held responsible for the outflow of profits from the exploitation of the host country's natural riches. It was also charged with depriving local competitors of the best opportunities to set up viable production lines and reap the gains from exporting to an expanding world market. According to a Burmese scholar, FDI had a 'decapitating' impact on the indigenous Burmese entrepreneurship (Aung 1989: 43, 68). The economic nationalism throughout Southeast Asia during the immediate post-war decades can only be understood against the background of this resentment of virtually any FDI on the part of the indigenous population.

Work in Burma was resumed in January 1946 and the output of logs reached prewar levels within a couple of years. Yet the unrest in the colony persisted and grew ever more intense, especially after the assassination of designated first president Aung San in 1947. Insurgents captured storage depots and logs were set adrift. Nationalization of the foreign forest concessions was a prime objective of the government of Sao Shwe Taik that took over as independence was acquired in January 1948. An agreement was negotiated with Bombay-Burmah Trading which turned over all assets, including inventories, elephants, equipment and up-country properties, to the Burmese state in exchange for some 44,400 tons of logs. The company transferred personnel to Thailand but soon found out that foreign teak operations were discouraged at the new destination also. New possibilities in logging soon materialized in Sabah and a new subsidiary, North Borneo Timbers, was incorporated at Sandakan. Eventually, this firm was to be taken over by the Malaysian government (Pointon 1964: 101-4, 108, 115). The gradual exodus of Bombay-Burmah Trading from Southeast Asia mirrors the change in the climate for FDI throughout the region as a whole.

British capital interests lingered on in other sectors. In 1951 one-quarter of Burma's tin production was still controlled by Anglo-Oriental (Malaya), flagship in the LTC group. Numerous rubber estates in Mergui did, however, change hands and become Burmese property at this time. The area held by British-owned estates declined from 14,000 hectares in 1936 to 6,200 hectares by 1950 (Tin 1959: 161; Lim Chong-Yah 1967: 69; Voon 1973: 224-5). Uneasiness multiplied among European businessmen during the 1950s as successive governments expressed anti-Western rhetoric.

The final reckoning with FDI came after the coup of 1962 under the communist dictatorship of Ne Win who styled himself a 'Buddhist Socialist'. Local branches of Imperial Chemical Industries were nationalized in August 1962, Burma Oil followed suit in January 1963 and the banks became public property in February. The Enterprise Nationalization

Law of 1963 stipulated appropriation of all major industries whilst the People's Stores Corporation was set up in September that year to take over consumer industries and trading firms (Steinberg 1981: 31).

Thailand and Burma represent two extreme cases where conditions of FDI changed fundamentally and permanently. It was gradual change against abrupt intervention and social revolution against decolonization. The points of departure looked much alike but the outcome was very different. In Thailand the basis was laid for a later partnership between strong domestic investors and foreign firms whereas Burma was effectively sealed off for Western capital and influence for decades to come.

5.2   IN SEARCH OF CONTINUITY

The Philippines was the only country in Southeast Asia where decolonization virtually coincided with not only post-war reconstruction but also, and more importantly, with an official attempt to restore investment by private firms from the former mother country. War damage payments were linked to American investment through a controversial amendment on American-Filipino parity to the constitution of the Philippines. The amendment was vigorously defended by President Mañuel Roxas but it met with vehement opposition from nationalist quarters. The intention of Roxas was to persuade American firms to use their war damage payments for investment in the Philippines and hopefully to add some of their own funds as well. Substantial interests were at stake with the American Congress authorizing payments of $125 million in total to indemnify property losses in the Philippines. The parity amendment did pass the referendum with a wide margin but the heated discussion about it had exposed anti-American sentiments that were there to stay, occasionally even slipping into presidential rhetoric, for instance when President Carlos Garcìa took office after Ramon Magsaysay's death in 1957 (Hartendorp 1958: I, 159; Gleeck 1975: 108). The settling of old accounts with the onetime metropolitan mother country was a common feature in major former colonies in Southeast Asia. This section surveys the Philippines, Indonesia and Malaysia. This allows us to contrast cases of continuity (the Philippines and Malaysia) with a situation where discontinuity prevailed (Indonesia).

At first American investment in the independent Philippines retained its traditional emphasis on extraction and estate agriculture but not for long. There was a shift towards manufacturing in the early 1950s that coincided with the imposition of new import and exchange controls. As a result, the emphasis in foreign American investment shifted from export orientation to import substitution. Colgate-Palmolive opened a factory in downtown Manila in 1950, Vick's followed in 1953 with a factory in Makati and the new large Caltex refinery came into operation in 1954.

Filipinization was strongly favoured by successive governments and several joint ventures were set up. In 1955 Goodrich supplied 44% of equity in the tyre plant of the Tuason family, promising to help the Philippines to attain self-sufficiency in rubber and, in return, being promised that no other foreign rubber firms were to be invited. The first promise was kept but not the second one. In 1958 Firestone appeared on the stage in a joint venture with the Ortigas family. Some years later, a controversy with Filipino shareholders about dividend payments in the subsidiary eventually induced Goodrich to turn its minority holding into a majority share thus taking an action that ran counter to both official policy and its own original intentions.

Another famed joint venture took place in one of the rare experiments with heavy industry in the Philippines. In 1956 Union Carbide combined with a successful Filipino lawyer, Guillermo Guevara, to erect a carbide and ferro-alloy plant next to the Maria Cristina Falls in Mindanao. The American parent company withdrew in 1970 as it, allegedly, could not exercise sufficient control over its subsidiary, Maria Cristina Chemical Industries (Gleeck 1975: 109–11, 129–30, 138–9, 140–42; Yoshihara 1985: 60–5, 68).

Filipinization also occurred in the wake of American withdrawals and not only for reasons of dissatisfaction with internal communications as with Union Carbide. Many American firms chose not to await the expiration of the Laurel-Langley agreement in 1974 but withdrew in anticipation of changing conditions. This applied to sugar mills dating from the early twentieth century and also to mining where American corporations were exempted, under the Laurel-Langley stipulations, from the requirement that exploitation be carried out by firms with a Filipino share in equity of at least 60%. The transfer of mines to Filipino owners started in 1968 with the sale of a controlling interest in Lepanto Consolidated, successful in both copper and gold, a transaction which, incidentally, was made possible by a loan from a New York bank. Filipinization in mining eventually turned out very costly for the state as heavy financial support was often needed, at first in the form of loans and later, after defaulting payment, as equity holdings (Gleeck 1975: 104; Yoshihara 1985: 65–7; McKern and Koomsup 1987: 273–4).

Cumulative American investment, defined as net equity and outstanding loans to subsidiaries actually controlled, increased from $150 million in 1950 to $230 million in 1955, $400 million in 1960 and $530 million in 1965, all in current prices which thus also reflects some inflation (Tsuda

1978: II, 30–34). In the final analysis, new augmentations exceeded withdrawals by far. The differences in the increase by five-year period, 53% in 1950/55, 73% in 1955/60 and 33% in 1960/65, mirror first the rise of import-substituting investment in manufacturing and later increasing Filipinization. American investment in the Philippines expanded but the growth soon slackened off. By and large, however, American predominance in FDI in the Philippines did remain intact. In the 1960s eight of the ten largest foreign corporations in the Philippines were still American: Caltex, Esso, Atlas Consolidated Mining, Mobil, Granexport, Bataan Refining, Procter & Gamble and Lepanto, in that order. The other two were the Royal Dutch/Shell in the second rank and the Chinese tobacco manufacturer La Suerte, ranking sixth (Cagampang-de Castro 1977: Table VI).

It is tempting to explain the growth pattern of American investment in the Philippines immediately after independence in terms of responses to an investment climate riddled with ambivalence: overt encouragement as opposed to President García's slogan 'Filipino First'. A rigid statistical analysis, however, brings us much closer to the hard facts of business results. By way of regression analysis, it can be demonstrated that the rate of return was the single most important factor explaining variations in American corporate investment, the dependent variable, as it had been accumulated up to 1971. Measures of general economic growth, monetary stability, tariff protection and wage rate differentials all explain less of the build-up of assets in the Philippines by American multinationals (Subido 1974: 243–4, 258). Yet, profit maximization cannot be considered entirely in isolation from the investment climate. The expected rates of return express an unmistakeable optimism with respect to the consequences of anti-American rhetoric and Filipinization. After all, withdrawals of American capital were voluntary and above all conditioned by the nearing expiration of the Laurel-Langley agreement.

The quest for continuity between the colonial and post-colonial situations was very strong in the Philippines, both among American corporations and within successive Filipino governments. Continuity as such was not the issue. It was more a matter of negotiating a mode of investment acceptable to both parties. The situation in Indonesia was very different.

Dutch firms were, in general, bent on staying on in Indonesia. During the confusing years of the late 1940s considerable effort was devoted to setting up production anew. The installations at the oil refineries had suffered much damage during the war with some, e.g. at Balikpapan in East Kalimantan, in fact having been destroyed twice, first by the Dutch in 1942 in the face of approaching Japanese, then in 1945 as the Japanese armies left. Extensive areas of land at the tobacco and rubber estates in

East Sumatra had been occupied during the war. Many of the new cultivators were less than inclined to take leave as the European supervisors returned. Uncertainties for the future were aggravated by the very fact that the archipelago was now partly controlled by Dutch colonial authorities, and partly by the young Indonesian Republic (Reid 1979: 148–77; Lindblad 1988: 115).

Problems multiplied for foreign firms in the early 1950s. Exchange controls limited the possibilities of importing equipment and high duties were levied on exports. In 1954 the Sukarno government imposed a tax of 66 2/3% on all profits to be remitted abroad. Agricultural estates were confronted with restraints on foreign land ownership. There was a proliferation of labour disputes, thefts and illegal occupations. In addition, the rate of inflation rose and 'exorbitant' wage demands were raised. One reaction was to shut down and leave altogether which is what happened with, for instance, the General Motors plant at Tanjung Priok near Jakarta (Allen and Donnithorne 1957: 135; van der Kroef 1955). Dutch firms tried to stay in operation as long as possible. Yet there was a greater tendency than before to repatriate profits as opposed to reinvesting in production facilities in Indonesia. It has been estimated that returns averaging ƒ200 million ($53 million) were dispatched from Indonesia to the Netherlands during the years 1954–1957 (Meijer 1994: 529).

Diversification was a common strategy of adaptation. Statutory modification at, for instance, Michiels-Arnold opened up the possibility of moving into economic activities other than agriculture in Indonesia. Billiton expanded into mining outside Indonesia and major trading companies started exploring markets in Africa or South America. The sugar company Handels–Vereniging Amsterdam (HVA) attempted to transplant the experiences with Java cane to Ethiopian soils but this met with little success (Goedkoop 1990). There was a growing appreciation of the necessity to spread risks, especially as the conflict between the Dutch and Indonesian governments about the future of New Guinea (Irian Jaya) escalated. The long-run perspective of investment, so much cherished in colonial days, was gone for good.

The Dutch-Indonesian conflict reached its climax in December 1957 and early 1958 when all Dutch properties were nationalized. The nationalizations affected 489 Dutch corporations, including 216 plantations, 161 mining and industrial establishments, 40 trading firms and 16 insurance companies. One of the nationalized firms was the Deli Company which was henceforth to be operated as an Indonesian state enterprise. Eventually, it was acquired by the American United Leaf Tobacco. Lengthy negotiations resulted in a promise of the Indonesian authorities to pay $167 million as indemnification starting in 1965. Oil received preferential treatment as the Indonesian authorities realized that the input of foreign-controlled technology was indispensable in keeping the refineries in operation. Special arrangements were made to secure a continued stay of the Royal Dutch/Shell in Indonesia (Creutzberg 1977: 32–5; Carr 1978: 117; Pangestu and Habir 1989: 20).

An immediate outcome of this first wave of nationalizations in Indonesia was the very substantial reduction of accumulated FDI in the country. In addition, the composition of remaining FDI was dramatically altered in favour of American investors in particular. Traditional strongholds of American capital in Indonesia, oil and rubber in Sumatra, now formed the backbone of FDI. American investment had been growing fast during the 1930s, the late 1940s and continued to do so after 1950. The estimated aggregate value of American-owned investment rose from $130 million in 1949 to $262 million in 1954 and $401 million in 1959. Meanwhile, the position of oil within American commitments grew even more pronounced. The share of oil in the American total rose from 69% in 1949 to 89% by 1959 (Gould 1961: 79). The foundation of today's predominance of American oil in the Indonesian export economy was laid during the reshuffle of FDI in the 1950s.

Standard Oil had been able to expand rapidly in the late 1920s and throughout the 1930s as its subsidiary in colonial Indonesia, the Koloniale, acquired a concession near Palembang in South Sumatra which, ironically, had been discarded as worthless by the Royal Dutch. Shortly after the war and not without foresight, the name of the subsidiary was changed into Stanvac, short for Standard Vacuum Petroleum Co. P.T., and under this label the facilities at Palembang were enlarged. Caltex joined shortly after 1950 exploiting rich oil fields near Pekan Baru in Riau. Caltex grew faster than its rivals and its new refinery at Dumai on the Straits of Malacca was soon the largest in the country. In 1957 Caltex accounted for no less than 47% of the total crude output with Shell delivering 23% and Stanvac 20%. Upon the nationalization of Dutch properties, a joint venture, Permindo, was formed between Shell and the Indonesian government to replace the joint venture set up in the 1920s between the Dutch state and the BPM for the exploitation of the oil resources in Jambi (van der Kroef 1960; Gould 1961: 68–77; Esmara 1975: 36–7; Ooi 1982: 10).

The concluding years of Sukarno rule brought an ever harsher climate for foreign investors and there was even a shift favouring incoming capital flows from the Soviet Union. Joint ventures with COMECON companies followed but the accompanying inflow of FDI remained modest. In 1966 COMECON participation in the main joint ventures was valued at only $12 million or one-sixth of the foreign capital employed through production-sharing in the oil sector (Gibson 1966: 81, 85). The *Konfrontasi* with Malaysia

(1963/65) brought about a second wave of nationalizations, now directed against American, British, Malaysian and Belgian possessions. The marketing facilities of Stanvac and Caltex were appropriated in June 1965 and in December Pertamina purchased the Shell properties for $110 million (Shakow 1962; Oei 1969: 35–41). A major difference with the first wave of nationalizations lies in the more temporary effect of the second one since much of the nationalized property was returned already in 1967. This, however, did not apply to the Royal Dutch/Shell. In the final analysis Dutch investment was permanently squeezed out of independent Indonesia.

In 1957 accumulated FDI in Indonesia was still valued at $1.1 billion or one-half of the level which had prevailed at the end of the 1940s. The further decline in the early 1960s brought the value of the total FDI stock down to a mere $254 million (Oei 1969: 42; Carr 1978: 111; Wong 1979: 177). Such a steep decline reveals that replacements lagged badly behind and that some disinvestment in fact took place. This was the true abyss of FDI in modern Indonesia.

The desire to remain in business under almost any circumstances prevailed among British managing agencies in Malaysia. The Emergency (1948-1957) meant fear, casualties and widespread banditry. Substantial loans were released to repair war damages in the European tin mines in particular, on average M$650,000 ($213,000) per dredge, but aggregate output declined as life at remote production sites became unsafe (Yip 1969: 27; Loh 1988: 68). The rubber estates encountered difficulties as well. Killings in and near the estates controlled by Guthrie were particularly frequent in 1950/52 and 1954/55. Casualties during the Emergency were reported at 93 European planters and 218 Asian staff members for the entire European estate sector.[3] A major difference with the colonial period concerned the prospects of FDI involving large outlays in installations or products with a gestation period. Foreign investors in Malaysia in the 1950s did not have the time to wait for rubber trees to become mature and productive.

Yet the Emergency was not a time only of stagnation. Harrisons & Crosfield seemed more troubled by working in Sumatra than by the constraints to enlarging estate areas on the peninsula. The agency house consolidated its position in Malaysia through a series of merges and consolidation. As a result, three groups of rubber firms evolved within the Harrisons & Crosfield concern, namely Golden Hope, Pataling and London Asiatic (Allen and Donnithorne 1957: 53–5; Pugh *et al.* 1990: 178–9). Meanwhile, there was a dramatic increase in establishments of foreign firms in Singapore, many of whom were fleeing the insecurity in

Malaysia. During the first three years of the Emergency alone, no fewer than 88 new foreign firms opened offices in downtown Singapore (Report 1951: 1–2).

The impact of the Emergency on the operations of foreign firms in Malaysia may be illustrated by a case study pertaining to the Guthrie-controlled United Temiang estate company during the years 1946–1959 (Figure 5.2).[4] Turnover was very low in the late 1940s but climbed towards a peak in 1951. Disruptions put their mark on output and revenue especially in 1953 and 1954 but conditions improved as the Emergency drew to a close. The extraordinary times induced the authorities to impose an export tax which severely reduced rates of return from 1952. The pretax rate only fell below 20% during the 'bad' years of 1953 and 1954 but, if we account also for the export tax, the rate of return stayed below 10% throughout the rest of the Emergency, even touching zero in 1953. The troubles of the day were probably more intensely felt at the local level of production than in headquarters abroad.

Malaysia became independent but the power of the leading managing agencies was largely intact. Five leading firms, Harrisons & Crosfield, Guthrie, Boustead-Buttery, the Borneo Company (later Inchcape) and R.E.A.-Cumberbatch, controlled 220 firms in Malaysian manufacturing

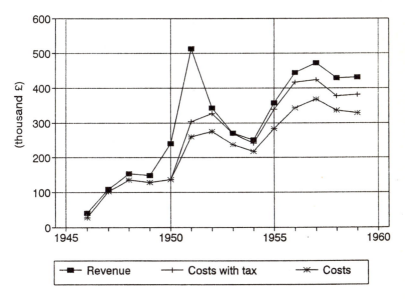

Figure 5.2   FDI results in Malaysia: United Temiang, 1946–1959

alone as of 1965. Annual average rates of return on non-oil assets held by British investors in Malaysia and Singapore during the first half of the 1960s were reported at 15–30% (Davies 1969: 55; Saham 1980: 115). The major form of adaptation to the new situation was the separation of British and Malaysian branches of the original agencies. This was done, for instance, at Boustead in 1960 and Guthrie in 1961. The increasingly local base of British firms facilitated continuity into the immediate post-colonial period.

Foreign ownership in the Malaysian economy thus remained far more widespread than in Indonesia. In the late 1960s accumulated total FDI was reported at M$3.6 billion ($1.2 billion) which corresponded to as much as one-half of gross fixed assets (Saham 1980: 34). The strikingly high share of rubber in this total, 49%, does, however, suggest that much of these assets consisted of holdings dating from colonial days and that little of new kinds had been added since then. In Singapore, foreign assets amounted to an unimpressive S$157 million ($51 million) when the city state gained full independence in 1965. Two-thirds of this was in oil and 45% was British-held (Hughes 1969: 190; Doshi 1989: 5).

There were no forced nationalizations in Malaysia but the traditional predominance of British capital in major lines of export production gradually vanished as the New Economic Policy (NEP) was implemented from about 1970. The NEP aimed at bolstering indigenous Malay (*bumiputra*) control over productive assets. Even if Chinese businessmen formed the foremost target of the NEP, a continued British hegemony in tin and rubber was clearly at odds with the aims of the policy. The Malaysian government adopted a strategy of takeovers. Newly established state enterprises purchased equity from British capital owners, thus achieving the combined aims of indigenization and Malayanization. The transactions were financed by profits made by state enterprises, e.g. by Petronas in oil, and also by extensive foreign credits easily extended since the growth perspectives for the Malaysian economy appeared very favourable (Faaland, Parkinson and Sanisman 1990: 78–80). The takeovers in the name of NEP formed a protracted aftermath of decolonization.

LTC was acquired in stages. In 1973 a Singapore firm, Haw Par Bros. International, bought 29% of the LTC equity and in 1975 the major agent of Malaysian state business, Pernas, purchased 21%. Resistance among British shareholders was broken as LTC was no more majority-controlled from London and it did not take long before Pernas acquired the rest of the equity through a complicated partnership with Charter Consolidated as a minority holder. By 1977 the Pernas subsidiary Malaysian Mining Corporation (MMC) was already making substantial profits from operating the former LTC mines. In total, Pernas paid M$170 million ($68 million) for LTC (Thoburn 1981: 82–3, 157).

Principal rubber holdings dating from colonial times were localized and the national capital corporation, Permodalan Nasional Berhad (PNB), gained a controlling interest in several groups, including Guthrie (60%), Sime Darby (60%, augmented by 18% held by MMC) and Harrisons & Crosfield (58.5%). But the Malaysian state wanted to get one step further and the interest of British shareholders in retaining the Malaysian possessions was waning. It was now more a question of the price at which the final takeover was to be realized. In 1981 the remaining shares in the Guthrie subsidiary (40%) were raided on the London Stock Exchange and the Malaysian state became the sole owner of the country's largest estate conglomerate. At the same time Sime Darby merged the economic realm of the Malaysian authorities.

The joint venture between Harrisons & Crosfield and the Malaysian state, the Harrisons Malaysian Plantations Berhad, was set up only after five years of tedious negotiations and guaranteed a minority voice for the British agency house (Clad 1989: 58; Pugh *et al.* 1990: 214–17, 248–52; Keiko 1991: 376). The negotiations were retarded by the slogan 'Buy British Last', much in vogue at the time in Malaysia, and also by the exceedingly complex ownership arrangements within the Harrisons & Crosfield concern, a web of cross interests between subsidiaries and parent companies that was likened with an 'incestuous relationship' (*Financial Times* 24/1 1978). The Malaysian government reportedly paid £150 million ($73.5 million) for its participation. The equity still held by the Harrisons & Crosfield parent company, however, came up for sale in 1989 at a price of $240 million. Buyers were the Malaysian government and a Kuwait/Abu Dhabi combination (*FEER* 16/3 1989). The alternatives to nationalization could turn out rather costly for the host country.

The transition at mid-century from enclave settlements under the protective umbrella of colonialism to today's negotiations with independent nation states formed the most profound disruption of continuity in the history of FDI in Southeast Asia during the twentieth century. Economic nationalism served as a uniting force but for the rest there was a variety of experiences by host country, ranging from the gradual rise of domestic capital formation in the Philippines to outright hostility as in Indonesia in the latter half of the Sukarno period. Malaysia occupied an intermediate position, only ridding itself of British predominance during the aftermath of decolonization in the 1970s and 1980s. The foreign investors generally attempted to accommodate and make the best of the situation. This held equally true for American corporations in newly independent Philippines, Dutch estates in Sukarno's Indonesia and British managing agencies in Malaysia. But it was largely in vain because they fought for a forlorn cause. A new dawn neared in FDI in Southeast Asia.

5.3   A CHANGE OF CLIMATE

Policies with respect to FDI were altered under Sarit in Thailand (from 1959), Abdul Rahman in the Malaysian federation (from 1963), Lee Kuan Yew in independent Singapore (from 1965), Marcos in the Philippines (from 1965) and Suharto in Indonesia (from 1966). All had in common that there was a tradeoff between attracting as much fresh FDI as possible and priorities of national economic policy such as economic growth and self-determination. Four of the five, Thailand, the Philippines, Indonesia and Malaysia, opted for a mix of incentives and restrictions. Singapore chose the most liberal path of all by refraining from specific legislation with respect to FDI while offering numerous incentives for multinationals entering the city state. Actual developments of incoming capital flows have induced the former four to revise their attitudes and to improve actual enforcement. Increasing deregulation since the mid-1980s has implied a convergence of policies. Singapore, however, has ever since enjoyed a solid reputation for providing the most favourable FDI regime of all. In this section we shall review the changes in the climate for FDI in each of these five host countries, i.e those ASEAN member states experiencing a resurgence of FDI since the 1960s.

In Thailand existing legislation at the time of the Sarit coup expressed the legacy of Phibun's economic nationalism with the Investment Promotion Act of 1954 putting a ceiling to foreign equity ownership at 49%. This requirement was soon relaxed as the Board of Investment, founded in 1959, started its task of promoting private industrial enterprises with domestic as well as foreign ownership. The Board issues promotion certificates to investors that favour resource development, exports and employment. Under the revised Investment Promotion Acts of 1962 and 1977 firms with promotional status are eligible for exemption or reductions in import duties on foreign raw materials and equipment and may also enjoy tax holidays during the initial stage of operation (at first five years, later three to eight years). There are no restrictions on the repatriation of investment capital and profits and additional deductions are allowed for investments improving local infrastructure. Registration with the Board of Investment is not compulsory. It is advised for convenience and in order to obtain promotional status. Foreign investors have been know to shun Board involvement, possibly out of fear of having a requirement imposed of a future transfer of ownership into Thai hands. Such firms have foregone the benefits of promotional status but also avoided much red tape. As a result, Board of Investment data fail to offer a complete picture of FDI commitments. In addition, holdings by Sino-Thai combinations are registered as 'domestic investment' which blurs the overall picture anyway (von Kirchbach 1983: 70–84; Lauwerier & Schermer 1987: 101; Country Report 1990: X, 8; Investing 1991: 110–30).

The Thai Act on Promotion of Industries of 1959 distinguished between three categories of exemption or reduction in payment of import duties and taxes. Vital and necessary industries, e.g. metal manufacturing and chemicals, receive full exemption, less vital and necessary industries, e.g. assembly manufacturing, only pay one-half whereas industries with promoted status of lesser urgency pay two-thirds. Yet another three-tiered classification, by foreign share in equity, was created with the Alien Business Law of 1972. The first category consists of reserved areas in the primary and tertiary sectors, e.g. rice farming and construction, for which at least a Thai majority (on occasion even 60%) is required. A foreign majority, up to 100%, is allowed in the second and third categories embracing respectively firms where this was already the case by 1972 and manufacturing firms producing for foreign exports (Ingram 1971: 288–90; Lauwerier and Schermer 1987: 104; Suehiro 1989: 181; Lim and Pang 1991: 47).

In the 1960s, when the scale of activities of the Thai Board of Investment was still rather modest, about one-half of the promotion certificates went to foreign firms, primarily engaging in joint ventures with Thai enterprises. Japan was the prime source of foreign capital accounting for one-third of all foreign equity capital committed whereas United States and Taiwan taken together were responsible for another one-third of the total. The emphasis was on labour-intensive manufacturing serving to substitute imports with many industries scarcely counting as 'vital and necessary' by the classification of 1959 (Ingram 1971: 292; Viravan 1972: 232; Tambunlertchai 1977: 111; Suehiro 1989: 181). By 1985 the Board of Investment had granted promotional status to 1670 individual firms of which 809 had foreign equity but only 48 were fully foreign-owned. Foreign equity represented only 28% of total equity involved. Japan, United States and Taiwan, in that order, still supplied the bulk of the foreign capital registered. The foreign equity share was especially high in oil and gas exploration and in the most diverse branches of manufacturing (Chunanunthatham *et al.* 1987: 47, 125).

Persistent criticism regarding inefficiency and corruption at the Board of Investment in Bangkok brought reform of the institution in the course of the 1980s. Investment Service Centres were set up to aid foreign investors and procedures were speeded up to the extent that processing at the Board of Investment is now likened to the separate bus lanes in the congested Bangkok traffic. Current priorities include decentralization outside the Greater Bangkok area and additional local-ization incentives are available but actual accomplishments in this vein have so far stayed far below the targets (Jungnickel, Gerberding and Maenner 1986: 73; Business and Investment 1987: 34; Schlossstein 1991: 147).

Thailand only completes and reinforces our impression of FDI at un-impressive magnitudes in the immediate post-war decades. Incoming FDI amounted to $38 million in 1954 and an average of 927 million baht ($45 million) in the second half of the 1960s (Yoder 1957; Suehiro 1989: 187). A cumulative total of initial paid-up foreign capital was quoted at merely 5039 million baht ($241 million) for the 1970s but this figure apparently covered only firms that had received promotional status which was by no means a prerequisite (Pongpissanupichit 1985: 168, 179). Still there were signs of change. FDI flows were diverted from their traditional stronghold in trading in the 1950s to manufacturing in the late 1960s. Significantly, of the 5700 foreign-controlled firms, including all joint ven-tures of whatever size, operating in the Bangkok-Thonburi area around 1960, less than one in ten had been established before the war (Brief Information 1960: xi–xv).

Selectivity marked legislation on FDI in the Philippines from the start on the liberal path. Under the Investment Incentives Act of 1967, as modified by the Foreign Business Regulation Act of 1968, foreign partici-pation was generally limited to 40%, on occasion even 30%, of equity. Only pioneer status would qualify for full foreign ownership during the initial stage of operations. Some service branches, e.g. banking, retail trade and public utilities, were reserved for Filipinos altogether. All foreign investors had to register with the newly established Board of Investment. Japanese firms in particular soon complained that they were eligible for a mere token share of equity and only moderate reductions in payments of duties or taxes. More could be attained only under excep-tional circumstances, e.g. when Kawasaki Steel bought back the steel factory it had once set up and sold to the Philippines government a few years earlier because the factory was now running at a loss (Yoshihara 1978: 87; von Kirchbach 1983: 199; Yoshihara 1985: 73).

Yet fresh FDI was slow in forthcoming, especially as the expiration date of the Laurel-Langley agreement (1974) drew nearer and the internal situa-tion deteriorated. Public policy was more effective in lifting controls and reducing uncertainties at election times than in offering incentives. However, shortly after martial law had been declared, in 1972, new incentives were added to attract more FDI including tax credits on interest payments, tax reductions on dividends and income and also exemptions from the unpopular export tax (Subido 1975: 213, 222–3; Yamada 1978: 102–3). Foreign firms were not convinced by these rather marginal improvements of the FDI climate. They were more likely to be held back by the political situation and the poor performance of the Philippine economy at large. From 1986 the Aquino administration made a deliberate effort to turn the downward tendency in FDI. The Omnibus Investments Code of 1987 illustrates how more flexibility is provided by a number of exemptions to the existing regulations. Firms producing exclusively for foreign exports can be fully foreign-owned and firms with pioneer status may take 30–40 years in reducing the foreign share from an initial 100%. Registration with the Board of Investment is no longer required unless the foreign share exceeds 40%. The foremost incentive is an income tax holiday of four to six years for firms with pioneer status under the newly formulated Investment Priorities Plan (UNIDO 1988: 55; Investing 1991: 7–89).

Soliciting of new FDI was explicitly tied up with solutions of the acute debt crisis inherited from the Marcos regime. This implies a strong preference for export orientation in granting pioneer status and also a direct subsidy on inward investment through the debt/equity scheme introduced in August 1986. Under this scheme creditors may receive shares, usually at a discount, in Philippine corporations instead of repayments in cash. By 1988 almost $1500 million of debt capital had reportedly been converted into equity in this fashion with no less $945 million (63%) involving foreign capital owners (European Companies 1987: xv–xvi; Bowe and Dean 1990: 24–6; *FEER* 28/6 1990). Such subsidization of FDI underscores that full liberalization in the Philippines was only achieved under pressure of external circumstances and considerably later than elsewhere in the region. The liberalization of the Philippine climate for FDI has been bearing fruit since about 1991.

The most dramatic turnabout in FDI policies took place in Indonesia. The Foreign Investment Law of 1967 first and foremost provided guarantees against nationalization and expropriation. Property was returned to several multinationals, e.g. Unilever, Bata, Goodyear, British and American Tobacco and Heineken, and agreements were concluded with Dutch firms in particular about the payment of compensations for the nationalizations under Sukarno in 1957/58. Generous tax holidays were offered and so were exemptions from payment of import duties and allowances for accelerated depreciation of newly acquired equipment. The first major contract was concluded in April 1967 with Freeport Copper committing $75 million to its giant copper mine at Tembagapura in Irian Jaya and offering a share in profits of 36–42% to the Indonesian state (Arndt 1967: 30–31; McKern and Koomsup 1987: 168–9; Hill

1988: 29–31). During the first three years projects worth about $1100 million were approved under the new regime, primarily in mining. Billiton returned to its onetime tin concession on the island of Singkep and a fully-fledged mining enclave arose around the INCO nickel exploitation at Soroako in Central Sulawesi (Clapham 1970; Thoburn 1981: 80; Robinson 1986: 29–35, 265–74).

But the honeymoon for foreign enterprise in Indonesia was short. The Tanaka riots in Jakarta in January 1974 prompted the Suharto government into immediate action to unequivocally pursue national economic interests above those of foreign capital. Indonesianization was prescribed in all industries under the administration of the BKPM which had been set up only in the preceding year. A domestic majority share of equity had to be realized within ten years. In addition, the requirements for hiring Indonesian personnel were stiffened and tax incentives were curtailed. The more restrictive investment climate in Indonesia coincided with the massive influx of foreign revenue as a result of the first round of drastic increases in world oil prices (Rosendale 1974: 23; Hill 1988: 30–31). The Suharto regime could afford to respond to popular resentment of excessive foreign control over the economy.

The shift towards a more restrictive stance reflected the intention of the Indonesian government to make the most of its bargaining power with respect to multinationals. This must be considered against the background of the colonial past and applies in particular to the arrangements concluded in the exploitation of the country's natural riches, both in oil, mining and forestry. The concession system, much in vogue during the colonial period, had been terminated by Sukarno and replaced by contracts of work including provisions for the Indonesian state to share in profits. Similar arrangements applied to Caltex and Stanvac from 1963 and also to the first comers in mining in 1967, e.g. Freeport Copper and INCO. Contrary to what the term suggests, the foreign firm did not operate as a subcontractor to the Indonesian state but functioned independently, just as under the previous concessionary agreements. Such an aloof involvement on the part of the Indonesian state was deemed less than desirable and the late 1960s and early 1970s saw the gradual introduction of production-sharing in oil, a new type of arrangement designed to let Indonesia benefit more from its prime asset that also set an example for neighbouring countries wishing to get a better bargain (Kusumaatmadja 1974: 21–3; Johnson 1977: 36; Lukman and McGlinchey 1986: 75; McKern and Koomsup 1987: 178–9, 200–203).

In Indonesian production-sharing the state, i.e. Pertamina, controls management whereas the foreign firm executes the work programme. Two-fifths of the final product are used to recover costs and the remainder is split between state and contractor. The proportions of the split form the most clear-cut indication of how liberal the arrangement is. It began with 65% for the Indonesian state and 35% for the foreign oil company. Numerous contracts were concluded and the new arrangement was considered 'not unattractive'. The subsequent change to a 70/30 split met with little opposition but the shift to 85/15, or even 88/12, in 1975 caused an outcry among the large American oil companies operating in Indonesia. The pace of expansion in Indonesian oil slowed down. The Indonesian state had apparently reached beyond its maximum bargaining power (Hunter 1971: 98, 101–4; Chia 1983: 228; Khong 1986: 37–50, 147).

Even if production-sharing arrangements are not directly comparable across countries, it is instructive to take a brief glance at the percentages in the split elsewhere. At first sight the foreign oil company often appears to be more favoured than in Indonesia, e.g. in the Philippines (60/40) or in Malaysia (70/30) (Khong 1986: 197–204; McKern and Koomsup 1987: 235–7; Beredjick and Waelde 1988: 242). The most extreme case of a liberal investment climate in oil in Southeast Asia is represented by Brunei where conventional 50/50 profit-sharing still applies and Royal Dutch/Shell is permitted to make very generous deductions before calculating profits (Hamzah 1981). Indonesia under Suharto seems to have maximized gains from its powerful bargaining position in oil.

In Indonesia the old concessions system is retained in forestry where joint ventures were increasingly established from about 1970 between foreign multinationals and local participants, often military. There are wide variations in profitability and an urgent need to strengthen enforcement and combat corruption. Foreign observers have recommended the Indonesian government to rely on corporate taxes rather than on royalties from concession agreements (Ruzicka 1979: 61, 73; Dickie and Layman 1988: 103–4).

The tendency towards a more restrictive investment climate in Indonesia continued until 1984 when even the tax holiday on new projects was abolished. For a long time, however, the tightening was less than effective. FDI continued to increase. Annual incoming FDI, including equity and intercompany loans but not reinvested earnings, rose from $1.2 billion in 1974 to $3.2 billion in 1983. Then, in the mid-1980s, came the worldwide slump in both oil and trade in general. Incoming FDI in Indonesia stagnated at an annual average of $2.7 billion. This appeared all the more alarming since oil prices were falling at precisely that time and the need was widely felt in Indonesia to reduce dependency on oil and gas exports. This brought a return to liberalism.

A series of deregulation packages came into effect during the years 1986–1990. The most striking novelty was the relaxation of the requirement for Indonesianization of equity ownership. Foreign firms fulfilling one of three conditions, i.e. large scale, high export content or remote location, could now start out with an Indonesian share in equity of just 5% and firms exporting all of its product would be exempted from any subsequent increase in the share of the Indonesian partner. The major incentive was a two-year exemption from payment of import duties and value-added taxes. In addition, administrative procedures were shortened and made more transparent through simplified versions of the *Daftar Skala Prioritas* (list of priorities) which served as a guideline for decisions by the BKPM. This list was later replaced by a negative list, a *Daftar Negatif* (Dickie and Layman 1988: 131–4; Halim 1988: 196; Hill 1988: 32–3; Simandjuntak 1989: 323; Investing 1991: 34–51). Results soon materialized with cumulative approvals at BKPM climbing from $15.4 billion in 1986 to $28.4 billion in 1989 (*Indonesia Development News* 1990: no. 6).

The successive swings from liberalism to restriction and back again in the climate for FDI in Indonesia illustrates, perhaps better than anything else, the perpetual host country dilemma in much of today's Southeast Asia. Foreign capital is badly needed to speed up economic growth and the path must be eased for multinationals but domestic capital should not be squeezed aside and as much as possible of benefits accruing from FDI ought to remain in the host country. In this respect the Suharto regime obviously contrasts markedly with the preceding Sukarno administration but there has been less continuity than what might appear at first sight. In fact, the attitude of the authorities has been perceived of as lukewarm, at best, throughout most of the *Orde Baru* (New Order). The need for still further deregulation is frequently voiced in the current discussion on FDI in Indonesia.

Malaysia displays fewer swings of the pendulum than Indonesia. It is rather a peculiar special case where incentives to foreign investors have been overshadowed by the NEP and its ambitious targets of radically altering ownership patterns in the economy. The Investment Incentives Act of 1968 combined five-year tax reliefs with pioneer status, a construction borrowed from Singapore that corresponded to promotional status in Thailand and found application in the Philippines as well. Pioneer status was granted in accordance with national priorities and tax holidays could under certain circumstances be extended for another five years. A coordinating body, the Malaysian Industrial Development Authority (MIDA), was set up in 1970 and the FTZ in Penang started operations in 1972. The usual incentives were offered with tax allowances depending upon export orientation, local content of inputs, employment generation and location in 'promoted industrial areas'. There were promotional activities to attract more FDI from Japan, in particular in the early 1980s, but the initial enthusiasm surrounding this 'tango with the Japanese' soon soured into disenchantment. Just as in Indonesia, deregulation emerged as the panacea of reform in the late 1980s (Schlossstein 1991: 236; Tan and Lim 1992: 89–98). Judged exclusively from the viewpoint of legislation pertaining specifically to FDI, the climate in Malaysia appeared no better and no worse than in other Southeast Asian countries (except Singapore).

The NEP, launched in 1970 by the ruling party United Malays National Organization (UMNO), was a reaction to the crisis following the anti-Chinese riots of May 1969. The twin main objectives of the NEP were rapid economic growth and a more equitable distribution of economic power among ethnic groups of which the latter was difficult to reconcile with attracting much new FDI. According to original targets, foreign equity in the corporate sector should not to exceed 30% by 1990. The redistribution of equity was to be attained through a more active involvement of state enterprise and a reshuffling of shares to the benefit of *bumiputra*. The Foreign Investment Committee was established in 1974 to supervise such operations and authorized to intervene in individual enterprises if need be whereas the Industrial Coordination Act of 1975 sharpened requirements in terms of the ethnic distribution of employees (Lim 1983; Yew 1988: 25; Jesudason 1989: 79, 137; Faaland, Parkinson and Sanisman 1990: 49). Even if the NEP was primarily aimed at a redistribution of ownership among domestic subjects, it was from the very start unpopular with foreign firms. Almost one-half of the respondents in a survey among American multinationals in the 1980s identified the NEP as the single most important disincentive to investing in Malaysia (Schlossstein 1991: 237).

The sluggish performance of FDI in the 1970s and 1980s, in combination with economic stagnation, forced the Malaysian government to reconsider priorities. The Mahathir administration opted for a pragmatic implementation of the NEP sacrificing a quick realization of redistributional targets to the promotion of economic growth. Requirements for *bumiputra* ownership of equity were relaxed and under the Promotion of Investments Act of 1986 equity may be fully foreign-owned if more than 80% of the product is exported. There was even a special offer, valid up to the end of 1990, allowing 100% foreign ownership at a lower export content (minimal 50%) provided there was no domestic competition and at least 350 jobs were created for Malaysian subjects (Investing 1991: 52–69).

Meanwhile, the NEP has given way to the NDP, effective from 1991, in which the pragmatic approach to implementation has been institutionalized. The NDP avoids specifications of targets for *bumiputra* participation thus offering a more liberal and, above all, more flexible framework for shaping the actual climate for FDI in the near future (Ariff 1992: 13). Malaysian policy has showed a cyclical pattern vaguely reminiscent of the one in Indonesia, i.e. from initial liberalism to rigid restrictiveness, pragmatism and a renewed liberalism. But the underlying considerations were widely different and so was the outcome.

Singapore prides itself on offering the most liberal investment climate in all of Southeast Asia. Since the entry of foreign capital is totally unrestricted there was no need for any specific legislation or even formal approvals. By implication there are no restrictions on repatriation of funds nor are there regulations concerning ownership distributions. The main form of encouragement, for foreign and domestic investors alike, remains the pioneer status as introduced by the Pioneer Industries Ordinance in 1959 and reformulated under the Economic Expansion Incentives Act of 1967, i.e. shortly after full independence had been attained. From the outset pioneer status has carried tax holidays of five to ten years that may be extended depending upon possible additional income generation due to the expansion of activities. Special benefits are available for a high share in manufacturing exports and if new technologies are implemented in production (Yoshihara 1976: 25–7; Ariff and Hill 1985: 20; Investing 1991: 90–109).

By the early 1970s pioneer status had already been awarded to several hundred companies, both foreign and domestic, but annual average inflows of foreign capital, including reinvested earnings, were still below S$500 million ($179 million). This figure was to rise above S$2 billion ($935 million) only from 1979 even exceeding S$5 billion ($2.4 billion) after 1986, long after favourable conditions for FDI had been created. This lends some credence to the belief, already expressed in the late 1960s, that pioneer status and tax holidays played only a secondary role in the decision whether or not to invest in Singapore (United Nations 1992: 263; Hughes 1969: 183).

Deregulation has swept through Southeast Asia since the mid-1980s as a panacea to the problems of red tape and excessive bureaucracy that abounded. But not all paths have been eased and striking differences still exist between host countries that may be of some importance, however secondary, in inspiring enthusiasm among investors. In 1990 the required time of processing applications for FDI was the shortest in Singapore, almost always less than three months, and the longest in Indonesia, frequently above six months. The number of bureaucrats involved in each procedure was the smallest in Singapore, virtually always three or fewer, and the largest in Indonesia, often more than ten. In Thailand about one-half of the respondents said that three to six months passed before the administrative procedure was completed while two-thirds of the investors had each entertained contacts with three to ten officials. Malaysia and Philippines occupied intermediary positions on both accounts (*Asian Business* 1990: no. 12). Efficiency in dealing with FDI thus appears to be strongly related to the degree of liberalism in government policy.

Each of the five original ASEAN member states designed a unique solution to the problem of maximizing attractiveness for foreign capital at a minimum infringement upon national priorities. Thailand chose for long-run stability from an early point whereas the Philippines needed long to catch up with the rest. Indonesia and Malaysia both switched back and forth between openness and self-assertion but for different reasons. In both countries ethnic tensions played a part in redesigning FDI policies whereas the existence of rich natural resources offered opportunities to try out the host country's bargaining position vis-à-vis the foreign multinational. Singapore stayed open all the time. A ranking by the degree of liberalism in the FDI climate can be intuitively inferred from host country strategies as they have evolved since the mid-1980s. It would place Singapore first followed by Thailand, Malaysia, the Philippines and Indonesia, in that order. Compared to a ranking by investors around 1980 this represents a marked improvement for Thailand (Chia 1982: 264–8). The low rank for the Philippines on this scale coincides with a slow or stagnating influx of FDI but the same logic does not hold true for Indonesia. Even if a liberal regime and all sorts of incentives may make little difference in the final analysis, it is obvious that an unfavourable climate does act as a major deterrent to new FDI.

Prevailing conditions of FDI could not be sustained when colonialism came to a close, even if many investors thought they could go on doing business as usual after the political conditions had changed. The profound break with the past had been anticipated before the war and its aftermath was felt long after the change of policies in the 1960s. Only after this discontinuity could the pendulum swing back towards more liberal FDI policies. The return to liberalism was marked by movements in both forward and backward direction but, in the end, all major host countries jumped onto the worldwide bandwagon of deregulation. Continuity was restored in FDI in Southeast Asia but the face of capital had changed beyond recognition.

6 The New Investors

1994 data from the Japan External Trade Organization (JETRO) show that Mitsui, Mitsubishi and Marubeni between them had 42 subsidiaries or branches in the five original ASEAN member states. Hitachi, market leader in electrical appliances and electronics, conducted its business in Southeast Asia through 37 plants and offices throughout the region. In total JETRO listed more than 3000 firms in Southeast Asia in which the share of Japanese owners amounted to 10% or more (JETRO 1994: 41–66, 85–280). Japanese firms of all dimensions, *sogo shosha* and large manufacturers as well as medium- and small-sized enterprises, played first fiddle during the resurgence of FDI in the region and continue to do so during today's penetration of virgin territories, for instance in Myanmar (formerly Burma) and Cambodia (*FEER* 1/2 1996). This chapter is about the emergence of new patterns of FDI in Southeast Asia since the 1960s.

An investor-specific approach is adopted which aids us in focusing on motivations and strategies on the part of the foreign investor rather than on the impact of FDI on the host country economy. Compared with our discussion of the inception and implementation of FDI during the late colonial period, the emphasis here is on the aggregation of multinationals hiding behind the statistics rather than on individual case studies. The reason for this is twofold. In part it is a matter of the accessibility of information. However shaky and mutually contradictory they may appear, aggregate statistics on FDI in Southeast Asia do exist for the contemporary period whereas interesting company records are likely to be confidential and unavailable. In addition, the context of FDI in the host country has changed fundamentally. Aggregate FDI in the colonial period was reviewed in conjunction with the emergence of a Western-style corporate network which in itself formed a major impact of FDI on the host country economy. The collective experience of contemporary FDI, however, should be disentangled from domestic developments precisely because FDI takes place in a context which could only come into existence by virtue of decolonization and varying degrees of economic nationalism. This calls for a global treatment and a differentiation by type of investor. Our principal aim is to identify pattern facilitating a comparison with FDI before the Pacific War.

Today's foreign investors come in many guises and for various reasons. This makes FDI during its post-war resurgence more intricate than the conventional search for vital raw materials and new overseas markets which by and large characterized FDI before the Pacific War. The recent literature on FDI in Asia abounds with typologies of FDI that alternately stress comparative advantages, the supply and demand sides of FDI and management strategy (e.g. Suehiro 1989: 199–204; Phongpaichit 1990: 6–20; Fukushima and Kwan 1995: 8–10). The following crude differentiation by rationale behind FDI offers a convenient point of departure:

(1) FDI based on firm-specific comparative advantage in securing supplies of raw materials and gaining access to foreign markets. This generalized version of the conventional perception of FDI is, in Southeast Asia, likely to apply in particular to American investment which offers the most obvious representation of continuity in FDI between the late colonial period and the present day (section 6.1).

(2) FDI as a means of reallocating resources in accordance with changing comparative advantage against the background of differentiated paths of industrialization. This type of FDI has been depicted in terms of product cycles and a 'flying geese' mode of economic development. It applies in particular to the so-called 'old wave' of Japanese investment in Southeast Asia which predominated during the 1970s and first half of the 1980s (section 6.2).

(3) FDI as a vehicle for shifting production abroad in the face of rising wages and appreciating currencies. This type of FDI presupposes that cost-reducing measures by investors fit into strategies for industrialization in host countries. It is the type of FDI generally associated with 'new wave' Japanese investment, since 1985, and the more recent NIC investment in Southeast Asia (section 6.3).

(4) FDI as a bandwagon effect of a success performance by host countries and earlier investors alike. Such an approach stresses tactics above long-run strategies and applies especially to the urge among EC investors to share in the benefits from the rapid economic growth in much of today's Southeast Asia, thereby on occasion reentering onetime colonies (section 6.4).

One or two comments must be added to this classification. The distinction between 'old wave' and 'new wave' Japanese investment follows the terminology suggested in some of the recent literature (Phongpaichit 1990). In addition, aspirations of foreign investors may overlap. Not only American but also Japanese and NIC investors are obviously keen on securing access to the supply of scarce raw materials. These four categories should therefore not be taken too literally. They serve above all as a device to enhance clarity in the presentation.

There is a bewildering proliferation of aggregate statistics on FDI in Southeast Asia since the 1960s comprising both annual flows, cumulative stocks and distributions by industry, size or nationality. The cumulative data are of limited use unless adjusted for price changes, ideally for relative changes in rates of exchange as well. On the whole, aggregate statistics are used here only sparingly and with caution. The information on American investment is probably of the best quality. The key position identified for Japanese investment in Southeast Asia in this period does, however, warrant separate attention to be paid to statistical material of Japanese origin (section 6.5).

6.1   RANKING BY PREFERENCE

In the late 1980s two giants in computer hardware, Seagate Technology and National Semiconductors, counted among the top ten American corporations operating in both Singapore and Thailand. For the remainder, the highest ranks of American investors in either of these two host countries contained a variety of company labels such as Mobil Oil in Singapore against Caltex in Thailand or General Motors and Black & Decker in Singapore against Pepsi Cola and Kodak in Thailand (Singapore 1989: 137–60; Million Baht Business 1991). This section focuses on American investment in Southeast Asia which in turn constitutes the single most important manifestation of a continuity in FDI patterns in the region between the late colonial period and today.

The worldwide upsurge of American investment after the Second World War occasioned the development of theories of FDI stressing the technological superiority of the individual multinational. The theory of firm-specific comparative advantage was formulated in the 1960s by Hymer who, as is perhaps less well known, thereby drew on older theories of firm positions in markets anticipating today's emphasis on transaction costs (Horaguchi and Toyne 1990). This paradigm basically prescribed a micro approach to explaining FDI stressing business strategies to safeguard the competitive edge by internalizing transaction costs incurred during the development of new technologies. The internationalization of production is, therefore, accompanied by retained oligopolistic advantages enjoyed by large multinationals. This is the type of FDI that we commonly associate with overseas investment by major American corporations in Southeast Asia.

A comparative advantage carries the seeds of success in terms of building up substantial capital interests abroad for the benefit of shareholders at home. Yet the extent to which the comparative advantage is exploited will obviously depend on the conditions in the host country economy, or more specifically, the resource endowment and the investment climate. This section argues that either of these two was a necessary and sufficient precondition for FDI to materialize on an appreciable scale in Southeast Asia after the Second World War. This is done by surveying traditional and new destinations of American investment in the region as well as by assessing the investment climate in general as perceived by corporate observers.

The early 1970s were tumultuous in the Philippines, the stronghold of American capital with the longest standing. Street rioting and ambushes provoked Marcos to declare martial law. Anti-American sentiments mounted and American investors grew uneasy as the long-awaited expiration of the Laurel-Langley Agreement neared in 1974. The years 1970–1973 saw a steady outflow of investment capital, especially of American origin (Doronila 1992: 160–70). The Philippines thus became the (non-Communist) host country in the region with the most outspoken resentment of FDI and the least impressive inflow of FDI.

The stock of primarily American investment built up in the Philippines by the time of the expiration of the Laurel-Langley Agreement can be inferred from an exceptionally elaborate statistical investigation undertaken by a joint research team from the University of the Philippines at Diliman near Manila and the Asian and Pacific Development Administration Centre of the United Nations. This survey covered all foreign affiliations among the top 1000 firms in the Philippines as listed in 1976 by the Securities and Exchange Commission (Tsuda *et al.* 1978: vol. I). The Tsuda report, as the four-volume publication of the survey is called, contains a systematic comparison between the situations in 1970 and 1976. The most conspicuous finding was the rising degree of Filipinization of large corporations in the Philippines between these two years. In 1970 some 46% (415 out of 900) of the largest firms in the country contained some foreign equity whereas in 1976 this applied to only 32% (324 out of 1000). The American share in total accumulated foreign equity (including both paid-in capital and retained earnings) declined from almost 80% in 1970 to 65% in 1976. The composition of accumulated foreign equity by industry, however, remained largely same with manufacturing accounting for at least 55% already by 1970 and mining declining below 15% in 1976 (Tsuda *et al.* 1978: I, 1–4, 8–10; II, 23–7).

Foreign equity was found more than proportionately in larger companies in the Philippines (Figure 6.1; Tsuda 1978: II, 18, 29–30). Almost one-half of foreign-controlled firms figured among the odd first 300 on the list of 1000 largest. The first half of the ranking, i.e. the 500 largest,

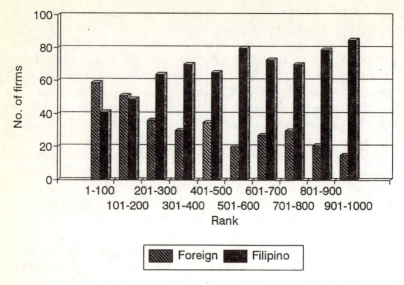

Figure 6.1   Top 1000 firms in the Philippines: ranking and nationality, 1976

included two-thirds of the 324 foreign-controlled corporations. Fourteen of the twenty largest foreign-controlled firms were American multinationals such as Caltex, Mobil Oil, Goodyear, Goodrich, Procter & Gamble, Colgate-Palmolive, International Harvester and Firestone. In addition, three-quarters of all firms with majority ownership by foreigners were of American origin. The large size and the tendency towards majority control were both reminiscent of FDI as it had developed in general in Southeast Asia already during the late colonial period.

Yet another characteristic feature of a traditional FDI pattern concerned profitability. Returns in American subsidiaries were satisfactory at an annual average of 16–18% of invested equity during the years 1966–1976. In this connection the Tsuda team of researchers presented an argument to the effect that every $1 invested in the Philippines eventually gave rise to $2 of outflowing capital and reinvested earnings of $1.58 (Tsuda *et al.* 1978: II, 15, 21). This reasoning is nonsensical since capital outflows should be related to accumulated totals, not to simultaneous inflows. Even if such an argument probably served a propagandistic purpose more than anything else, it is clear that American investment in the Philippines in the late 1960s and early 1970s was still quite profitable. This in turn may, at least partially, be considered as rewards accruing to a comparative advantage enhanced by scale effects and a solid foreign control over business operations.

But things went from bad to worse in the Philippines and incoming FDI continued to fall. Eventually, during the final years of Marcos rule, it amounted to less than 10% of what the country received by way of remittances from its numerous citizens choosing to work overseas (*FEER* 29/2 1996). The Philippines thus became a special case among recipients of FDI in the region, the one potentially promising host country which continuously lagged behind. The Philippines ceased to function as the American gateway to Southeast Asia. Out of the 35 largest American corporations operating in the Philippines in the 1990s, only four established themselves there after the expiration of the Laurel-Langley Agreement in 1974. American firms had accumulated at least twice as much equity in Indonesia as in the Philippines already in the 1980s. Singapore had also emerged as a new major destination for fresh American capital (United Nations 1992: 267; OECD 1993: 249).

The demise of the Philippines and the ascendancy of Singapore in particular as a prime destination for outgoing capital reflect a general reorientation in American investment in the region, a shift away from the heritage of political ties and onto a more detached assessment of the investment climates in presumptive host countries. This, however, does not at appear to apply to the same extent to Indonesia where Caltex and Stanvac expanded precisely at the time, in the 1950s and early 1960s, when the Royal Dutch/Shell was gradually losing ground. The high American stakes in the Indonesian oil sector today represent the continuation and elaboration of a trend with its origin in colonial times.

The investment climate in the host country counts as a set of intangible variables that can be studied through surveys and questionnaires each producing its own statistics and impressions. Such surveys are notoriously subjective. Outcomes should always be treated with the utmost caution and it is essential to confront their evidence with preferences as revealed by actual FDI flows. Still, such personalized perceptions do matter in decision-making about FDI and should be taken into account when explaining the kind of reorientation that did take place over the years in flows of American capital directed towards Southeast Asia. By relying on surveys among an English-language readership of Asia-oriented businessmen, it appears possible to capture the main trends in views held by presumptive American investors which, incidentally, must not be taken to imply that non-American respondents thought very differently on these matters.

Rankings in the literature, traditionally based on subjective ratings, usually position Singapore at the top followed by Malaysia. In rankings during the 1980s the Philippines fell from a third to a fifth position and was thus surpassed by both Indonesia and Thailand. The latter challenged

Malaysia, on occasion even Singapore, as the 1990s neared (Tambunlertchai 1991: 19). This brings us to a final tripartite clustering: Singapore first, Thailand and Malaysia in the middle, Indonesia and the Philippines last.

The monthly magazine *Asian Business* has carried out surveys of opinions about the investment climate in Southeast Asia since 1988 through a succession of telephone interviews over a protracted period of time. Six criteria are applied to express confidence in the future: local market perspectives, export potentials, turnover, profits, firm expansion in general and host country economic perspectives at large. In 1991 Indonesia scored strikingly high on almost every account (except export potentials), Malaysia did well in terms of turnover, both at home and abroad, and Singapore and Thailand emerged as the most competitive host countries in sales in foreign markets. The Philippines ended low by any criteria (*Asian Business* 1991: nos. 1, 2, 3, 9, 10; Baltussen 1993).

Four years is a short historical perspective but the very continuity of the surveys conducted by *Asian Business* throughout the years 1988–1991 permits us to identify some changes over time. Confidence in the host country appears to have improved, not only for Thailand but also for Indonesia. The relative position of Malaysia in the middle range has hardly changed and the same goes for the final slot with the Philippines. Singapore may have had to relinquish some of its original lead (*Asian Business* 1990: no. 10).

Chats over the telephone and boxes blackened on questionnaires are susceptible to radical revision as new information becomes available or conditions in the host country change. What counts in the final analysis are preferences as revealed by FDI actually materializing. Accumulated FDI in Southeast Asia by 1989 displays a pattern of preferences among major suppliers of investment capital which positions first-ranking Singapore and fourth-ranking Indonesia far ahead of all other host countries (Figure 6.2; United Nations 1992: 149, 165, 225, 267, 322–3). It should be noted that at this stage, at the end of the 1980s, the recent increase of FDI in Thailand was yet to gain momentum and Vietnam was barely opened up for FDI. In addition, accumulated NIC investment had then not yet reached its current dimensions.

Actual American preferences were instrumental in catapulting Indonesia into a lead above Singapore. This can without doubt be ascribed to the heavy American commitment to the Indonesian oil and LNG sector. The American nationality applies to six out of seven major foreign concerns engaged in extracting and processing Indonesian petroleum and LNG. Caltex and Stanvac ushered Riau in central Sumatra into becoming the newest centre for the Indonesian oil industry already under the Sukarno

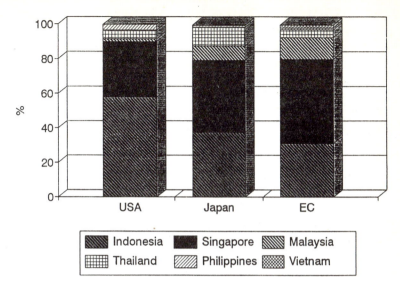

Figure 6.2   Accumulated FDI in 1989: host country preferences by investor

regime when most other potential investors shunned this host country. The two veteran oil firms have since then been joined by Exxon which is rumoured to be responsible for the largest accumulated capital investments by a single foreign corporation operating in Indonesia. Mobil Oil is a major participant in the international consortium developing the rich LNG fields in Aceh in northern Sumatra whereas Huffco Oil has grown especially important in the Balikpapan region in East Kalimantan, near the rich reserves which brought success and fame to both Shell and the Royal Dutch around 1900 (Lukman and McGlinchey 1986; Lindblad 1989b).

American multinationals apply sophisticated technology in exploiting natural riches elsewhere in the mining sector in Indonesia. The most spectacular example is the huge and at times controversial copper mine of Freeport Copper on the top of the Gunung Bijih in Irian Jaya where the ore is transported by aerial tramway cars through clouds and breathtaking mountain passes. The strong presence of American multinationals in Indonesian mining, including oil and LNG, shows how a technological lead in exploiting rich natural resources may take precedence above a less than favourable assessment of the investment climate in the host country.

In their choice for Singapore as a major destination for investment capital, however, American investors have stuck to the same secure path as their rivals in Japan and Western Europe. Accumulated American investment in Singapore manufacturing increased from about $1 billion in 1980 (S$2091 million) to $2.4 billion (S$5147 million) by 1986 and was reported at no less than $8.15 billion in 1992 of which the latter figure may include some plans that never reached implementation (*FEER* 12/10 1995; Pang Eng Fong 1995: 113). The production process in American-affiliated manufacturing in Singapore has become increasingly sophisticated since the early 1980s. This applies in particular to the electronics industry where the emphasis is now shifting towards computer systems, telecommunications and office automation equipment as well as display devices. The quantitative increase and the qualitative upgrading both underscore the attractiveness of the investment climate at Singapore for American business.

Few precise figures are disclosed on profit rates for the Indonesian operations of American oil and mining corporations but repeated reports in the press about huge investment schemes reveal a strong confidence in expected returns. For American firms operating in Singapore, however, levels of profitability can be inferred from stated profits compared to equity. The range in the late 1980s and early 1990s was 20–24% (Singapore 1989: 137–60; Foreign Equity 1992: 9). Such profit rates compare very favourably with those cited by, for instance, Japanese investors in the region.

Technological superiority and the large scale of operations traditionally account for much of the relatively high profitability achieved abroad by American multinationals. Both explanations apply to American investment in Indonesia and Singapore. American oligopolies are the rule rather than the exception in Indonesian mining. American firms constituted one-fifth of all foreign corporations in Singapore in 1989 while boasting 40% of all foreign equity (Singapore 1989: 137–60).

Caltex and Seagate Technology together symbolize the persistence in Southeast Asia of FDI born out of firm-specific comparative advantage factors. The comparative advantage may be realized either if the resource endowment of the host country is rich or if the investment climate is very favourable. Either of these two conditions is necessary and sufficient for FDI to materialize. Technology plays a crucial role since that is precisely where the foreign multinational possesses an advantage.

6.2   FLYING GEESE AND GIANT FIRMS

Tides turn and in the very long run points of gravity change as well. The Industrial Revolution brought British supremacy in the nineteenth century and an American lead in the twentieth just as mercantile capitalism moved from the Mediterranean region in the sixteenth century to the Dutch Republic in the seventeenth. East Asia, with Japan at the helm, is seen as the most likely candidate for world economic leadership in the twenty-first century. There is nothing strange, it is said among economists of our time, about different economic systems acquiring, enjoying and eventually relinquishing technological superiority at different times with factors of production being reallocated accordingly. This section considers FDI in Southeast Asia against the background of the worldwide economic ascendancy of Japan.

In the event, however, the most direct incitement to the dramatic rise of Japanese overseas investment stemmed from institutional change rather than technological superiority. The massive outflow of Japanese investment capital could only materialize after the exchange controls in Japan had been lifted in the early 1970s. Foreign exchange controls were lifted in 1972 and a gradual deregulation of interest rates on deposits of foreign currencies followed. The pace of deregulation was relatively slow so as to assure orderly credit conditions and interest rates on time deposits only became fully subject to bank discretion by the early 1980s (Kitagawa 1995: 155–6). The deregulation coincided with an ever larger surplus on Japan's current account. The push at home coincided with a pull in Southeast Asia where investment climates improved again whereas decolonization had left a vacuum in overseas sourcing of investment capital. This section argues that this juxtaposition of push and pull factors produced the massive Japanese capital commitments in the region during the 1970s and 1980s. At a slightly later stage the share of Southeast Asia in the Japanese total started to fall as more Japanese capital was targeted for investment in Europe or North America.

The first Japanese to arrive were the *sogo shosha* which by virtue of their very diversification possessed unique advantages in penetrating new markets. By the end of the 1970s four large *sogo shosha*, i.e. Mitsubishi, Mitsui, Marubeni and Itoh, had invested for $225 million in the ASEAN member states. The share of eleven large *sogo shosha* in total Japanese investment was 20% in the Philippines, 24% in Indonesia, 30% in Thailand and 33% in Malaysia (Katano 1981: 70, 76, 91, 127). Japanese investment in the region rose to prominence along a broad frontier during a short period of time. This new phenomenon in FDI patterns in Southeast Asia is considered with the aid of the controversial 'flying geese' model of economic development. In doing so we make elaborate use of empirical Japanese data pertaining to the situation by 1986. Although rather dated, at least by the standards of economists, this benchmark is useful since it allows us to focus on 'old wave' Japanese investment, i.e. FDI implemented prior to *endaka* or rapid yen appreciation since 1985.

Akamatsu's concept of *ganko keitai* dates from the time of Japanese political and economic expansion in the 1930s. It has acquired a controversial or mysterious ring among economists. Yet its undertone is essentially optimistic. Each country moves up the ladder of industrialization participating in the international division of labour according to its stage of development at that particular time. The import-substituting country at a lower stage may thus concentrate on goods for which production is becoming too costly for the export-oriented country at a higher stage. Actual production may then be relocated from the more developed to the less developed participant, to the benefit of both, and this is where we encounter the juxtaposition of push and pull factors (Kojima 1977; Arndt 1989: 21; Chowdury and Islam 1993: 101–2).

An international system of division of labour thus emerges allowing dynamic growth to pervade throughout an entire region as is indeed conceived to be the case in East and Southeast Asia during the concluding decades of the twentieth century. The economic gap is said to be 22 years between Japan and Korea and another 24 years between Korea and, for instance, Indonesia, i.e. a total of 46 years or a little less than two generations separating Tokyo and Jakarta (Fukushima and Kwan 1995: 14–15).

The combination of *ganko keitai* with Vernon's product cycle was easily accomplished since the successive phases in a product life, i.e. introduction, growth and standardization, may coincide with the more global stages of the 'flying geese' model. The highest level of technological sophistication is required at the time of introduction, the lowest when standardization occurs. The *ganko keitai* is mirrored within the individual production line or even single firm by a 'billiard ball' style of production shifts. In computer electronics mass production of semiconductors moved out of Japan, first into NICs, then from there to a country with 'near-NIC' status such as Malaysia. Similarly in colour televisions, Toshiba manufactures cathode ray tubes in Thailand whereas assembly is in Singapore and new designs are devised at home in Japan (Ohta, Tokuno and Takeuchi 1995: 45, 51, 57). FDI, in particular of Japanese origin, obviously has a key role to play in linking the various stages of technological sophistication into one integrated system of production and marketing. The most important difference of this paradigm in analyzing FDI compared to conventional wisdom based on firm-specific comparative advantage is the strong emphasis on mutual benefit.

The normative side of the argument has been especially defended by the Japanese economist Kojima. This in turn has already given rise to a substantial literature. Kojima argues that American and Japanese investment differ fundamentally and thus will have a widely different impact on the host country economy. Kojima depicts Japanese firms as investing industries where they were losing their comparative advantage in production for exports. Therefore, Japanese investment is trade-oriented and likely to have a positive impact, not only on employment, but also on the balance of payments of the host country. Japanese-style FDI complements, creates and enlarges foreign trade of the host country rather than forming a substitute to it. American investment, on the other hand, is by firms retaining their comparative advantage by relying on their market power. According to Kojima, subsidiaries of such multinationals will form no complement to the existing structure of production in the host country but will rather crowd out local competitors and total exports may even decline. Japanese investment is likely to be either resource-oriented, labour-oriented or market-oriented whereas American investment remains oligopolistic (Kojima 1973: 4–7; Kojima 1978: 84–90; Kojima 1985/86: 79–81).

Critics of the Kojima hypothesis have not always been readily inclined to view Japanese investment as intrinsically 'better' than American investment. Arndt and Lee both point at the shortcomings of the Kojima model as a theoretical construction whereas Sekiguchi and Krause assert that only the timing of Japanese investment made it unique, i.e. in due course it would resemble American investment anyway. Hill and Johns demonstrate that the predicted sales orientation, i.e. biased towards foreign exports, are not borne out by the statistics. Japanese-affiliated firms were even found to be more oriented towards domestic markets than American rivals (Arndt 1974; Sekiguchi and Krause 1980: 436–9; Lee 1984; Hill and Johns 1985: 366–7).

Empirical evidence has also been gathered on specific host countries. The Kojima hypothesis is, for all intents and purposes, rejected for both the Philippines and Indonesia but, at first sight at any rate, upheld for Malaysia (Alburo and Sicat 1983: 106–7; Thee 1984: 104; Cable and Persaud 1987: 103–5). Working within a sophisticated theoretical framework, Pangestu calculates so-called indices of investment intensity and bilateral complementarity. She argues that there is a closer association between FDI and bilateral trade in Japanese flows to Southeast Asia than in investment made by American firms (Pangestu 1986: 305–6, 322). This is an important finding since it shifts our attention towards less tangible factors such as geographical and cultural proximity as opposed to any 'intrinsic' nature of FDI.

According to Kojima, Japanese investment is potentially more beneficial to the host country economy, not only because of its trade orientation, but also because it was to a higher extent undertaken by small and medium-size firms inclined to enter into joint ventures with domestic partners and also to integrate with the local economy to a higher degree than large American oligopolists. Although perhaps too bright a picture, this has not been found to be at variance with actual experience. Interestingly, however, this feature of Japanese investment in Southeast Asia does not appear to be unique for Japanese corporate commitments but applies to NIC investment in the region as well (Kojima 1973: 5; Hill and Johns 1985: 366; Thee 1993: 447–8).

Recent discussion on the nature of FDI in Asia has probably to an undue degree centred on the Kojima hypothesis. The hypothesis itself has indeed been proven to be basically wrong. Nevertheless, even if less than useful as a tool of historical explanation, the Kojima hypothesis has undeniably revitalized the discussion about the nature of FDI thereby calling attention to the way in which FDI fits into the economic development of host countries. This theme has been pursued in a perhaps more forceful fashion by other Japanese economists such as Ozawa and Yoshihara.

Ozawa, writing shortly after Kojima, stressed the historical coincidence of the shortage of labour and space in Japan with the abundance of cheap labour and land in Southeast Asia. It was therefore logical to transplant the labour-intensive and more traditional segment of Japanese manufacturing to locations abroad but still within easy reach. Yoshihara, who has since gained a certain notoriety in parts of Southeast Asia for his concept of *Ersatz* capitalism, was one of the very first explicitly to incorporate also the demand side of FDI into the explanatory model. Host country priorities with respect to economic growth and industrialization can prove decisive in the decision-making about FDI when no country-specific endowments are at stake. The rise of Japanese investment in Southeast Asia should thus be viewed as the outcome of simultaneous developments in Japan itself and in the region (Yoshihara 1978: 179–204; Ozawa 1979: 76–110).

Objectives stated by investors often tell us more than theoretical constructions about why and how FDI is undertaken. It is revealing that local sales formed the most often cited rationale of Japanese-affiliated companies for being in business in the ASEAN member states by the mid-1980s (Figure 6.3; Japanese Overseas Investment 1986: 49–114).[1] In no host country, except Singapore, did expectations for future exports come anywhere near local sales as an objective of importance. Marketing considerations as a whole clearly outweighed possibilities to cut production costs by utilizing cheap labour whereas the resource endowment was almost nowhere of more than marginal importance. Policy incentives accounted for scarcely more than low wages, i.e. considerably less than any responses pertaining to market perspectives. The following relative frequencies apply to the various objectives stated:

- local sales 51%
- policy incentives 32%

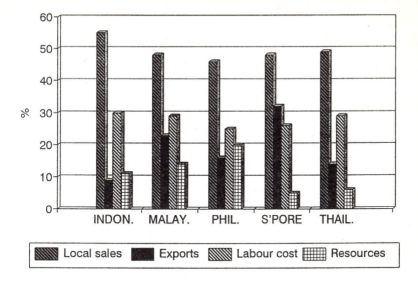

Figure 6.3   Japanese firms in ASEAN: motivations by host country, 1986

- labour costs 28%
- foreign exports 22%
- resource endowment 10%.

Total market orientation (local sales and/or foreign exports) varied by host country:

- Singapore 83%
- Malaysia 64%
- Thailand 64%
- Indonesia 63%
- Philippines 54%.

These results agree surprisingly well with tentative findings dating back as far as the early 1970s (Allen 1974: 5–6).

The preoccupation with local sales may be generalized into an urge to reap the benefits from the process of economic development in the host country by participating in precisely that process. FDI then becomes part and parcel of an intra-regional 'virtuous cycle' with industrialization occurring according to the 'flying geese' pattern from which all may profit (Primo Braga and Bannister 1994: 111). The new theoretical paradigm inspired by Japanese investment and surveys of investors' motivations point in the same direction. Opportunities for an integration into host country economic development may be designated as a necessary precondition for Japanese investment in Southeast Asia. This is precisely the point where both the supply and demand factors behind FDI merge in a region characterized by substantial differentials within the same process of industrial restructuring.

Empirical evidence on Japanese-affiliated firms in Southeast Asia unveils the unique character of Japanese corporate commitment in the region, not only on an aggregate level but also with respect to individual host countries. The rest of this section first gives an overview of the penetration of the region by Japanese investment capital between the 1950s and the mid-1980s. Then Japanese investment in individual host countries is characterized with the aid of three selected variables: sheer numbers of firms, employment and equity capital.[2] This enables us to compare capital and labour intensities by industry. Thus an impression is rendered of the 'typical' Japanese-affiliated firm in each host country.

The breakthrough of Japanese investment in the region came in the 1970s when three out of five Japanese-affiliated firms in operation by 1986 had started out (Figure 6.4; Japanese Overseas Investment 1986: 49–114). Most of the attention was initially given to Indonesia, up to the Tanaka riots in January 1974, then the emphasis shifted to Singapore and Thailand. Malaysia lagged behind until Mahathir's 'Look East' policy was launched in 1981 as a means of countervailing the restraining impact of the NEP. Japanese enthusiasm was markedly less for investing in the Philippines.

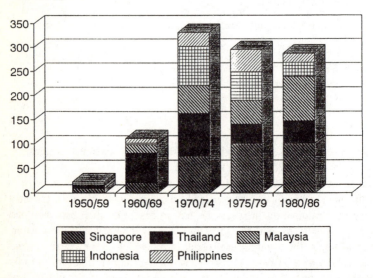

Figure 6.4   Japanese firms in ASEAN: chronology of establishments, 1950–1986

Networks of Japanese-affiliated firms emerged in all major host countries of the region. Local businessmen were officially encouraged to seek cooperation with Japanese corporations not only in Malaysia but also in Thailand and the Philippines. Yet despite converging policies and similar motivations on the part of the Japanese investor, each network looked different. Singapore counted the largest numbers of Japanese-affiliated firms, 29% of the total, but offered less employment than any other host country. Malaysia was noted for the largest aggregation of equity, about one-third of the total for the region's Japanese subsidiaries. This did not result in more employment than, for instance, in Indonesia where aggregate equity amounted to much less. Thailand offered the most employment, 27% of the total labour force of a quarter of a million persons working for these Japanese-affiliated firms. Here aggregate equity was less impressive than anywhere else. Each network of Japanese-affiliated firms was, as it were, tailormade to the environment of the host country. This may be demonstrated by constructing a profile of Japanese investment as of the mid-1980s by host country.

Indonesia became the testing ground for Japanese investment on a massive scale. This host country alone accounted for two-thirds of all fresh Japanese investment in Southeast Asia in the years 1970-1977. By the time of the Tanaka riots Japan had already surpassed the USA as the largest source of FDI outside oil, which of course makes all the difference (Sekiguchi and Krause 1980: 428, 434). The Asahan project illustrates particularly well how the influx of Japanese investment capital also became a matter of political reorientation and prestige. Agreement on the huge dam, hydro-electric power station and aluminium smelter was only reached, in 1975, after the original American participants, Alcoa and Kaiser, had backed out and the Japanese government had provided very large loans on relatively soft terms. The total worth of the investment was eventually to exceed the $2 billion. Two-thirds of the aluminium production was earmarked as exports to Japan. Initially, the Indonesian government held only 10% of equity in the aluminium smelter but this was to rise to 35% by 1985. The dam is to become full Indonesian property by 2005 (Ozawa 1979: 98-103; Hill 1988: 89–90).

Japanese investment in Indonesia was from the outset geared towards manufacturing outside oil. Nine of the ten largest investors in manufacturing during the initial years of resurgence of FDI in Indonesia, 1967–1973, were Japanese. The list included several *sogo shosha* such as Mitsui and Marubeni, ranking highest, as well as Mitsubishi and C. Itoh (*FEER* 15/11 1974; Panglaykim 1977: 163). By the 1980s all top groups of Indonesian business conglomerates had entered into joint ventures with Japanese giants, both *sogo shosha* and industrial concerns. Examples include the Salim (Liem Sioe Liong) group with Marubeni and Suzuki, Rodamas with Asahi Glass, Astra with Sumitomo and Toyota, Lippo with Mazda, Bob Hassan with Nissan, Pembangunan Jaya with Fuji Bank, Damatex with Mitsui and Toray (Panglaykim 1979: 89–90; Steven 1988: 47; Kano 1989: 153).

Three branches of non-oil manufacturing predominated among Japanese-affiliated companies in Indonesia by 1986: textiles, metals and the automotive industry (Figure 6.5; Table 6.7; Japanese Overseas Investment 1986: 103–14). Textiles ranked particularly high in terms of aggregated equity and employment whereas the automotive industry contained a very large number of different Japanese brands. Scale economies were above all realized in textiles whereas most of the metals production remained rather small-scale. The single largest enterprise listed in 1986 was Toray's joint venture in the production of polyester–rayon fibres dating back to 1972. Other manufacturing, on occasion, also attained the very large scale of the textile industry as, for instance, in the joint venture of Asahi Glass with Tan Siong Kie which alone offered work for more than 1700 persons or more than five times the average for all Japanese-affiliated firms in the country. The emphasis on consumer goods and large-scale labour-intensive production suggests a tendency towards import substitution by gaining control of ever larger segments of the increasing domestic market.

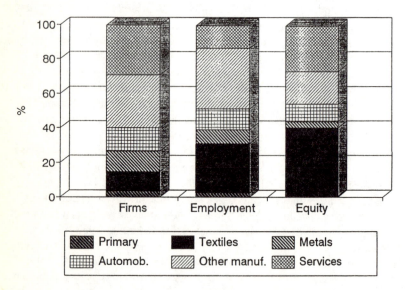

Figure 6.6   Japanese firms in Malaysia: distribution by industry, 1986

Table 6.7   Equity and employment in Japanese firms in Southeast Asia, 1986

	Firms (numbers)	Equity (million $)	Employment (thousands)
Indonesia	176	750.5	53.6
Primary	3	1	2
Textiles	11	40	29
Metals	12	4	8
Automobiles	14	10	12
Other manufacturing	31	19	35
Services	29	26	14
Malaysia	220	1430	55.4
Primary	2	1	1
Textiles	3	6	18
Metals	6	24	11
Electrical	12	6	25
Other manufacturing	32	33	30
Services	45	30	15
The Philippines	109	778.2	37.5
Mining	4	8	26
Other primary	3	0	9
Metals	4	13	18
Other manufacturing	55	14	30
Trade	17	32	4
Other services	17	33	13
Singapore	306	949.6	36.5
Chemicals	9	12	5
Metals	7	17	12
Electrical	12	12	32
Other manufacturing	14	11	19
Trade	34	12	21
Other services	24	36	11
Thailand	243	590.6	67.0
Textiles	10	22	46
Metals	8	10	4
Automobiles	10	7	10
Other manufacturing	27	21	23
Trade	24	7	12
Other services	21	33	5

Source: Japanese Overseas Investment 1986: 49–114.

In Malaysia electrical and electronic equipment figured prominently next to traditional strongholds of foreign-controlled manufacturing such as textiles and metals production (Figure 6.6; Table 6.7; Japanese Overseas Investment 1986: 72–85). The production of textiles and electrical and electronic equipment was very large-scale in terms of employment whereas aggregate equity in the metals industry was exceptionally large. Average employment per Japanese-affiliated firm amounted to 1400 employees in textiles and more than 500 in electrical and electronic equipment whereas the general average for Japanese-affiliated corporations was no more than 250. The single largest wholly-owned Japanese subsidiary was formed by the twin polyester plants operated by Toray in Penang employing 6300 people in the region. Another very large Japanese employer was the neighbouring semiconductor plant of Hitachi in Penang to which we shall have occasion to return in due course.

Furukawa and Sumitomo were important in metals production whereas the electronics industry contained numerous well known labels such as Hitachi, Sanyo and Toshiba. Most large Japanese investors in these industries preferred majority holdings but this was not the case everywhere. Mitsubishi, for one, also participated with minority shares in leading Malaysian enterprises such as the exploitation of LNG in Sarawak or the giant ULBON steel plant employing 3300 persons in Johor Baru. The

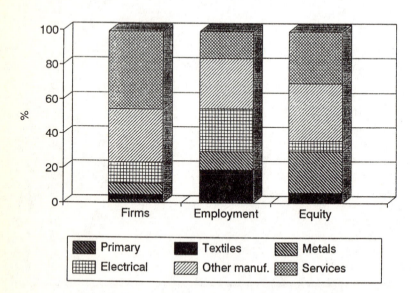

Figure 6.6   Japanese firms in Malaysia: distribution by industry, 1986

emphasis on large-scale production and technological sophistication combined with the modest size of the domestic Malaysian market betrays an orientation towards exports of goods that were demanded in the region but could be more cheaply produced outside Japan itself.

Capital-intensive mining and labour-intensive trading activities threatened to squeeze traditional manufacturing aside among Japanese-affiliated producers in the Philippines as of the mid-1980s (Figure 6.7; Table 6.7; Japanese Overseas Investment 1986: 49–56). Small-scale production was the rule in most firms with a Japanese interest operating in the Philippines, e.g. chemicals, electrical equipment and automobile parts, where average employment was barely more than half of the average for all Japanese subsidiaries, 185 employees against 345. The largest single wholly-owned Japanese subsidiary was Kawasaki Steel with its extraordinary history of having been once both sold and bought back by the Japanese mother concern. Mitsubishi reported a minority participation in the managing company and investment bank of Ayala, renowned for its Spanish tradition during pioneering in colonial times. A rare case of Japanese involvement in high technology was found in a minority-owned Fujitsu subsidiary specialized in computer maintenance in metropolitan Manila. On the whole, however, the link with industrialization in the activities of Japanese-affiliated companies was weaker than in other major host countries in Southeast Asia.

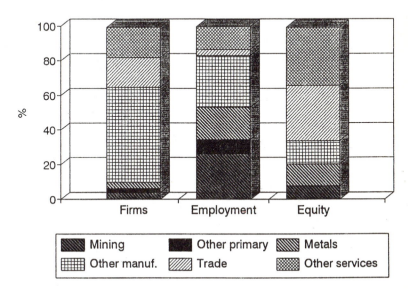

Figure 6.7　Japanese firms in the Philippines: distribution by industry, 1986

The Singapore government under Goh Chok Tong was particularly keen on forging alliances with foreign multinationals, including Japanese ones. This was not confined to manufacturing at a high level of techno-logical sophistication but applied equally to a wide spectrum of commer-cial and financial services (Figure 6.8; Table 6.7; Japanese Overseas Investment 1986: 85–103). As of the mid-1980s, the fabrication of electrical and electronic equipment offered by far the most employment and ranked second, after metals, in terms of aggregate equity. In addition, chemicals were important as well with Mitsui Toatsu and Nippon Paint at the forefront. The largest majority-controlled Japanese subsidiaries were the Jurong shipyard, partly owned by Ishikawajima-Harima, and Mitsubishi Singapore Heavy Industries. Wholly-owned Japanese subsidiaries included Hokoriku in electrical appliances, Matsushita in electronics, Mineba-owned Pelmec and Nomura Securities.

The largest scale of production was found in electrical and electronic manufacturing where the number of workers per firm exceeded 300, far above the average for all Japanese-affiliated firms listed at 120 employees. Aggregate equity was apparently very high in services other than trade and in the chemical industry. The Singapore network of Japanese-affiliated corporations displayed the highest degree of diversification and techno-logical sophistication in the region. Government encouragement has been more instrumental in its formation than elsewhere. This underscores the

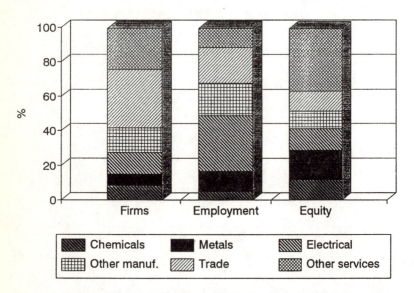

Figure 6.8   Japanese firms in Singapore: distribution by industry, 1986

strong link of Japanese investment in Singapore with official strategies aiming at industrial restructuring and rapid economic growth.

In Thailand Japanese firms counted among the pioneers as soon as the investment climate had started to improve in the 1960s. In the 1980s four out of five firms looking back on a history of foreign capital involvement were Japanese (Pornavalai 1989: 149). Textiles formed the traditional stronghold with Marubeni, Toray, Teijin and Shikibo leading the way. Meanwhile, the automotive industry gained ground as well with early factories set up by Mitsubishi and Mitsui soon being followed by the assembly of Hino, Isuzu, Mazda and Nissan. There was a strong preference for joint ventures with Japanese minority holders expecting to exercise a decisive influence as domestic shares were distributed over numerous Thai hands (Phipatseritham and Yoshihara 1983: 22; Tambunlertchai 1993: 136).

By the mid-1980s the traditional Japanese bias towards textiles still remained intact but it was successively being challenged by an increasing diversification in other manufacturing (Figure 6.9; Table 6.7; Japanese Overseas Investment 1986: 56–71). The share of electrical and electronic manufacturing was still very modest at only 5% of total employment generated by Japanese-affiliated enterprises. The largest Japanese interests were the joint ventures of Isuzu, Toray and Taisei, an engineering firm in Bangkok. Major wholly-owned Japanese subsidiaries included Honda, Toyo Ink and Fujikura, an electronics manufacturer in Bangkok.

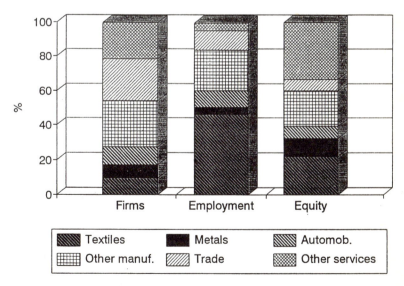

Figure 6.9   Japanese firms in Thailand: distribution by industry, 1986

Capital intensities in manufacturing displayed a considerable variety with metals production ranking far above and textiles far below the overall average. Much of manufacturing, with the notable exception of metals production, was very labour-intensive which contrasted starkly with the relatively limited employment created by Japanese investment in services. The heavy reliance on cheap unskilled labour in combination with economies of scale being realized suggests that Japanese investment in Thailand up to that stage had been primarily geared towards import substitution and local sales rather than making a substantial contribution to an industrial upgrading for the benefit of exports.

This section has in great brevity portrayed Japanese investment as the true novelty in FDI patterns in Southeast Asia since the 1970s. Japanese investment rose quickly throughout the region not only because of push factors at home but above all because of its capability to respond to the new opportunities emerging in the thrust for industrialization in the host countries. Such opportunities constituted a necessary precondition for massive Japanese investment to materialize. Networks of Japanese-affiliated firms emerged possessing a different profile dependent on the stage of industrial restructuring prevailing in the host country. The differentiated approach to FDI embraced technological sophistication in Singapore, increasing export orientation in Malaysia, import substitution in Indonesia or Thailand and few illusions about restructuring at all in the Philippines. Such was the character of 'old wave' Japanese investment in Southeast Asia.

6.3   A VARIETY OF WAVES

During the three years between August 1985 and August 1988 the value of the Japanese yen increased by 46% against the dollar whereas the New Taiwanese dollar and the Korean won gained 27% and 14% respectively. This phenomenon, in the literature known as *endaka*, occasioned a dramatic expansion of FDI of East Asian origin in neighbouring Southeast Asia. It is a type of FDI that has swept through the region in successive waves in response to rising costs of labour and appreciating currencies in the East Asian economies. Production at ever higher levels of technological sophistication is shifted to overseas locations which usually guarantees a warm welcome in host countries bent on rapid industrialization. It is no coincidence that the deregulation of FDI legislation in most of Southeast Asia has been intensified precisely at the time of the influx of so-called 'new wave' Japanese investment and NIC investment in the late

1980s and early 1990s. This section depicts *endaka*-inspired flows of capital as a special case of converging supply and demand factors determining incoming FDI. Two complementary waves of such FDI are distinguished, Japanese 'new' wave and NIC investment.

The Plaza Accord in August 1985 was a watershed in the development of Japanese direct investment in Southeast Asia. Outflows of Japanese investment capital to the six ASEAN member states increased threefold between 1985 and 1988, from $940 million to $2.7 billion, only to reach an annual average at almost $3.7 billion in the years 1990/93 (Table 6.4; Chia 1990; Fukushima and Kwan 1995: 6). During the second half of the 1980s Japanese investment rose five times in Malaysia, six times in Singapore and as much as 25 times in Thailand. Meanwhile, the accumulated value for the region was bolstered by at least $10 billion (Fallows 1994: 264–5). The massive scale in absolute terms is an important characteristic of Japanese 'new wave' investment.

Rankings of recipient countries all over the world changed. The combined share of East and Southeast Asia in total Japanese capital outflows increased from 12% to 18% between 1989 and 1993 but this above all reflects the rise of mainland China as a rival location for labour-intensive Japanese production. Within Asia, the ASEAN region (without Singapore) has successively gained at the expense of the four NICs. The ASEAN share in the Asian total rose from 35% in 1988 to 52% in 1991 while the share of the NICs fell from 59% to 37%. This reorientation brought the share of the ASEAN (excluding Singapore) to 7% of worldwide Japanese investment in the early 1990s (Jun 1993: 15; Fukushima and Kwan 1995: 6). Southeast Asia benefits more than others from Japanese 'new wave' investment because the region, with the exception of Singapore, offers precisely what 'new wave' Japanese investment capital is looking for, i.e. a convenient escape from appreciating currencies and rising wages.

The year 1988 already saw a switch towards more investment in electrical and electronics manufacturing in Thailand. Newly arrived Japanese investors were exceptionally quick to acquire promotional privileges for their projects. New arrivals frequently involved *sogo shosha* with extensive experience in Thailand. Mitsubishi, for instance, claimed to locate 40% of its new overseas Asian projects in Thailand alone (Tourret *et al.* 1989: 96–7; *FEER* 3/5 1990). In Malaysia numbers of Japanese manufacturers using advanced technologies increased rapidly. The *bumiputra* equity ownership requirements were less stringently applied and 100% ownership proved possible in 40 out of 250 Japanese manufacturing firms. The expansion continued unabatedly through 1989 and 1990 despite labour conflicts at Toray and Hitachi and a much-publicized criticism of

Japanese aloofness with respect to Malaysian demands for more influence on management (*FEER* 28/3 1991).

Japanese 'new wave' investment has brought a further division of labour within manufacturing industries requiring different capital and technology intensities at different stages of production. The electronics and electrical industry provides the best illustration. Here, sophisticated technologies are applied in the highly capital-intensive development of new products and fabrication of specialized parts whereas standardized production at the assembly stage is, above all, labour-intensive. A vertical division of labour then becomes sensible, as in the case of Sony colour televisions where the cathode ray tubes are manufactured in Singapore while the television sets are assembled in Malaysia with research and development being retained in Japan. In addition, there is an increasing horizontal division of labour with little technological difference between the various production sites within Southeast Asia. Actual production moves to the overseas location possessing the most attractive wage and currency conditions while the base at home is adjusted so as to retain its technological lead. Such chain reactions in the production process have in the literature been labelled 'billiard ball' shifts in FDI (Ohta, Tokuno and Takeuchi 1995: 54–5).

A survey conducted by MITI in 1991, six years after the Plaza Accord, cited access to low wage labour as the single most important motive of Japanese manufacturing subsidiaries in Asia. This motive was followed by the expectation of increasing local sales, amongst others by circumventing the high costs of the yen in the case of exporting directly from Japan. Strikingly, however, the possibilities of exporting cheaply to Japan were at that time still deemed to be of even less importance than, for instance, promotional policies pursued by the host country. This hierarchy of motivations, which did not explicitly include the wish to avoid the effects of yen appreciation, was especially pronounced for the electrical and electronics industry. A slightly different pattern was signalled in the motor car industry where opportunities for increasing local sales ranked above all other motivations. Here, very substantial gains were clearly to be reaped from lower wages at the assembly stage as well as from circumventing the expensive yen (Jun *et al.* 1993: 25).

The 'billiard ball' style of relocating production has resulted in an increasing emphasis within manufacturing on industries such as electrical machinery and electronics where production is likely to possess a higher degree of technological sophistication. By virtue of its large-scale standardized assembly it has almost automatically also led to a stronger orientation towards foreign exports. Export propensities have been rising consistently since the Plaza Accord for Japanese-affiliated manufacturing in Indonesia, Malaysia and Thailand. Exports to Japan have also increased markedly. The ASEAN share in electrical home appliances imported into Japan from Asia rose from 5% in 1988 to 31% in 1994. The change was even more dramatic in the case of colour television sets that had been assembled elsewhere in Asia. In 1988 none came from Southeast Asia (except Singapore) but in 1994 the region's share had risen to almost 50% (Ohta, Tokuno and Takeuchi 1995: 48). This reflected a relocation of Japanese-affiliated manufacturing from NIC locations to Malaysia, Thailand and Indonesia in particular.

A more expensive yen not only urges Japanese manufacturers to move export production overseas but it also means that higher prices have to be paid for parts and components from suppliers in Japan. This in turn forms a strong incentive to enhance the local content or third country imports in overseas production. Therefore, the relocation of labour-intensive stages of the production process has been supplemented by procurement networks involving sourcing of parts and components from elsewhere within the Southeast Asian region. Singapore has often become a natural hub in such networks. As a result the local content in Japanese-style production in Southeast Asia has increased considerably at the time of the 'new wave' of Japanese investment. A few examples may suffice. The proportion of locally available parts in total value of the finished product exceeds 80% for stereo equipment or air conditioners from Malaysia while amounting to 50% for cassette recorders from Indonesia or computer peripherals from Singapore (Ohta, Tokuno and Takeuchi 1995: 50). The higher local content is particularly important when assessing FDI effects in terms of technology transfer to the host country economy, a matter to which we shall return in due course.

Large enterprises predominated in the older wave of Japanese investment, i.e. during the 1970s and first half of the 1980s, even if the Japanese-affiliated corporate structure in each host country displayed a wide range of different types of subsidiaries. The 'new wave' of Japanese overseas investment has furthered the involvement of smaller and medium-size companies. This applies specifically to recent Japanese commitments in Southeast Asia as opposed to overseas investment elsewhere (Chia 1990: 30). It is tempting to associate this 'regional' characteristic to the emergence of supply and service networks for the benefit of Japanese production throughout Southeast Asia. It is also likely that these types of investors have benefitted more than large multinationals from the deregulation policies implemented in most host countries of the region. Investors with less financial reserves value full ownership more than giants capable of playing first fiddle in joint ventures.

In the late 1980s NIC investment, i.e. originating in one of the four 'tiger' economies of Hong Kong, Korea, Singapore and Taiwan, in Southeast Asia corresponded to only 16% of the accumulated total for ASEAN member states (except Singapore). Moreover, it was largely confined to Indonesia (48%) and Malaysia (36%) with less attention given to Thailand (13%), let alone the Philippines (United Nations 1992: 149, 165, 225, 322–3). Although these figures represent the most authoritative information on accumulated FDI in the region, they are less useful for assessing NIC investment. The United Nations aggregates are stock data which by definition understate the significance of incoming flows of the youngest vintage. Precisely the years since the compilation of authoritative United Nations data have witnessed a dramatic upsurge of NIC investment. Our impression of NIC investment, therefore, must remain incomplete and preliminary as it can only be founded upon scattered evidence about flows of a questionable quality reflecting approvals rather than realizations and often displaying unexplainable short-run fluctuations.

Indonesia offers a case in point. NIC investment climbed, as a percentage of total approvals as registered by the BKPM, from 12% in 1987 to 34% in 1988, then settled at 25–30% in 1989 and 1990 only to rise above 40% in 1991. No individual NIC investor predominated throughout this rapid expansion. Taiwan was responsible for the largest slice in 1988 and again in 1991 but Korea and Hong Kong took turns in furnishing most in 1989 and 1990 (Thee 1993: 444).

There is little doubt that the breakthrough of NIC investment in this region occurred around 1990, i.e. after a gestation period of about half a decade compared to the 'new wave' of Japanese investment. In 1990 NIC investment in Malaysia no longer consisted merely of Singapore capital crossing the causeway to Johor Baru. Taiwan already accounted for 70% of all NIC flows entering Malaysia and some very large investment projects were materializing including the huge petrochemical plant of China General Plastic in Johor, a long-term project worth M$8.5 million ($3.1 million) in total (*FEER* 26/4 1990; Wong Tai Chee 1990: 112). Net incoming flows entering Thailand averaged 58 billion baht ($2.3 billion) in 1990/91 of which almost 40% originated in Hong Kong, Singapore and Taiwan, in that order. The level of net inflows was about ten times the one prevailing in the mid-1980s whereas the combined share of NIC investors was at least one and a half times as high.[3] Throughout Southeast Asia the pace of FDI accumulation has quickened but the rate of increase of NIC investment has been higher still.

The situation in the mid-1990s tells us how much has changed in a preciously short time span. In 1994 Taiwan supplied the largest flow of FDI entering Malaysia, $1.15 billion out of an aggregate approaching $3.8 billion. In the same year Hong Kong ranked first and Korea fourth among approvals as registered by the BKPM in Indonesia accounting for respectively $6.1 billion and $2.1 billion out of a staggering total of some $22 billion (which obviously is only to be partially implemented). Hong Kong and Taiwan, the two nearest NICs, figured with a combined inflow of $670 million immediately after the USA in the ranking of foreign investors in the Philippines, where the total amounted to $2.2 billion's worth of investment capital. In 1995 Singapore was reputed to rank second in Thailand and fourth in Vietnam (*FEER* 12/10 1995, 25/4 1996). The wave of NIC investment forms the most spectacular recent development in FDI patterns in Southeast Asia.

NIC investment can only be properly understood against the background of the 'East Asian model' of industrial development which as such forms a generalization covering disparate paths of growth. According to this so-called model, the process of industrialization embraces five stages: import substitution to reduce outlays of foreign currency, labour-intensive export production to earn foreign currency, capital goods production to support further industrialization, capital-intensive export production at a higher level of technological sophistication and, finally, technology-intensive export industries to retain the industrial momentum. This model was first tried out in Japan and is now successfully applied by the NICs (Chowdhury and Islam 1993: 88–106; Inoue 1993: 11). In addition, it provides an example and a guideline for industrial policy in the 'near-NICs' and those hoping to reach that status shortly in Southeast Asia.

The repeated restructuring of industries within a short period of time makes the application of the 'East Asian model' in today's NICs into a special or accelerated case of the 'flying geese' type of economic development. As today's NICs move up the ladder of industrial restructuring, the urge to relocate industrial production at lower stages to Southeast Asia will become stronger. Rising wages in the NICs reflect important productivity gains whereas the appreciation of currencies, also apart from international agreements, testify to the greater competitiveness of production at a higher level of technological sophistication. The NICs can only retain their comparative advantages by shifting parts of the production process to overseas locations. 'Near-NICs' and 'would-be NICs' in Southeast Asia now fulfil the same function with respect to today's four NICs as these did, less than a generation ago, with respect to Japan.

The time is not yet ripe for a full assessment of NIC investment in Southeast Asia as the information is still too piecemeal and fragmented. Only an occasional observation can be made on each of the four NICs. In addition, it is important to emphasize the role of networks of overseas Chinese in NIC investment since three out of the four investor countries are predominantly Chinese. Little is known with certainty about the true extent of investment holdings of overseas Chinese in the major host countries of Southeast Asia. A rare estimate dating as far back as to the mid-1970s cites $2.7 billion for Thailand, $1.9 billion for Malaysia and $1.6 billion for Indonesia (Limlingan 1986: 3, 5). It is quite clear that these figures have multiplied since the 1970s and that overseas Chinese capital today fuels much of the industrial production throughout Southeast Asia.

Among the NICs, Hong Kong initially counted as the foremost exporter of capital. It was the largest 'developing country' investor up to 1987 when Taiwan took the lead. Singapore has remained somewhat in the shadow of the other two Chinese-dominated NICs, at any rate by the sheer magnitude of FDI outflows. Korea started late. Capital exports only reached an appreciable scale during the second half of the 1980s when the financial regime at home was relaxed. Interestingly, however, Korea provided the very first NIC investment in Southeast Asia, a lumber project in Indonesia undertaken already in 1968 (Chen 1992: 69–73). It is necessary to touch briefly on each of the four NICs in relationship to FDI in Southeast Asia. Individual NICs are discussed in order of geographical proximity to the region.

Singapore is unique in this context. It is at once a major destination for incoming FDI and a recent exporter. Singapore investors emerged around 1980. Total foreign commitments amounted to S$470 million ($220 million) in 1982. The firms involved had often begun as offshoots of joint ventures with foreign capital and started going abroad themselves as soon as they had grown large enough. In the early 1980s two-thirds of the Singapore outstanding total was still to be found in Malaysia. The emphasis was on developing sales in local markets rather than on exports. The organizational structure of early Singapore investment was allegedly determined by a small number of families such as Chang, Chia and Yeo (ESCAP/UNCTC 1985b: 94–5; Lim and Teoh 1986: 342, 348).

Annual outflows averaged $1.6 billion in the 1980s. This corresponds to 70% of annual average inflows. However, the average outflow for the 1980s is inflated by the upsurge towards the very end of the decade, for instance in 1989 when outflows doubled. The dramatic increase in 1989 may be associated with the launching of the SIJORI (Singapore-Johor-Riau) Growth Triangle. Since then Singapore has become the single largest source of foreign investment capital in manufacturing in the EPZ on Batam (Indonesia), just across the waters from Singapore. By 1993 total assets held abroad were reported at S$16 billion ($9 billion) of which 38% in Malaysia and 11% in Indonesia (Pang Eng Fong 1995: 115–17;

Thee 1995). Even so Singapore's involvement in investment activities in the immediate economic region has been far less pronounced than Hong Kong commitments in mainland China.

Singapore investments in the region explicitly serve to complement domestic manufacturing by providing an 'external wing' within easy reach. Much recent investment, especially in Thailand, Vietnam and Myanmar, may be connected with the increasingly important function of Singapore as the focal point in regional supply networks. Two characteristics should receive special attention in a more thorough study of Singapore investment in Southeast Asia today. The first one concerns the link between incoming and outgoing FDI. Inflows of FDI facilitate higher intensities of capital and technology whereas outflows serve to relocate labour-intensive production lines. The second characteristic refers to the ever widening geographical scope of action by Singapore investors, from Johor and Batam to Bangkok and Yangon (formerly Rangoon). Such a shift marks the emergence of new industrial procurement networks extending throughout the region.

Hong Kong is slightly closer to Southeast Asia than is Taipei. The small city state with its extraordinary status expired in 1997, has grown entangled in financial transactions among largely Chinese firms operating in Singapore, Taiwan and various ASEAN countries. For instance, Hong Kong-based corporations are known to take a keen interest in services in Singapore but such investments are next to impossible to separate from domestic investment in Singapore (Chia 1990: 12–13). There has been a spectacular increase of Hong Kong direct investment in Indonesia which also should be associated with the multinational character of large corporations run by overseas Chinese in Indonesia. Recorded inflows from Hong Kong into Indonesia approached $1 billion already in 1990 which was more than the one noted for Korea and only marginally less than the slice held by Taiwan. In Thailand links with domestic investors of Chinese origin are even more difficult to recognize since most overseas Chinese have adopted Thai names and the Thai nationality. Significantly, Hong Kong ranked first among NIC investors in Thailand around 1990 and accounted for the largest net inflow from a NIC origin also in 1994 (Yeung 1994: 1943–4; *FEER* 12/10 1995; see also Suehiro 1989: 8–9).[4]

Hong Kong investors initially focused on low-level technology manufacturing, especially textiles and footwear. Indonesia became a favoured destination in Southeast Asia in the 1980s but in absolute terms it was dwarfed by mainland China. Since the late 1980s the emphasis in Hong Kong investment in Indonesia has shifted towards chemicals and services such as real estate and hotels. The attitude of the Indonesian government with respect to 'Chinese' NIC investors can best be described as 'benign neglect'. The deregulation, from 1986 onwards, witnessed little overt encouragement which can only be ascribed to Indonesian sensitivity concerning the 'overpresence' of overseas Chinese in the economy as symbolized by the Liem Sioe Ling empire and the Bank of Central Asia in particular. It has been demonstrated that personal connection, *guanxi*, through the business and social networks of overseas Chinese have been decisive in channelling Hong Kong investment to Indonesia in particular (Thee 1995).

The search by Hong Kong investors for cheap unskilled labour did not long remain confined to Indonesia but was soon extended to Thailand. Access to local institutions and markets through networks of overseas Chinese was again combined with the utilization of comparative cost advantages of the host country in labour-intensive types of production that were becoming increasingly difficult to retain in Hong Kong itself, were it not for constraints in physical space alone. The interest of the Hong Kong Chinese in investing in Southeast Asia is today being slowed down by alternative opportunities materializing on the South China coastline and the uncertainties about what will happen after 1997.

Taiwan started investing heavily abroad after 1985. A first peak was reached by 1991. The prime motivation was to reduce costs in manufacturing for exports in the light of rising wages at home and an appreciating New Taiwanese dollar. There was, therefore, a strong emphasis on labour-intensive production, especially on the part of larger Taiwan investors. The textile industry thus became the foremost area of operations of Taiwan investors in Southeast Asia, possibly also in order to gain access to unutilized quotas under the Multi Fibres Agreements (Pangestu and Hasni 1991: 223). In the late 1980s textiles alone accounted for more than one-half of Taiwanese commitments in Indonesia whereas the share of this industry oscillated between 30% and 40% in Thailand and the Philippines (Chen, Chen and Ku 1995: 95). Taiwan offers a rather clear-cut case of overseas relocation of production in response to a successful industrial restructuring at home.

Taiwanese investment in Southeast Asia possesses several of the same features as investment originating in Singapore and Hong Kong. Transactions among overseas Chinese across borders tend to blur the distinction between foreign and domestic investment. In the late 1980s there were already signs that Taiwanese investment in Thailand was in fact considerably larger than what was registered, as *guanxi* bonds permitted corporate control to be exercised informally at the level of management rather than through ownership shares and boards of directors (ESCAP/UNCTC 1988: 467–581). On the other hand, mushrooming Taiwanese capital commitments in Malaysia were suspected of incorporating investment by overseas Chinese in Malaysia through roundtrip constructions, i.e. setting up a subsidiary in Taiwan which subsequently may benefit from promotional status as a foreign investor entering Malaysia (Fukushima and Kwan 1995: 10).

Taiwanese investment also shares some characteristics with 'new wave' Japanese investment in the region. This applies specifically to the increasing importance of small and medium-size manufacturing firms following in the wake of industrial giants. The smaller firms benefit from the experiences and contacts of the larger ones and tend to focus more on specific niches of production that often form an intermediate stage in a chain of export production. This may mean a higher degree of local entrenchment achieved by making more use of locally available materials and skills as compared to the large forerunners merely seeking access to cheap unskilled labour on a massive scale. It is believed that the part played by small and medium-size Taiwanese manufacturing firms in Southeast Asia is underrated in a both quantitative and qualitative sense due to respectively underreporting in the statistics and the potentials for effective transfers of technology (Chen 1995; Chen, Chen and Ku 1995: 89).

Korea has experienced a spectacular growth performance and industrial restructuring in a matter of one or two generations but outward investment flows remained small until the second half of the 1980s. Corporate strategies were initially geared towards realizing economies of scale through taking advantage of lower labour costs on overseas locations in combination with the application of standardized technologies of production. There was an early interest in relocating assembly operations of electrical and electronic appliances to Southeast Asia. In addition early Korean investors showed a great interest to invest in an exploitation of natural resources without much further processing, e.g. in logging in Indonesia (Euh and Sang 1986).

The early 1990s saw a gradual transition in the outlook of major Korean investors. The policy regime with respect to outward investment then came to favour a more active marketing and penetration of host country economies. Networks are since then set up to facilitate vertical divisions of labour reminiscent of 'new wave' Japanese investment. Diversification and more use of local technology signify a greater attention for economies of scope as opposed to those of scale. Several types of firms are involved in building up Korean-controlled production in Southeast Asia. Large *chaebol* such as Samsung and Goldstar manufacture colour television sets in Thailand, refrigerators in Indonesia and microwave ovens in Malaysia whereas small and medium-size firms specialize in components and accessories in the same or neighbouring host countries (Lee 1995: 70–73, 83). Recent Korean investment in Southeast Asia appears to more closely mirror the experiences of Japanese predecessors, both those of the original type and those belonging to the 'new wave', than do the other three NIC investors.

NIC investors are generally supposed to adapt more easily to local circumstances of production in the host country as compared to multinationals from the United States, Japan or Western Europe. They are reported to more willingly enter into joint ventures and allowing a more substantial participation by host country nationals. The technology applied is said to be of a lesser sophistication so that transfers of technology more readily materialize. In addition, there is supposedly a stronger export orientation in production which implies more tangible benefits in terms of foreign exchange earnings for the host country (Hock 1990: 124–5; Panchareon 1990: 174–8; Guisinger 1991: 36). It is tempting to argue that current NIC investment better illustrates the Kojima hypothesis than does Japanese investment. Yet perhaps it is more a matter of difference in bargaining power vis-à-vis the host country and less an inherent feature of NIC investment.

Successive waves of FDI have swept over Southeast Asia during the last decade. The experiences are still too recent and the evidence too hazy to allow much of a conclusive assessment. Suffice it to say that the Japanese 'new wave' and mushrooming NIC investment can be considered mutually complementary forming a special case of the juxtaposition of supply and demand factors behind FDI in which rising wages and appreciating currencies become decisive. In addition, there is marked contrast between 'Chinese' NIC investment founded upon informal networks across boundaries on the one hand and Korean-style NIC investment which more faithfully reproduces the Japanese pattern. This is where cultural identity and tradition enters into an equation otherwise determined by macro-economic variables.

6.4   THE YOUNGEST PARTNERS

Nothing breeds success like past success. Recent advancement in terms of integration and performance of the economies inside the European Union has made other European nations queue up for membership just as new foreign investors flock to share in the benefits from rapid growth in Southeast Asia. This final section on identities of foreign investors in Southeast Asia since the 1960s briefly considers the recent attraction of the region for West European capital seeking profitable investment outlets. It is a historical irony that three out four of these newest arrivals among foreign investors in the region are, in fact, oldtimers reestablishing flows of capital familiar from the colonial period. This applies to Britain, the Netherlands and France, leaving only Germany as a 'true' newcomer in the region.

Southeast Asia today boasts a reputation as the fastest growing economic region in the world. In the late 1980s average real rates of growth ranged from 9% in Thailand to 5.5–6.5% in Singapore, Malaysia and Indonesia, whereas the debt-ridden Philippines scarcely got beyond 3% (IMF 1991: 286–9, 350–53, 432–5, 470–73, 518–23). Halfway through the 1990s Singapore, Malaysia, Thailand and Vietnam remain just a little short of securing two-digit annual rates while both Indonesia and the Philippines are comfortably above 7% and 5% respectively (Asia Yearbook 1996: 140, 168, 196, 204, 217, 222). Such growth rates easily exceed those achieved by the West European economies during the 1950s and 1960s and do not fail to impress observers in these countries. Recent years have witnessed a lively discussion about whether Western Europe has missed a golden opportunity to participate in the spectacular growth of the Southeast Asian economies. The 'new wave'-type of attention given to Southeast Asia is best interpreted as an effort to catch up with investors from the United States, Japan and the NICs. A bandwagon effect seems to be in force of the kind which was originally formulated for multinationals following each other into the same new markets (Knickerbocker 1973).

Two factors are of importance in explaining why the investors from Western Europe have been lagging behind during much of the resurgence of FDI in Southeast Asia since the 1960s. The first one refers to the colonial heritage. The violent break with the colonial past in Indonesia under Sukarno discouraged Dutch enterprises to such an extent that a return was, in fact, ruled out, even when the investment climate had improved under Suharto. Significantly, the New Order government in Indonesia did restore British and American property nationalized during the 'Crush Malaysia' campaign in 1963–1965 but not the Dutch assets confiscated in 1957/58. The disruption of continuity was, of course, even more violent in the case of the British in Burma and the French in Vietnam. In Malaysia, where the rupture was less violent, British willingness to invest again was restrained by the persistent efforts of the Malaysian government at the time of the NEP to gain hold over assets dating back from the colonial hegemony, if need be with the aid of newly acquired oil revenues.

The second factor explaining the West European lag concerns the internal developments in the European Community. The process of economic integration within the European Community underwent an acceleration in the mid-1980s precisely at the time when the liberalization of investment climates in Southeast Asia began. The Single European Act of 1986 aimed at creating a region with no internal frontiers, a construction feared to become a 'fortress Europe' for outsiders. Whatever its effects for those on the outside, it certainly served to redirect attention of insiders towards the emerging large internal market and to make the EC member states more inward-looking in their strategies than they already were. The heavy concentration on other industrialized countries among capital exports inside the EC was reinforced and Southeast Asia failed to increase its appeal as an attractive destination (Wagner 1989: 3–17). EC investment remained in the shadow of American or Japanese investment.

In 1988 EC Commissioner Cheysson declared more EC investment in the ASEAN to be a high priority. Effects were less than impressive which was above all ascribed to the preoccupation with the internal matters of the common market just mentioned. This changed only during the early 1990s. Dutch firms reentered Indonesia and by 1993 cumulative approvals, as registered by the BKPM, were on a par with those of Hong Kong or Singapore investors. This increase in incoming capital flows was not adversely affected by the disruption of official Dutch aid to Indonesia in 1992. British firms returned to the region but chose locations in Indonesia rather than Malaysia and soon overtook their Dutch rivals. German commitments were widened to embrace also manufacturing in Indonesia, Malaysia and Thailand. Meanwhile, France emerged as one of the largest foreign investors in Vietnam, claiming by 1994 to have secured approvals worth some $750 million which was only surpassed by some of the NICs and Australia. In Singapore continuity still reigned supreme. The traditional Anglo-Dutch combination here accounted for $8.2 billion out of a total $39 billion of foreign assets reported to have been accumulated up to 1992 (*FEER* 22/9 1994; 12/10 1995; Thee 1995).

In the 1980s the sectoral composition of EC investment in Southeast Asia reflected the lag with respect to American and Japanese firms. British and Dutch capital was concentrated on oil with the establishments of British Petroleum and Royal Dutch/Shell at Singapore. German investment in manufacturing was said to fit into the import substitution policies of Malaysia in particular but were, in terms of volume, overshadowed by commitments in banking and commercial services in Singapore (Hiemenz 1987: 124–5; Wagner 1989: 13). Links with the export-oriented industrialization in progress throughout the region were less pronounced than in the case of American or Japanese investors. More detailed study of the available evidence is required in order to ascertain whether this has changed during the early 1990s.

The question whether EC investors have missed opportunities in Southeast Asia cannot be answered unequivocally. It is true that the former European colonies in Southeast Asia did not obtain the same preferential treatment in trading relations as, for instance, the former French colonies in Africa, a fact that may be ascribed to the timing of the Yaoundé and Lomé treaties and the powerful voice of France in effecting these arrangements. Yet this argument is only valid to the extent that mutual trade and FDI flows reinforce one another. It is also true that EC investors have lost much of their traditional comparative advantages in the stiffer competition with, for instance, NIC investors. Yet in the final analysis much depends on what the presumptive investor can offer in terms of technology transfer which is a key topic of the next chapter.

This chapter has identified a number of new patterns of FDI in Southeast Asia as they have materialized since the 1960s. American investment represents the strongest continuity with the prewar past. It can still be largely explained from the supply side of the FDI equation and it flourishes whenever natural resources can be profitably exploited or if the investment climate is exceptionally favourable. Japanese investment of the type dating back from before the Plaza Accord is better explained by a convergence of push and pull factors which implies tailormade networks of affiliates by host country rather than overriding preferences for certain environments. 'New wave' Japanese investment since 1985 and NIC investment since about 1990 constitute complementary flows within a region-wide 'flying geese' pattern of industrial restructuring where relocations of production are induced by specific changes in labour and currency costs. These waves also give rise to two types of regional networks, a Japanese-Korean version based on procurement hierarchies and a Chinese one based on informal contacts. The difference may also reflect different stages of economic development in the capital-supplying countries concerned. The most recent EC investment, finally, is best conceived as a bandwagon effect, at times combining belated returns of onetime predominant capital suppliers with fresh arrivals. Whatever these rough trends may imply for future developments, it cannot be doubted that the character of FDI in Southeast Asia has changed profoundly. Its impact on host country developments is likely to differ as well.

6.5 ON JAPANESE STATISTICS

There is a bewildering variety of statistical data on FDI in Southeast Asia since the 1960s. The most authoritative set of data appears to be the one

compiled around 1990 by the Centre for Transnational Corporations at the
United Nations/ESCAP office in Bangkok (United Nations 1992; section
2.3). The level of aggregation in this source is too high to allow a more
penetrating insight into the structure of FDI in various host countries. For
this purpose details by investor are required. The best available information of this type is provided by the list of Japanese-affiliated subsidiaries
prepared annually in Tokyo and on rare occasions rendered into an
English-language version.[5]

The 1986 issue used here reports the outcome of a survey conducted by
way of both questionnaires and telephone interviews (Japanese Overseas
Investment 1986). The survey covers companies listed on the stock
exchanges of Tokyo, Osaka and Nagoya, as well as a number of leading
unlisted firms in Japan. The information is arranged by host country and
parent company and always includes names of Japanese investors and subsidiaries, date of starting operations, total equity capital of the subsidiary
expressed in domestic currency, foreign capital ratios, numbers of employees, major business lines and locations of production. Investment objectives are stated in most cases whereas annual sales and a qualitative
assessment of business results are given only on rare occasions. The 1986
issue enumerates 1057 individual firms with a Japanese interest in the
ASEAN member states (excluding Brunei). The distribution by host
country runs as follows: 307 firms in Singapore, 245 in Thailand, 220 in
Malaysia, 176 in Indonesia and 109 in the Philippines.

A major advantage of the Tokyo survey derives from its very compre-
hensiveness which enables us to review Japanese investment of every
extent and type, i.e. minute participation by the Bank of Tokyo in the
Development Bank of Singapore or the Industrial Finance Corporation of
Thailand as well as wholly-owned subsidiaries of Toray or Hitachi. The
wide coverage facilitates a full appreciation of the extent of Japanese
influence on business in Southeast Asia but, by the same token, the source
does not readily lend itself to estimations of the total Japanese capital actually invested in the region. Therefore, the emphasis has to be on relative
distributions and comparisons across lines of production rather than on
absolute figures or individual firms. Some of the information is presented
in Table 6.7.

7 The Ideals of Industry

On Monday 10 May 1993 a fire swept through the toy factory of Kader Industrial in downtown Bangkok, killing 189 unskilled workers and eliciting an outcry about labour conditions prevailing in foreign-owned manufacturing in Thailand. Some 2000 Thai labourers lost their jobs during the aftermath of the fire while the complex ownership structure of the factory made it exceedingly difficult to establish who was to assume responsibility for the casualties. Kader Industrial (Thailand) appeared to be a joint subsidiary of Taiwanese investors and KCP Toys which in turn was owned by Lyre Terrace in Hong Kong together with the Sino-Thai conglomerate Charoen Pokphand (*FEER* 24/6 1993). The calamity at Kader Industrial highlighted the dark side of what was supposed to be yet another example of how FDI could make a substantial positive contribution towards the industrial restructuring of the Thai economy. Here, standardized production for exports took place under the most deplorable of labour conditions precluding any other lasting benefits than sizeable profits for the primarily foreign owners. This chapter considers contemporary FDI in Southeast Asia within the wider context of the regional quest for economic growth and industrialization.

The focus of analysis now shifts from the identity and character of FDI as it has reemerged since the 1960s to its impact on the host country economy. An exhaustive coverage of all possible effects of FDI on the recipient will not be given as the discussion is confined to economic effects and directed specifically towards the role played by FDI in the process of industrialization taking place throughout the region at this time. In this way FDI is explicitly linked to the major change occurring in the region during the current generation, just as FDI before the Pacific War was connected with the process of colonial state formation, the major change experienced by that generation (Chapter 4). It should also be stressed that this chapter cannot possibly offer a complete review of the huge international 'linkages and leakages' literature on the implications of FDI. Our aim is rather to present a number of observations deemed to be of particular relevance for a systematic comparison of FDI in Southeast Asia in the early as well as the late twentieth century. That is, after all, the general theme of this book.

Several classifications of effects of FDI are applied in the literature (Hill 1990). From the various alternatives we distil a list of the seven major effects:

(1) Income effects through the contribution of FDI in total capital forma-
    tion in the host country. This effect is positive to the extent that the
    newly generated investment raises gross domestic product and
    national income.
(2) Employment effects, i.e. job opportunities created by FDI which did
    not exist before.
(3) Balance of payments effects embracing not only the balance between
    increased exports and the rise in imports required to support new pro-
    duction but also the inflow of fresh capital against remittances and
    retrievals.
(4) Structural effects such as the emergence of new lines of production
    for facilitating or further processing, i.e. backward and forward link-
    ages. A generalized structural effect refers to the sectoral composi-
    tion of the economy as a whole.
(5) Technology transfer through the application of more sophisticated
    knowhow in production. The transfer may be effected through the
    technology embodied in FDI and also through the upgrading of skills
    associated with FDI activities.
(6) Market effects which may be either positive when FDI sets a good
    example for domestic entrepreneurs to follow or negative when
    domestic businessmen are crowded out by foreign ones.
(7) Taxation effects appearing as a logical corollary to rising corporate
    and personal incomes. Benefits accruing to host country governments
    on this account are often significantly reduced by tax holidays and
    other incentives to attract FDI, at least during the initial stage of
    building up FDI.

There are no generally accepted criteria for the assessment of these effects.
Exercises in this vein tend to opt for pragmatism concentrating on comparisons over time, between types of investors or across host countries
thereby making use of the most recent available empirical information,
however piecemeal it may be. As a result, scarcely any study renders a
comprehensive overview of all major effects. Malaysia forms an exception
as it is singularly well endowed with systematic analyses of FDI, especially with respect to the 1970s when the NEP was first implemented.
Much of the more general and theoretical discussion has been devoted to
different linkages between FDI and other economic activities (Hirschman
1977; Thee 1977: 122, 129; Ariff and Hill 1985: 49–53).

Traditional distrust of foreign multinationals coloured many concep-
tions of FDI effects in the newly independent host countries of Southeast
Asia, with the exception of Singapore, at the time when the resurgence of

FDI began in the 1960s. Since then there has been a successive improvement in the image of both expectations and achievements of large-scale incoming FDI. The decisive change of attitude and appreciation came in the mid-1980s, significantly coinciding with the general shift towards deregulation and more liberal investment policies. The most positive sound was voiced, to cite just one example, in a comparative study of Japanese car manufacturing in Indonesia, Malaysia, Thailand and the Philippines. This study signalled a tendency to overrate the bargaining power of the foreign multinational, in this case Mitsubishi, and to underestimate potential benefits for local manufacturing following the Japanese lead (Doner 1987).

Assessments have become ever more favourable in the 1990s. One observer has bluntly generalized that 'the role of FDI in Southeast Asia has been benign' (Fry 1993: 57). FDI was considered to have an equally positive effect on economic growth and domestic investment. The only drawback was a lower propensity to save at home but this was considered to be unimportant. Japanese transnational corporations in particular enjoy a better reputation than before as their investment 'accommodates sequenced industrial development of the host countries' (Ostry and Harianto 1995). At the same time, however, the need is also felt for more differentiation by host country even if the overall score remains positive. A ranking of three host countries positions Singapore first in terms of capacity of gaining from FDI followed by Malaysia and Thailand, in that order (Natarajan and Tan 1992: 59–64).

Effects of FDI are intertwined and must not therefore be examined independently of one another. This necessitates the argument of this chapter to be arranged by host country rather than by issue. The survey is restricted to the five major host countries of the region that can all look back on a relatively long history of incoming FDI, i.e. Singapore, Malaysia, Thailand, Indonesia and the Philippines. A full treatment of the impact of FDI is not yet feasible for host countries that have only recently been opened up, notably Vietnam. The logical point of departure is Singapore where the common ideal of the region, a mature industrial nation, has already been achieved. Here a link is established between different types of foreign-affiliated firms and achievement in manufacturing (section 7.1). The electronics industry is generally held to possess the richest potential for rapid industrial growth at an advanced level. Such prospects are especially relevant to Malaysia, the host country in Southeast Asia that is most closely associated with 'near-NIC' status (section 7.2). Industrial restructuring is proceeding at an especially rapid pace in Thailand and it becomes feasible to associate different kinds of foreign investors with changes in the size and composition of manufacturing sector (section 7.3). Indonesia is one step further down the ladder of industrial progress, so far. Here, industrialization serves to reduce dependence on oil revenues. The decisive shift from labour-intensive production to applying advanced technology still has to take place (section 7.4). The Philippines, finally, is really a separate case within the regional spectre where highest priority is given to overcoming the legacies of the Marcos regime so as fully to join the path chosen by the region at large (section 7.5). This chapter makes use of several complementary approaches drawing on aggregate statistics on foreign-affiliated firms (Singapore and Thailand), one individual case study (Malaysia) and a multitude of empirical findings reported in the secondary literature (Indonesia and the Philippines) among other things. Selected statistics on macro-economic performance are added to the chapter (Table 7.9).

7.1   ENGINES OF ASSERTION

Goh Keng Swee, Minister of Finance under Lee Kuan Yew, once remarked about the Singapore government that 'we imported entrepreneurs in the form of multinational corporations' (Huff 1994: 320). Such an assertion is indicative of Singapore's strategy to employ FDI for its own purposes of i.e. rapid growth and fast industrialization, without ever fearing that the foreign multinationals may pocket the returns without occasioning much sustained economic development. Singapore's unique self-confidence in bending FDI to its own benefit has upset all conventional theories about FDI drainage (Chong 1986: 64). This section looks more closely at the immediate link between rebounding FDI and industrial achievement in Singapore since the late 1960s. It is a rather clear-cut case of success in which FDI functions as an engine of accelerated growth. A further elaboration requires that we consider first the general pattern of FDI and then some effects of FDI on the domestic economic development.

Oil traditionally played the foremost role within manufacturing, the sector which, for obvious reasons, formed the economic core of the newly independent city state. Stanvac (preceding Esso or Exxon) was operating a refinery on Pulau Minyak in the 1930s whereas Mobil set up installations in Jurong in the 1960s. Shell arrived in Pulau Bukom after its departure from Indonesia in 1965 and was the single largest foreign investor in the country in 1993. These three giants were joined by Caltex and British Petroleum and Singapore soon ranked as the world's third oil refining centre, after Houston and Rotterdam. Oil refining and petroleum products accounted for more than 60% of FDI in manufacturing in Singapore during the late 1960s but by 1975 this share had already dropped to about 40%, only to fall towards one-third in the 1980s (McKern and Koomsup 1987: 301–2; Doshi 1989: 5, 89–91; *Singapore Investment News*: April 1993). The oil firms kept growing but other branches of manufacturing expanded even faster.

The Singapore government engineered a change of strategy by pushing a 'Second Industrial Revolution' stressing automation and information technologies rather than the capital-intensive processing of petroleum. Incentives and cost advantages were provided and new arrivals during the early 1980s included Hewlett-Packard and National Semiconductor as well as Hitachi and Asahi. The electrical and electronic industry emerged as the leading branch of manufacturing, capturing almost one-half of all new investment in manufacturing by 1988. Foreign involvement was high with four computer firms out of five having a majority foreign ownership (Mirza 1986: 167; Rodan 1989: 175–80, 209–11; Lim and Pang 1991: 59). Between 1981 and 1987 the contribution of electrical and electronic products in aggregate manufacturing value-added doubled, from 20% to 40%, whereas the industry's share in total manufacturing exports climbed from 48% to 62% (Wong Poh Kam 1991: 169). Foreign sales of integrated circuits, to mention just one example, rose threefold between 1982 and 1988 (Huff 1994: 313).

The increasing level of technological sophistication in incoming FDI implied high capital intensities in production and heavy concentrations of equity capital. This may be further explored by a statistical analysis of major foreign-controlled corporations operating in Singapore. A list of the 500 largest companies, as measured by sales volume, was consulted with reference to 1988. This year was chosen so as to better incorporate the changes in manufacturing investment associated with the 'Second Industrial Revolution' in Singapore. Specifications of foreign ownership, above a threshold of 60% of equity holdings, facilitated the selection of the segment of total manufacturing built up by accumulated FDI (Singapore 1989: 137–60).[1] A foreign nationality applied to 318 out of the 500 largest corporations which gives an immediate clue to the overriding importance of foreign capital in implementing the industrialization of Singapore.

The high degree of concentration of foreign capital in Singapore is apparent from a glance at the list of the 318 largest firms by turnover reported over 1988. Fifty large firms were responsible for 67% of total sales where 73% of all equity was vested with only 28 firms. The computer hardware producer Seagate Technology ranked among the top five on either account. Less than one firm in ten (30 out of 318) in Singapore was classified as 'small' in terms of sales. Average annual sales amounted to $75.5 million (S$151 million).

There were marked differences by nationality among the large foreign enterprises in Singapore as of the late 1980s (Figure 7.1; Table 7.8). Japanese firms were generally smaller but reported larger sales volumes. American firms were the largest, possessing an accumulated equity that corresponded to two-fifths of the total for the largest 318 foreign-owned corporations. EC occupied an intermediate position and NIC companies were still, in 1988, rather underrepresented in the top echelons of the foreign-affiliated corporate network of Singapore.

The larger scale of operations of Japanese firms, relative to endowment, was not reflected in higher profit rates. Here American and EC firms scored better. This observation reaffirms a ranking by rate of return established by the Singapore Department of Statistics: American firms with an average of 24% during the 1980s followed by British firms (16%) and Japanese firms averaging 12.5% (Foreign Equity 1992: 9). The higher rate of return of the former two types of FDI may possibly be influenced by the inclusion of the highly profitable oil concerns (Chia 1982: 392–404). In addition, it is conceivable that Japanese firms were less inclined to report profits or more bent upon ploughing back revenue into the enterprise.

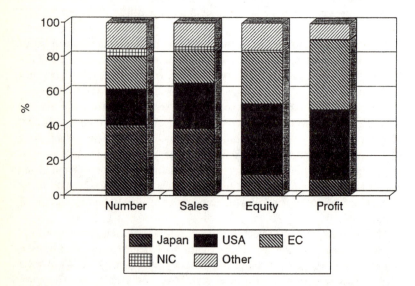

Figure 7.1   Foreign firms in Singapore: characteristics by nationality, 1988

Table 7.8   Characteristics by nationality of foreign-affiliated firms in Singapore, 1988.

(All values in S$ millions at current prices)

	Japan	USA	EC	NIC	Other	Total
Number	128	66	61	15	48	318
(%)	(40)	(21)	(19)	(5)	(15)	(100)
Sales	16947	11726	8203	1186	6128	44190
(%)	(38)	(27)	(19)	(3)	(14)	(100)
Equity	1895	6470	4715	175	2491	15747
(%)	(12)	(41)	(30)	(1)	(16)	(100)
Profits	285	1249	1229	17	287	3067
(%)	(9)	(41)	(40)	(1)	(9)	(100)

Note: The selection covers foreign-affiliated firms included among the 500 largest business corporations in Singapore.
Source: Singapore 1989: 137–60.

The shift of emphasis from oil to electronics in foreign-controlled manufacturing with its associated concentrations of capital has broadened the basis for potentially substantial contributions of FDI in terms of income and export revenue. Optimistic predictions with respect to new employment, linkages and skills development are more hazardous since so much depends on the manner in which the newly accessible technology is implemented in production. A 'Second Industrial Revolution' by definition implies a certain displacement of labour by capital whereas actual transfers of technology are difficult to measure. The literature contains numerous scattered references to FDI effects in Singapore which need to be reviewed in this context.

The share of FDI in gross capital formation was reputed to be very substantial by the late 1960s and early 1970s. Actual estimates, however, vary considerably depending on which definitions are applied and which sources have been consulted. The most extreme estimates cite very high percentages whereas use of officially registered incoming FDI flows reduces the contribution of FDI in capital formation down to about one-tenth but the latter figure is admitted to be a gross understatement (Hill and Johns 1985: 361). There is not even a consensus about the development over time. Reliance on IMF data on FDI flows produces an upward trend in the foreign contribution to gross capital formation towards annual averages at 22% in the 1970s and 25% in the 1980s. A combination of various kinds of balance of payments and international financial statistics, however, results in a downward trend, towards 18% in the late 1970s and 14% in the early 1980s (ASEAN-U.S. Initiative 1989: 96; cf. Yoshida *et al.* 1994; Huff 1994: 338). Yet even the lower figures are relatively high by international comparison. The persistence of a very sizeable share of FDI in capital formation is borne out by the fact that one-third of all equity investment stemmed from foreign-controlled firms at both the beginning and the end of the 1980s (Foreign Equity 1992: 2).

Import substitution is commonly considered to be the 'easy' initial stage of industrialization where the economy stays until the time is ripe for the shift towards export-oriented industrial production. In Singapore, however, the import-substituting phase was exceedingly brief with the emphasis being put on export production already by the late 1960s. Manufactured exports increased as a proportion of GDP from 17% in 1969 to 47% in 1979 and further to 63% by 1990 (Huff 1994: 305). The foreign share in exports was exceedingly high which testifies to the disproportionate participation of FDI in export manufacturing. The share of wholly-owned foreign subsidiaries had been a mere 33% in 1963 but climbed to 57% in 1970 and 71% in 1978. Inclusion of joint ventures pushes the percentage above 80% for 1970 and above 90% for 1975 (Yoshihara 1976: 146; Lim Joo-Jock 1977: 80; Wong 1979: 75; ESCAP/UNCTC 1985b: 275). The share of wholly- and majority-owned foreign firms in manufacturing exports stayed at the level of 82–85% during the 1980s and 1990s which underscores the high dependence on FDI as opposed to domestic firms in penetrating foreign markets (Chia 1985: 293; Huff 1994: 319).

Employment effects were substantial but showed a more erratic pattern than the persistent positive link between the accumulation of FDI and export growth. The initial expansion of labour-intensive lines of production implied a dramatic increase in new employment with, for instance, numbers of jobs in manufacturing doubling between 1965 and 1969 alone. The turning-point came in 1978 when Singapore shifted towards applying more capital-intensive types of production in manufacturing. Layoffs followed but in the long run the expansion of output and adjustment of the labour market brought another thrust of expansion of employment. Numbers of jobs in manufacturing increased substantially. By 1988, foreign firms were responsible for almost 55% of all employment in manufacturing (Chia 1980: 258; Kwan and Lee 1983: 158–60; Dunning and Cantwell 1987: 573–83; Rodan 1989: 113; Huff 1994: 319; United Nations 1994: 187).

The experience of Singapore shows that technological upgrading through FDI can be accompanied by substantial positive employment effects. It has been calculated that foreign-controlled firms accounted for three-quarters of all new employment in manufacturing over the entire period 1962–1982. Significantly, as much as 40% of the newly created employment was found in joint ventures between foreign and Singapore firms (Chia 1986: 103). A small case study embracing three multinational producers in the electronics industry of Singapore argues that as much as 40–60% of all new employment was attributed to multiplier effects, i.e. indirect employment materializing elsewhere as a result of the enlargement of the original capital-intensive line of production (Lim and Pang 1977: 186–7).

An extreme export orientation and high capital intensities in production among foreign firms carries two immediate risks for the development of the host country. There is a danger that foreign-controlled production will turn into virtual enclaves in the host country economy and also that domestic competitors will be overshadowed by the larger and more productive foreign firms. Both risks have appeared real enough in the case of Singapore. Early manufacturing growth in particular was foreign-dominated to an extraordinary degree and seemed to depend almost exclusively on imports of both foreign capital and foreign goods. Linkages with the local economy remained limited and local business did indeed feel crowded out (Chia 1984: 150; Lim and Pang 1991: 51–2). Much new investment involved turnkey transfers of technology, not in the least so as to speed up the start of operations of the local subsidiary. Local research and development was rumoured to lag behind. If true this could seriously impair the capacity of Singapore to absorb new technologies. In this regard there was little difference between oil refining, the traditional stronghold, and the youngest leading sector, electronics (Mirza 1986: 257–9).

The situation changed in the mid-1980s. This is associated with the accelerated expansion and technological upgrading of the electronics industry. Singapore became the world's largest producer of computer tape and disk drives and soon ranked among the five leading suppliers of semiconductors (after the USA, Japan, Malaysia and Korea). Exports of disk drives almost quadrupled in less than five years, between 1986 and 1990. The electronics industry alone contributed 12% of GDP in Singapore by the early 1990s, employing no less than one-quarter of all labourers in manufacturing. For Japanese electronics firms in particular Singapore developed into a regional centre of technology-intensive operations. Backward linkages were observed for major firms such as Aiwa, Hitachi, JVC, Matsushita, Sanyo and Sony. Such linkages were found to extend to the Southeast Asian region as a whole rather than to the economy of Singapore alone (Huff 1994: 313; Pang 1995: 121–5). Technology transfer due to FDI in Singapore is thus above all dependent on the regional dimension of the Singapore economy.

Separate mention should be made of the growing participation of FDI in the service sector which again is immediately related to the central position of Singapore within regional networks. Partnerships have been established between the Singapore government and foreign firms in developing telecommunication facilities as well as financial and accounting services. Transfers of advanced technology in information networks have been aided not only by official encouragement but above all by a rapid increase in public expenditure on research and development in recent years (United Nations 1995b: 234, 240). The 'new' mix of electronics and technologically sophisticated services was manifest in the group of foreign firms making large investment pledges for 1994 and subsequent years. This group included Asahi's plant for manufacturing colour TV glass panels ($211 million), Hewlett-Packard's factory for handheld information products ($168 million), a vast network to be set up by British Telecommunications (eventually worth $1 billion) and also disk drive and chips factories owned by Micropolis and National Semiconductor respectively (*Singapore Investment News*, February 1995).

Singapore constitutes perhaps the most 'pure' illustration of how FDI can make a decisive contribution towards attaining rapid economic growth. This happens if two conditions are met. First, FDI augments resources available for capital formation, i.e. FDI corresponds to a significant proportion of gross domestic capital formation. Second, FDI raises a higher efficiency of investment by making use of a more advanced technology than domestic investment. Both conditions were amply fulfilled in the case of Singapore. Such a causal relationship between FDI and economic growth has been substantiated and statistically verified for nine Asian economies, including Singapore, during the period 1965–1982 (Rana and Dowling 1988). The very open economy and the tough fiscal regime were both crucial in monitoring the success of Singapore. Growth is also favourably affected by increases in final demand elsewhere in the region, i.e. economic growth in Southeast Asia at large is transmitted to trading partners via multipliers and trade linkages (Toh and Low 1990).

Singapore today possesses probably the most heavily foreign-dominated manufacturing sector in the world. It has gained much as is witnessed by very sizeable income and balance of payments effects. The employment effect has in the long run also turned out favourable because of the sheer scale of output enlargement and the many new jobs in auxiliary branches.

Linkages and technology transfers lagged behind and only materialized when manufacturing was modernized so as to serve as a hub in regional procurement and service networks. Technological upgrading has compensated for the crowding-out of domestic entrepreneurs which is likely to have occurred in the early stages of industrialization. The high level of technological sophistication may, in due course, serve to reduce an excessive dependence on foreign capital.

7.2   TECHNOLOGY TRANSMITTED

Malaysia's charismatic prime minister, Datuk Seri Mahathir Mohamad, feels comfortable with his self-proclaimed mission of leading his country into the twenty-first century, literally and figuratively. 'Dr M.' believes strongly in the East Asian mode of rapid industrialization through technological upgrading. He used to be an outspoken admirer of Japan but he did become somewhat disenchanted after dealing with Mitsubishi in the Proton Saga episode (Jomo 1994: 289). By the mid-1990s 'near-NIC' status had been firmly rooted in Malaysia with per capita incomes above $10,000 (after correction for international differences in purchasing power). The Malaysian economy was growing at a rate of 8–9% per year (*Asia Yearbook* 1996: 168–9). This section sketches the role of FDI in the remarkable transformation of the Malaysian economy since the 1960s. Technology transfer forms a *Leitmotif* in the discussion since it appears as the most lasting impact of FDI on domestic economic growth. The review covers the changing conditions for implementing such transfers, i.e. the NEP and beyond, as well as one key branch of manufacturing, electronics. The latter theme is elaborated by looking more closely at one specific location, Penang, and even one individual foreign-controlled enterprise on that location, a leading Japanese producer of semiconductors.

With the NEP the Malaysian government tried to do two things at the same time. One was industrialization, at first through import substitution, later through export orientation. The other was to eradicate the ethnic imbalances in terms of ownership and control of economic resources. The Second Malaysia Plan of 1971 combined an accelerated industrialization through importing technology with specific targets for *bumiputra* ownership in corporate business. By 1990 it was stipulated that the Malay and foreign shares of ownership should both reach 30% which implied that the indigenous Malay share had to rise from the 4% actually held in 1970. The foreign share would have to be reduced to one-half of its original level at more than 60%. The proportion of the Malaysian economy controlled by overseas Chinese was to stay more or less than same (Wong 1979: 63–4; Khong 1986: 199; Jomo 1990: 118–23). From the outset it was clear that these two objectives were mutually inconsistent.

The intended wholesale reshuffling of ownership in the corporate sector could only be accomplished through strict regulation of incoming FDI and direct intervention by the government. Minimal Malay equity require- ments were introduced relating ownership distributions to the use of domestic resources and market orientation. Such arrangements effectively restricted majority-held FDI to selected parts of export-oriented produc- tion. The Malaysian government utilized windfall gains from the rising oil prices to take over major British-held assets, e.g. London Tin in 1975, Sime Darby in 1976, Guthrie in 1980/81 and Harrisons & Crosfield in 1982. The foreign share in total corporate equity dropped to 43% in 1980 and further to 26% in 1985 (Chee and Lee 1979; Ali and Osman-Rani 1987: 187; Jesudason 1989: 147–51; Lim and Pang 1991: 41). The outcome of a decade and a half of NEP implementation was indisputably a declining foreign share in the Malaysian economy. It is less clear if it also meant a significant rise in individual *bumiputra* equity holdings since so much of the ownership shift was effected through increased government participation. In addition, it is possible that equity holdings of overseas Chinese, whether official or through so-called 'Ali Baba' con- structions, increased as well.

In an evaluation of Malaysian economic planning undertaken in the mid-1980s, the United Nations Industrial Development Organization (UNIDO) pointed out that the objectives of the NEP posed constraints to one another. Equity ownership patterns changed but only at the expense of less incoming FDI and slower rates of growth. UNIDO recommended a relaxed application of NEP provisions, especially in the light of the tougher competition for foreign capital in the 1980s as opposed to the 1970s (Taylor and Ward 1994: 114–15). Eventually, in 1991, the NEP was replaced by the less restrictive NDP. At that time FDI was climbing to unprecedented levels. Our assessment of FDI effect under the NEP is above all coloured by the fact that the NEP itself restrained incoming FDI, thus also the scope of its total impact on the host country economy.

Malaysia is comparatively well endowed with assessments of FDI effects, both general impressions and partial observations applying only to individual effects. The most comprehensive work of this kind was under- taken by Hoffman and Tan who estimated actual effects of FDI over the period 1962–1970. According to their findings, the contribution of foreign-controlled companies was as follows:

- 18% of overall GDP growth (52% in manufacturing alone);
- 23% of gross investment;
- 6% of overall new employment (26% in manufacturing alone);
- about 45% of tax receipts.

In addition, Hoffman and Tan distinguish between two types of effects on Malaysia's balance of payments. The resource effect, i.e. accumulated inflows versus outflows of capital, was strongly negative due to sizeable remittances of investment income to foreign owners of rubber estates and tin mining corporations. The exchange effect, which is restricted to the current account of the balance of payments, was positive with a trade surplus accruing to foreign-controlled companies that was more than three times the size of the total trade surplus, at any rate during the second half of the 1960s. Foreign firms were clearly more effective in replacing imports and enlarging exports than were domestic corporations. No attempt was made to specify effects which do not easily lend themselves to quantification, e.g. linkages and technology transfer (Hoffman and Tan 1980: 219–53). The overall record of FDI performance was good in terms of stimulating manufacturing exports but less so when it came to employment and retaining profits for reinvestment.

The lead of Hoffman and Tan in measuring FDI effects in a comprehensive fashion has not been taken up by others. This is all the more regrettable since the study of Hoffman and Tan refers only to the 1960s when industrialization was just starting and the colonial legacy was still being felt in the economic life of Malaysia whereas the time was not yet ripe for the NEP. A whole host of partial calculations and observations may, when taken together, serve as a follow-up to the systematic analysis offered by Hoffman and Tan. The subsequent survey reviews some of the evidence pertaining to the 1970s and early 1980s and directs our attention in particular to less easily measured effects than Hoffman and Tan provided.

NEP discrimination against both foreign and non-Malay domestic investment was on occasion criticized for not differentiating carefully enough between investors sending profits out of the country and those who did not. A statement to that effect is even attributed to the Chinese billionaire Robert Kuok who is himself one of Southeast Asia's major investors abroad. Kuok said: 'For every ringgit of foreign investment, a few more ringgits are going to flow out of the country' (Lim and Pang 1991: 38). Popular belief in the negative balance of payments effects of FDI was traditionally associated with large British firms reaping excessive monopoly profits that were in turn remitted abroad rather than reinvested (Lindenberg 1973: 181; Saham 1980: 246, 309). An estimate over the first half of the 1980s reaffirmed that the resource effect on balance of payments was negative whereas the exchange effect was at best neutral. The final excess of outflows above inflows on the balance of payments averaged $1.8 billion (M$4237 million) per year (Yew 1988: 45–6). The balance of payments effect of FDI had thus grown even more disadvantageous than as estimated by Hoffman and Tan for the 1960s. Interestingly, however, this deterioration coincided with a drastic reduction of the British share in FDI assets in Malaysia.

Between 1968 and 1981, foreign-controlled manufacturing firms provided 114,000 new jobs for Malaysians corresponding to 30% of total new employment generated in this sector. The foreign share was slightly higher than the one cited for the 1960s but a very sizeable proportion of the employment effects of foreign manufacturing firms was confined to firms with pioneer status in the ten FTZs which had been established in Malaysia since 1972 (Yew 1988: 43). Foreign manufacturing firms were found to generate more employment than domestic competitors but this could be attributed to their larger scale of operations (Tan 1978). Amongst other easily measured effects of FDI, the taxation effect stood out as an example of a declining contribution from the side of FDI. The foreign share in tax receipts fell from about 30% in the latter half of the 1970s to less than one-quarter by 1982 (von Kirchbach 1983: 424; Yew 1988: 31). This probably reflects the slow rate of incoming FDI flows as well as the tax holidays enjoyed by foreign firms in the FTZs.

Foreign-controlled manufacturing was different from domestic establishments. More economies of scale realized, the production process was more capital-intensive and more advanced technology was applied (Sieh-Lee 1979: 73, 84; Bautista 1981: 7–10). Yet the more efficient techniques were scarcely, if at all, implemented by adjacent local producers. Little local adaptation of the imported technology took place. A notable exception to the rule was Malayawata Steel which was established as a joint venture between the Malaysian State and Nippon Steel. The huge integrated steel mill near Butterworth enjoyed the special protection of Tunku Abdul Rahman and became a showcase enterprise with its almost all-Malaysian top management and numerous new jobs being created in the region (Chee and Lee 1979: 43–63). But Malayawata Steel was atypical, not only because of the support from Malaysia's first prime minister, but also since it represented the orthodox emphasis on heavy industry in strategies for industrialization rather than the export-oriented manufacturing. The latter was to prove more conducive to rapid economic growth.

Several studies have pointed at the lack of linkages emanating from foreign-controlled manufacturing during the 1970s and the 1980s. Only a minority of foreign manufacturers procured some simple parts from local sources. Japanese firms in the electronics and electrical industry imported all machinery, 95% of the raw materials and 80–90% of the parts and components from abroad, often from the mother company in Japan. The ten FTZs became notorious for a virtual absence of backward linkages which in fact was in part fostered by the regulations surrounding production in the FTZs. Forward linkages were similarly ruled out by the very requirement to export virtually the entire output. Sizeable imports were often required for production in the FTZs. This on occasion even threatened to wipe out export revenues generated by the FTZs (Cheong and Lim 1981: 134–5; Osman-Rani, Toh and Ali 1986: 32–7; ESCAP/UNCTC 1988: 250–53; Jomo 1990: 137). The onetime enclaves controlled by British managing agencies seemed to have made place for Japanese-style assembly processes relying on package inputs imported from Japan.

New technology poured in, especially from the USA and Japan, but the only adaptation to local conditions was said to consist of a downscaling of operations to fit the smaller Malaysian market. Access was allegedly scarcely given to patented information and virtually no research and development was undertaken locally. Only knowhow sufficient for operation and maintenance was transferred. Transfers of technology were supposedly virtually absent in electronics and electrical manufacturing and did not amount to much also in the production of textiles or iron and steel. The failure of transfers to materialize was by foreign investors ascribed to the lack of perception of the importance of such transfers among Malaysian partners and employees whereas American and Japanese firms in particular were charged with not wishing to share their core technologies (Chee and Lee 1983: 81; ESCAP/UNCTC 1987b: 191–239; O'Connor 1989: 111; Fong 1990: 206). Overstating the argument a bit, it was asserted that Malaysia got 'the worst deal possible'. By insisting on joint ventures it forfeited (from a Malaysian point of view) the cost advantage of fully-owned capital investment while no additional advantage was reaped from the association with foreign firms as long as technology failed to be transmitted (Razak Abdul 1984: 291).

The poor performance in terms of linkages and technology transfer had repercussions for other types of FDI effects as well. The technological gap and difference in profitability could easily result in domestic capital being crowded out and this tendency would only be reinforced by NEP discrimination of domestic capital of non-Malay or Chinese origin (Lim and Pang 1991: 37). The extensive sourcing of raw materials and parts from abroad meant a reduction of the trade surplus, as was already mentioned with respect to the FTZs. In addition, it has enlarged opportunities for 'hidden' outflows of returns through transfer pricing, i.e. paying high prices for imports from the overseas mother company and selling finished products back at low prices. The adverse effect on balance of payments was aggravated by a sizeable outflow of royalty fees for use of the modern technology. More than 600 agreements for technology transfer were concluded in the 1970s and the outflow of fees doubled between 1975 and 1978 alone (Marappan and Jomo 1994; Ali 1994: 116–21; ESCAP/UNCTC 1984: 92–150). The Malaysian authorities could do little more than to recommend a short duration of such contracts and as low a fee as possible.

The latter half of the 1980s was a time of readjustment for the Malaysian economy. The stringent ownership requirements of the NEP were relaxed and priorities shifted towards rapid industrialization. The Industrial Master Plan (IMP) of 1986 urged a more efficient use of FDI in upgrading technology in manufacturing and FDI was more actively promoted by the Malaysian government from 1987 onwards (Jomo 1990: 136–7). The recovery of FDI was reflected in a steep rise in the foreign share in total equity investment, from 49% in 1986 to 74% in 1989. This percentage then declined but has stayed very considerable also in the early 1990s (Salleh 1995: 134–5). Newly arriving foreign investors responded to the greater leeway by insisting on more wholly-owned enterprises than before. Also NIC investment evolved as a serious contestant of the primacy of American and Japanese investment. During the years 1986–1988, for instance, equity investment from Taiwan and Singapore each exceeded American inflows while being equal to the Japanese total when taken together (Wong Tai Chee 1990: 112).

The character of FDI was also different. The electrical and electronics industry received the largest slice and became even more important in terms of output and export revenue. There was a greater participation by small and medium-size firms which is directly associated with the rising share of Taiwan with its conspicuous lack of conglomerates at home. There was a strong predomination of exports in the market orientation of FDI, significantly also including sales from Malaysia to the (Asian) home country of the investor. The capital intensity in foreign-controlled manufacturing rose, thus reinforcing the lead of foreign firms above domestic ones in terms of marginal productivity and efficiency. The scope for a substantial foreign contribution to the on-going industrial restructuring in Malaysia was enlarged and so was the potential for technology transfers (Ariff 1992: 7–10; Yokoyama 1992: 54–7). No comprehensive study has yet been made of the impact of this 'new' FDI on the development of the Malaysian economy. The impact can at this stage only be inferred from circumstantial evidence concerning individual industries. The electronics industry is here used as a case in point conveying some important trends in recent years.

If any branch of the Malaysian economy deserves the Rostowian epithet 'leading sector' in the first place, it must be the electrical and electronics industry (Figure 7.2; United Nations 1995a: 176).[2] Its contribution to expansion in manufacturing has been impressive on every count. Thousands of new jobs have been created and the high share in total manufacturing employment, relative to the industry's share in manufacturing output or fixed assets, testifies to the persistence of labour-intensive processes. Production has always been oriented towards exports to an extreme degree which is underscored by the wide gap between the high share in manufacturing exports and the industry's proportion of output or employment. This branch of manufacturing has appeared as the single most reliable earner of foreign exchange for the Malaysian economy.

Electronic components, notably integrated circuits, traditionally forms the most important branch of the Malaysian electronics industry (i.e. without electrical appliances). Its share in total output of electronic manufacturing was 84% in 1986 but since then other branches, such as consumer electronics (audio-visual equipment) and industrial electronics (peripherals), have gained importance, accounting for more than one-half of the industry's output by 1992. The intervening years, between 1986 and 1992, saw a spectacular growth with output increasing by 30% annually and 23% more employment each year up to a total labour force of almost

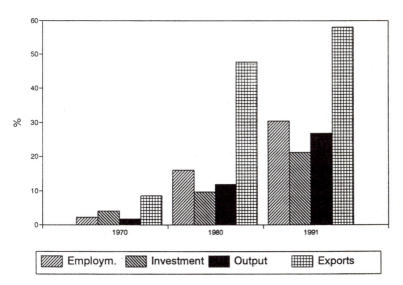

Figure 7.2   Electronics in Malaysia: share in manufacturing, 1970–1991

200,000 in 1992 (Salleh 1992: 72; Salleh 1995: 141–2). The capacity of rapid expansion and continuous diversification are sources of strength for the electronics industry in Malaysia. Weak spots include the extreme dependence on foreign capital and the vulnerability to sudden slumps which is characteristic of the electronics business at large.

In the early 1990s Malaysia became the world's third largest producer of semiconductors. The history of this type of manufacturing provides a good illustration of how the product lifecycle may induce a new international division of labour. A succession of innovations, e.g. the integrated circuit, the microprocessor and the Dynamic Random Access Memory chip (DRAM), has raised the technological sophistication of the production line and hardware performance has been enhanced by a factor of one million or more since the industry came into being in the 1950s. Several stages with very different capital and technology intensities have evolved and this is where opportunities for offshore locations of parts of the production process arise. The conventional classification of phases of production in the manufacturing of semiconductors runs as follows:

(1) Research and development, in particular design of integrated circuits through mask making;
(2) Wafer fabrication or the imprinting of batches of thin silicon wafers which are then sliced up into hundreds or thousands of individual chips;
(3) Assembly of chips into semiconductors;
(4) Testing of all packaged devices.

High levels of skill are required at the first, second and fourth stages. Capital intensities are the highest at the sensitive second stage whereas the third one is traditionally extremely labour-intensive (Morgan and Sayer 1988: 43–65; Todd 1990: 185; cf. Chang 1971: 14–15). According to the product lifecycle model, a Japanese parent company is likely to shift the assembly stage to a low-wage location in Southeast Asia and the testing, possibly also the production of simple wafers, to a NIC location while retaining research and design and complex wafer fabrication in Japan.

The semiconductor industry in Malaysia was established in the early 1970s and soon centred around the FTZ of Penang. The number of firms producing electronic components increased fast, reaching a total of almost 70 in the mid-1980s and approaching 120 by the end of the decade. Major investors included Motorola, National Semiconductor and Hitachi. Total employment in the semiconductor industry of Penang alone climbed from less than 3000 in 1972 to a peak at some 20,000 in the early 1980s but fell back again during the worldwide slump of the industry in 1985–1987

(Rasiah 1987: 185; *FEER* 1/11 1990; Salleh 1992: 74). Penang with its attractive location across the water from the western coast of the Malaysian peninsula quickly developed into one of the world's foremost production centres for semiconductors. It tasted the fruits of rapid expansion but also became vulnerable to the vicissitudes of a highly volatile branch of industry (Clad 1989: 179).

Initially, production in the Penang FTZ was exclusively geared towards labour-intensive assembly operations. The bonding of chips was done manually, a type of work requiring an infinite patience and much dexterity. Young women were preferred and the sex ratio in Penang's semiconductor industry stayed heavily biased in favour of females throughout the 1970s and 1980s. The introduction of this new element into the industrial labour force resulted in tensions within the workplace, complaints from village elders and even occasional outbursts of mass hysteria which did little good to the industry's reputation or to the reputation of FDI in general (Blake 1982: 154–9; Rasiah 1987: 185).

Positive economic effects in terms of export earnings and new employment were clearly realized but the pessimism about interindustry linkages, let alone technology transfers, was at least as outspoken as with respect to Malaysian manufacturing in general. A MIDA survey in the early 1980s reported that local firms supplied only 1% of materials needed in the semiconductor industry. No attempts were made to integrate semiconductor manufacturing with consumer or industrial electronics. A study focusing on FTZ in Penang cautioned that linkages were at best 'not negligible' for local firms starting out. As late as towards the end of the 1980s a sample of foreign-owned electronics firms in Penang reaffirmed that they had in fact no choice but to import all parts from abroad (ESCAP/UNCTC 1985a: 188; Rasiah 1987: 347–54; Rasiah 1988; Rajaghanttam 1991: 84–91). Penang had housed an industry at the forefront of technological progress for a protracted period of time but the record in terms of technological upgrading was disappointing.

Two crucial changes occurred in the mid-1980s. Stiffened competition in the field urged producers of semiconductors to raise efficiency targets. This was above all accomplished by automation at the assembly stage which vastly increased the quality of the chips, often for the simple reason that dust from the workers' clothes and bodies would not interfere with the production process. In addition, more of the final testing was integrated with the assembly stage which by definition also meant a higher level of technological sophistication in the offshore subsidiary (ESCAP/UNCTC 1987: 23–4; Rasiah 1988). Since then several empirical studies have stressed the gradual emergence of backward linkages, i.e. purchases from domestic suppliers, in the Malaysian electronics industry in general and among semiconductor producers in Penang in particular. Forward linkages, however, remained limited with only an occasional case of upstream activities connected to wafer fabrication being spotted (Rasiah 1991; Salleh 1992: 91–5; Salleh 1995: 146–53; United Nations 1995a: 207). Structural effects thus proved to be intimately connected with the mode of implementing FDI and this theme is further explored by taking a closer look at the experiences of one individual firm.

Hitachi was one of the very first foreign companies to arrive shortly after the Bayan Lepas FTZ had opened its gates next to Penang Airport in 1972. Like other manufacturers of semiconductors in Malaysia this company enjoyed pioneer status during the first ten years. It did not have to comply with rigid ownership requirements since it produced exclusively for foreign exports. Hitachi Semiconductor (Malaysia) Sdn. Bhd. (HISEM) was set up as a joint venture with the equity share of the Japanese mother country amounting to 90% and the remainder held by the Malaysian state through the PNB. The product range was gradually extended from transistors, diodes and digital integrated circuits to 16 Megabyte DRAMs. HISEM long remained the sole Japanese electronics manufacturer in Penang. It performed a pioneering function in more than one respect and was frequently included in samples constructed for surveys of FDI and its effects in Malaysian manufacturing (United Nations 1994: 50; United Nations 1995a: 183).

Changing conditions of production at HISEM are revealed by the development over time of output as compared to inputs of different factors of production (Figure 7.3).[3] Sales rose roughly parallel to employment during the initial decade of operations, 1973–1983, but accelerated towards the end of the 1980s in response to a dramatic increase in capital investment. Meanwhile, total employment stayed the same or even fell somewhat. This testifies to a significant increase in labour productivity which could only be accomplished through an automation requiring heavy investment in new machinery. By the mid-1990s total sales at HISEM climbed towards $500 million (M$1.2 billion) while the total labour force remained relatively constant at 2000. The tale of the behaviour of these economic variables can be corroborated by direct observation. The white HISEM factory building in Bayan Lepas today contains endless rows of fully automatic machines attended by a handful of operators in an antiseptically clean environment (cf. United Nations 1994: 54). Within two decades this production line was thus transformed from being highly labour-intensive into one using much capital and the latest technology.

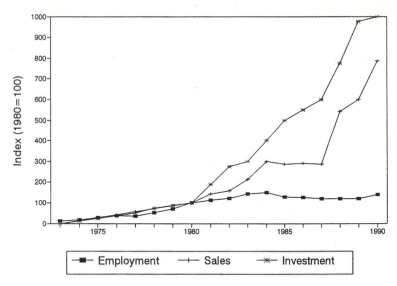

Figure 7.3   Electronics in Malaysia: Hitachi Semiconductor, 1973–1990

The higher capital intensity of production will undoubtedly inflate foreign exchange earnings through the greater value-added of the output. At the same time it dampens employment effects and might possibly also raise expenditures on purchases from abroad since the required machinery is not likely to be locally available. The key concern, however, is the extent to which the host country economy benefits from the sophisticated technology applied in the foreign-controlled plant. This in turn is dependent on the position of the subsidiary within the corporate hierarchy of the mother company and the means deployed locally to ensure a dissemination of technology. Illustrations may again be drawn from the HISEM plant in Penang.

In 1995 Hitachi ranked as the world's thirteenth largest private corporation, with total revenues approaching $85 billion. Semiconductors were responsible for more than one-tenth of total sales and counted among the most profitable products even if margins were threatened by a general excess supply in the world market (*Fortune* 5/8 1996). Production is organized along the lines of locational comparative advantage as suggested above for the semiconductor industry at large. Memory chips and DRAMs are designed in the research laboratories within easy reach from the Tokyo headquarters whereas wafers are fabricated at Takasaki in Japan and Landshut in Germany. Assembly and testing have both been concentrated to Penang which has thus become the concern's worldwide centre for this line of manufacturing.

The prospects of initiating also the technologically more advanced stages at the Penang locations do not appear realistic. A full-fledged wafer factory would require investment outlays of at least $400 million which corresponds to the total accumulated at the Penang subsidiary between 1973 and 1989. Even if the need for decentralized design centres closer to customers is readily acknowledged in Tokyo, actual intentions for such efforts had by the mid-1990s scarcely advanced beyond the planning stage. The input of HISEM at the concern headquarters is therefore confined to suggestions for new products and additional investment. The separation of tasks also applies to the day-to-day management of production. The Penang plant has a responsibility of its own when it comes to the details of cost management but totals must remain within the global framework as defined in Tokyo. The relative independence which HISEM enjoys should probably be connected with the outspoken satisfaction in Tokyo about performance in Penang.[4]

HISEM initially lacked substantial links with other industries in Penang precisely because its production process was so labour-intensive (Rasiah 1988). The shift to more capital-intensive processes was induced by rising wages. This shift allegedly coincided with a conscious effort to raise the level of local procurement. HISEM is free to choose the cheapest supplier of parts and machinery and Hitachi materials are only chosen when necessary because of quality requirements. Some machines are produced locally which in turn has stimulated local research. In addition, a small laboratory for chip design was established in 1990.

The group of Japanese employees at HISEM is strikingly small but does include the managing director and one of the four other members of the top management team. In 1993 more than one-half of the total labour force was Malaysian but the Chinese and Indian contingents were sizeable as well with shares amounting to 30% and 15% respectively. Four employees out of five were women, usually in their twenties. About 7% of the total labour force at HISEM consisted of indigenous technicians who had often been trained in Japan. One device to ensure Japanese-style cohesion in the factory at HISEM has been the formation of small groups of about ten members equipped with a unique logo and carrying fancy names such as 'Wafer' or 'James Bond'. These groups are invited to make suggestions for improvements in quality control and productivity gains. Local research on a limited scale as well as on-the-job or overseas training programmes, perhaps even the small group activities have come to provide concrete opportunities for technology transfer at HISEM. The scope of the technology transmitted obviously remains restricted to the art of manufacturing of semiconductors.

It is always hazardous to generalize from an in-depth study of one individual industry, let alone one single firm. There is no guarantee that signs of improving linkages and technology transfers apply to other major manufacturers of semiconductors, nor to other industries in Malaysia. Hitachi was chosen as a case study precisely because of its pioneering and leading role in Malaysian manufacturing. The high degree of specialization in accordance with locational comparative advantage and the relatively recent technological upgrading of the production process both make HISEM a good representative of the semiconductor industry in Malaysia. And, as also mentioned, the electronics industry was selected because of its increasingly important position in Malaysian manufacturing. Recent case studies, covering other branches of manufacturing in Malaysia, indicate that technology transfers are, at long last, improving. Malaysian employees are beginning to master the technologies applied by foreign firms and technology-intensive firms, such as electronics manufacturing, have in practice turned out to be less 'footloose' than critics had feared (United Nations 1994: 33–72; Athukorala and Menon 1996: 40–42).

Malaysia has come a long way since positive *bumiputra* discrimination and 'Buy British Last' campaigns held the day. FDI has rebounded in an unforeseen way and its effects on the host country economy have been enlarged accordingly. But, more importantly, these effects have changed character. FDI has become less effective in terms of employment creation. There are positive signs of a greater contribution in terms of a technological upgrading of production processes even if Japanese manufacturing firms have often been criticized for transferring advanced technology only sparingly. Downstream activities still remain subordinate and the semiconductor business has turned out almost proverbially volatile.

7.3 SPEEDING UP GROWTH

The 'flavour of the decade', to borrow an expression from Thai expert Peter Warr, has now also won acclamation by the World Bank. Thailand was nominated the world's top growth economy during the years 1985–1994 and is forecast to become the world's seventh largest economy in just another quarter of a century. The annual rate of growth has exceeded 8% every single year since 1984 and even the slowdown in the mid-1990s left Thailand with a growth performance which is very impressive by the standards of the region (Table 7.9; *FEER* 15/8 1996; World Bank 1996). The consistent rapid growth of recent years is intimately connected with structural change in the Thai economy. This section reviews FDI effects in Thailand since the 1960s in the light of a rapidly changing economic environment. It is necessary to touch briefly on growth patterns in general and FDI patterns in particular before identifying implications by type of effect.

Table 7.9   Selected indicators of economic growth performance in Southeast Asia, 1980–1993

	Singapore	Malaysia	Thailand	Indonesia	The Philippines
1980/93 growth (average percentage per year)					
GNP/capita	6.1	3.5	6.4	4.2	–0.6
Population	1.1	2.5	1.7	1.7	2.3
Real GDP	6.9	6.2	8.2	5.8	1.4
Agriculture	–6.4	3.5	3.8	3.2	1.2
Industry	6.2	8.2	11.0	6.3	–0.1
Services	7.4	5.5	7.7	6.9	2.9
Manufacturing	7.2	10.3	10.8	11.8	0.8
Exports	12.7	12.6	15.5	6.7	3.4
Imports	9.7	9.7	13.8	4.5	4.5
Money supply	13.5	12.6	19.2	26.3	17.4
Prices	2.5	2.2	4.3	8.5	13.6
1993 (% of GDP)					
Agriculture	0	*	10	19	22
Industry	37	*	39	39	33
Services	63	*	51	42	45
Manufacturing	28	*	28	22	24
Consumption	43	49	54	60	76
Investment	44	33	40	28	24
Government	9	13	10	10	9
Exports	134	73	29	23	21
Imports	155	71	37	19	35

Note: * = not given in this source. Per capita GDP differs less when considered in terms of purchasing power parities.
Source: Asia Yearbook 1996: 1–17.

Much has been written on the importance of foreign capital for the economic development of Thailand but the literature contains regrettably few systematic assessments. The most comprehensive endeavour predated the switch to rapid growth by at least a decade and Santikarn's pioneering monograph on technology transfer was based on data from the late 1970s. Many of the subsequent references therefore concern evidence with a limited empirical base. Generalizations are few and far between and will have to be inferred by combining scattered observations. Fragmentary evidence from the literature is supplemented by a statistical analysis of two selections of foreign-controlled firms in operation during the most recent decade. Pessimism was paramount among early observers. Tambunlertchai, who drew on a sample of more than 100 foreign-controlled firms, concluded that FDI was 'unable to render a significant contribution to the host country'. His information largely concerned the period 1963–1971 and he applied four criteria to test for FDI contributions referring respectively to national income formation, new employment generation, the utilization of domestic resources and foreign exchange earnings. FDI failed on every account. The poor record, in terms of technology transfer as well, was ascribed to the high capital intensity and high import dependence of foreign-controlled production (Tambunlertchai 1975: 247–70, 287–95). With benefit of hindsight we may assert that American and Japanese FDI at this stage did not fit very well into the prevailing growth pattern of the Thai economy. We will have occasion to return to this hypothesis in due course.

The evolution of priorities in the growth strategies of Thailand can be inferred from the five year development plans formulated by the Thai government from the early 1960s. The First Plan (1962–1966) was scarcely more than an elaborated public budget but the Second Plan (1967–1971) introduced structural change through its emphasis on import substitution. This was to be achieved through heavy protection and much foreign capital and results were indeed meagre. The Third and Fourth Plans (1972–1976 and 1977–1981), however, stressed distributional issues and the need for restructuring the entire. By the Fifth Plan (1982–1986) export-oriented industrialization had become the chief target. By the 1980s the composition of foreign exports did change in the intended direction, i.e. from being dominated by traditional primary commodities from agriculture to finished goods from manufacturing (Wong 1979: 78–9; Warr 1993: 30–34, 57–60). The movement to the 'difficult' export-oriented phase of industrialization constitutes the most important change of the environment in which FDI in Thailand is implemented.

Thailand only became a major recipient of FDI in Southeast Asia after 1987. This explains why the accumulated stock of FDI still appeared relatively modest in regional comparison at the time when the most recent authoritative estimates were made (United Nations 1992; section 2.3 above). The late 1980s was a transitory stage when traditional Japanese, American and West European investment were gradually supplemented by incoming flows from NIC sources (Lim and Pang 1991: 49; Warr 1993: 68; Pupphavesa and Pussarungsri 1995: 162). It is likely that official statistics do not fully capture the extent of FDI at that time, because of the increasing importance of combinations of foreign corporations with Sino-Thai business concerns. The pattern of FDI in Thailand at the time of the transitory stage may be further explored by surveying a selection of foreignaffiliated firms operating in Thailand.

The survey covers 461 individual firms chosen from a total of about
2250 entries in a leading Thai business directory for companies with
annual sales in excess of 100 million baht ($3.9 million). The edition consulted gives financial details by company for 1989 (Million Baht Business
1991). Almost one-half of the firms with a sizeable recognizably foreign
stake are of Japanese origin whereas most of the remainder, 38% of the
total selection, is taken up by West European and American subsidiaries,
in that order. NIC investment is seriously underrepresented for two
reasons. At this stage many newly established NIC holdings may not yet
have reached a sufficient scale of operations to be included in the directory
in the first place. In addition, since the source itself does not specify
nationalities, the researcher must rely on the recognition of foreign names
of companies and shareholders which inevitably implies that Chinese NIC
firms are next to impossible to distinguish from domestic Sino-Thai combinations (cf. Lim and Pang 1991: 45).

There were marked differences by nationality within the corporate
body of foreign-affiliated firms in Thailand at the conclusion of the
1980s (Figure 7.4; Million Baht Business 1991: 5–754).[5] American
firms were without doubt the largest with annual average sales per firm
at 70% above the level attained by Japanese or West European companies. Average equity, including Thai proportions, exceeded that of the
average Japanese enterprise by at least 50% whereas the West European
competitor occupied an intermediate position. Profits, calculated against
both total sales volume and total equity, seemed to be related above all
to firm size. American subsidiaries reported the highest percentages
whereas the Japanese ones ranked last again leaving the middle position
to EC firms.

Distributions by size were relatively uneven. A group of 38 large
foreign-affiliated firms accounted for 54% of all sales while the top
echelon in terms of equity consisted of only 14 individual firms holding
29% of all equity between them. Yet the largest sales volumes were not
always realized by the firms with most equity. Only two firms counted
among the top five on either account, the ubiquitous disk drive manufacturer Seagate Technology from California and the Thai subsidiary of
Shell. Asahi Glass was the sole Japanese member in the top five group as
defined by equity. The latter group also included the early pioneer, the
East Asiatic Company, i.e. Hans Niels Andersen's old Østasiatiske
Kompagni (cf. section 3.2).

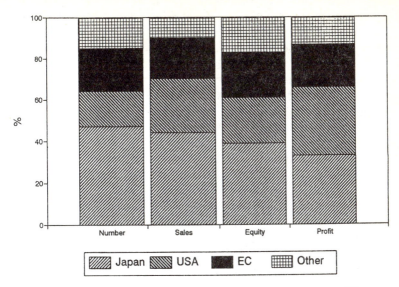

Figure 7.4   Foreign firms in Thailand: characteristics by nationality, 1989

By 1990 almost 80% of all FDI actually implemented in Thailand originated in Japan or one of the NICs, mainly Taiwan and Singapore.[6] American and European investors lagged behind in enlarging investments and starting out anew in the booming Thai economy. Combined with the salient features of FDI in Thailand as established at the end of the 1980s, this change of directions of FDI flows also meant less emphasis on scale and wide profit margins. It is tempting to revitalize the Kojima argument for more beneficial effects from Asian FDI, albeit in an entirely different setting, and to investigate whether effects of FDI did improve as patterns of FDI changed. This second hypothesis is discussed by examining various FDI effects by type.

Income effects of FDI should, in a case such as Thailand, be measured against the sheer size of the national economy which, with a total GDP of $125 billion (1993), corresponds to Singapore and Malaysia taken together (Asia Yearbook 1996: 14–15). A comparison between FDI inflows and statistics on domestic investment is also likely to understate the foreign contribution since inflows take no account of reinvestment of retained profits or outlays financed by domestic borrowing. Officially registered FDI represented only a very small part of total investment in Thailand, 5% or even less on average during the years 1970–1987 (von Kirchbach 1983: 139; Hill and Johns 1985: 361; Tambunlertchai 1993: 136). This percentage only climbed to an appreciable level, about 10%, during the general rapid increase of FDI around 1990 (Pupphavesa and Pussarungsri 1995: 160).

However, actual contributions of FDI in the enlargement of productive capacity were considerably higher than as indicated by the modest foreign share in gross domestic capital formation already before the FDI spurt had set in. In the 1970s foreign firms were said to account for no less than one-third of total investment in so-called 'modern' industries and foreign-held equity corresponded to 25% of total equity investment in promoted activities as of the mid-1980s (Intharathai 1974: 76–7; Khanthachai *et al.* 1987: 13; cf. Tambunlertchai and Chirathivat 1990: 203–11). FDI was concentrated to a small number of key industries, e.g. textiles, motor cars and consumer electronics, and here FDI accounted for very substantial proportions of total output and sales. The final FDI impact included indirect income effects which, on occasion, were estimated to be the equivalent of one-half of the original income effect emanating from the foreign-controlled enterprise (Yoshino 1976: 69; Pongpissanupichit 1985: 322).

Employment effects also easily appear rather marginal at first sight, in part because of the very large Thai labour force. In the late 1980s overall direct employment in foreign-affiliated manufacturing was put at about 180,000 by the International Labour Office, a number corresponding to a mere 9% of total manufacturing employment in Thailand. Indirect employment effects, however, were held to be almost twice as substantial but the labour multiplier varied strongly by industry (Sibunruang and Brimble 1988: 50). The recent upsurge of FDI has altered the orientation in manufacturing and this is likely to have important ramifications for new employment generated by FDI. For lack of conclusive judgements in the literature, we rely on a preliminary statistical analysis of foreign-affiliated firms in Thai manufacturing.

A selection of individual companies was made from a list drawn up by the Board of Investment in Bangkok in 1993, or shortly before that year. The total list embraced 600 firms that had indicated 'a concrete interest' in further cooperation with foreign firms. No less than 534 out of the 600 companies (89%) were classified in manufacturing (Directory 1993).[7] The selection criteria for the specific purpose of measuring employment effects were twofold. First, there had to be a more than marginal foreign share in equity; the threshold was set at 10%. Second, the firm in question should employ at least 100 people. Both criteria were met by about one-third of the listed firms in Thai manufacturing, 170 out of 534. This sample enables us to establish links between employment on the one hand and the nationality of FDI and the branch of manufacturing on the other.

Japanese and NIC firms predominated strongly in both numbers and employment effects in foreign-affiliated manufacturing in Thailand during the early 1990s (Figure 7.5; Directory 1993: 27–127). One important difference between the two refers to size. The Japanese share in total employment was larger than in terms of numbers of firms whereas it was precisely the other way around for NIC firms. These Japanese firms were about 60% larger than NIC ones with average employment amounting to 890 and 540 persons respectively. The low share of both American and European firms above all reflects that this analysis does not include oil companies nor FDI in the service sector. It can also be speculated that American and European manufacturing firms were less bent upon enlarging activities in Thailand and, therefore, did not end up on the list of the Board of Investment in the first place. Total employment at the 170 firms in the sample exceeded 126,000 persons or almost 750 in the average firm. This total should be compared with the 180,000 cited by the International Labour Office several years before but pertaining to the entire manufacturing sector, i.e. including also small and medium-size firms with fewer than 100 employees. The order of magnitude of such aggregates does not suggest a very dramatic rise in FDI-generated employment since the late 1980s.

Japanese employment effects were bolstered by a number of very large manufacturers such as Mineba's fabrication of fans and calculators in Lopburi (8160 employees), the Toyota assembly plant (8000 employees) and Thai Arrow's wiring harnesses factory (6000 employees) of which the latter two were both located in the metropolitan Bangkok region. More

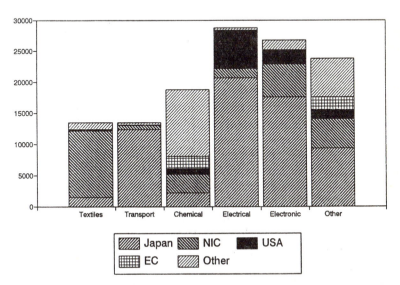

Figure 7.5   Foreign manufacturing in Thailand: employment by nationality, 1993

generally, Japanese manufacturing was strongly geared towards electrical machinery and electronic parts with brand names such as Toshiba, Fujitsu and Muramoto ranking especially high. Involvement in the textile industry was comparatively scant whereas two major food producers specialized in poultry.

NIC involvement significantly concentrated on textiles and electronics, two industries representing both ends of the evolutionary ladder from conventional low-level technology production with much labour to the application of advanced technology in conjunction with labour-intensive assembly work. In addition, NIC involvement often took the shape of a minority participation, especially in large enterprises. Only two manufacturers with more than 1000 employees cited a majority NIC ownership, the Taiwanese shoe factory J & D (2660 employees) and the Hong Kong-run PCB producer called Elec & Eltek (1130 employees). The largest American-held manufacturing establishments were Singer (6150 employees), turning out sewing machines since the late 1960s, and the IC plant of National Semiconductor (2260 employees). These firms all operated in the Bangkok region which underscores the extreme tendency towards centralization of FDI in manufacturing in Thailand.

Employment effects as such do not tell us the whole story, in particular when absolute numbers of jobs remain minute compared to the total labour force of the host country. Distributions of employment may also reveal changing directions in the technological content of FDI. Viewed from this perspective employment effects in fact anticipate a subsequent elaboration of interindustry linkages, possibly even of technology transfers.

Electrical machinery and electronics held the greatest promises for employment creation through FDI even when counted as separate industries within the manufacturing sector (Figure 7.6; Directory 1993: 27–127).[8] Three out of every five employees in larger foreign-affiliated manufacturing enterprises worked in one of these two industries. The Japanese share of employment was very high in both cases, two-thirds or more. The relatively large number of individual Japanese firms involved reflects a major feature of so-called 'new wave' Japanese FDI, i.e. a lower concentration of capital in the hands of a few very large investors. The share of Japanese firms was exceptionally high in the manufacturing of transport equipment, including motor cars and tyres. Here, the Japanese producers could draw on a long tradition with assembly operations of Nissan, Toyota, Daihatsu, Isuzu and Hino being established already before 1970 (Suehiro 1989: 209). The Japanese lead in terms of employment effects only failed to apply in textiles, where NICs prevailed, and in so-called 'other manufacturing' with its high participation of combinations of investors from several countries.

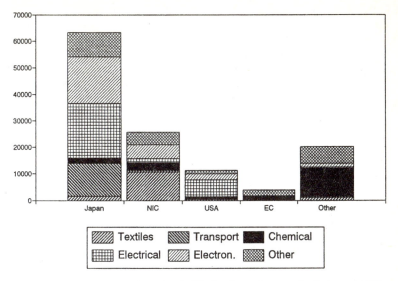

Figure 7.6   Foreign manufacturing in Thailand: employment by industry, 1993

It is not accidental that the most traditional labour-intensive type of manufacturing such as textile and car assembly and the most technologically advanced production lines like electrical machinery and electronics are so well represented in the brief review of recent employment effects of FDI. Thailand is in the midst of the transition from low value-added import-substituting or 'easy' export-oriented industrial production to the stage of high value-added manufacturing where competition in foreign export markets is stiff and comparative advantages, because of cheap unskilled labour, mean less. An export-oriented industrialization has been advocated with great emphasis since the Fifth Plan (1982–1986) and a key aspiration of the Thai government in inviting foreign capital has always been to enhance the capacity of the domestic economy to earn foreign exchange and alleviate the problems with the external balance. The actual record, however, has traditionally been a source of concern, particularly when broadened to encompass FDI effects on the balance of payments at large. It is also important to recall that Thailand never possessed special arrangements for foreign-controlled export-oriented production in EPZs in the same way as, for instance, Malaysia.

Throughout the 1970s and much of the 1980s complaints abounded about the high ratio of outflows as compared to inflows of FDI. In most years foreign firms remitted almost twice as much as the flows of FDI entering Thailand. British and American firms had the 'worst' record. Here the ratio of outflows to inflows averaged 250%. Only Japanese firms among the major nationalities of investors recorded inflows which on average exceeded outflows, albeit by a narrow margin. Japanese firms in export manufacturing, on the other hand, became notorious for an excessively high propensity to import raw materials and parts. This also held true for American offshore manufacturing in, for instance, electronics (Tambunlertchai 1975: 200; Chinwanno and Tambunlertchai 1983: 205; ESCAP/UNCTC 1985a: 219; Suehiro 1989: 217).

Some improvement was noted only in the late 1980s. The upsurge of FDI from 1988 is illustrative. In 1987 total FDI inflows at $360 million (9,045 million baht) were not even large enough to fully compensate for outflowing profits, dividends and interest payments on foreign loans, a total of $420 million (10,480 million baht). One year later, however, FDI inflows had climbed to more than $1.1 billion (28.2 billion baht) whereas total outward remittances stayed at $500 million (12.6 billion baht).[9] The problem of drainage, in its strictest sense, appeared to be solved.

In an interesting exercise along the lines of formal econometric analysis, Jansen has measured what would have happened if FDI had not started to increase rapidly around 1987. His conclusion is that incoming FDI did raise export revenues considerably in the period 1987–1991 while also occasioning a steep rise in imports. The high import intensity of FDI, together with outflowing income on investment, ultimately resulted in a deficit on the current account of the balance of payments (Jansen 1995). Significantly, Jansen established in passing that Thailand's good export performance did not lead to a 'Dutch disease'-type of effect, i.e. a currency appreciation not matched by the competitiveness of large parts of the export sector. Corroborating evidence reaffirms that more high value-added manufacturing exports mean more imports while also suggesting that increasing FDI in the service sector is likely to mitigate these effects (Pupphavesa and Pussarungsri 1995: 171).

There seems to be a time lag in the reduction of the import propensity of foreign manufacturing firms. The complaints of the 1970s and early 1980s concerned textiles and motor car assembly. Today, Toyota claims to have reached a higher local content ratio in its assembly of cars in Thailand than anywhere else in Southeast Asia. Backward linkages appear a lot less impressive in the much younger electronics industry. Local procurement of materials and parts is indeed gradually increasing but refers almost exclusively to standardized off-the-shelf products, not critical components which are brought in from Japan or one of the NICs (United Nations 1995a: 249–84). The most far-reaching structural effect of FDI in Thailand is probably the very diversification in manufacturing production which has emerged since the late 1980s. In this connection, mention should also be made of the widely criticized unfavourable consequences of industrialization on the environment in Thailand (ESCAP/UNCTC 1990: 320–65).

The extent to which technology transfers occur probably forms the best known source of conflict between Japanese multinationals and the Thai government. The Thai government accused the Japanese firms of 'jealously' guarding the secrets of its success (Tambunlertchai 1980: 307–8). The topic has attracted attention ever since Santikarn's case study, one of very few of its kind, focusing on the experiences in the Thai textile industry. She applies the conventional differentiation between four distinct stages of technology transfer: utilization on a new location, the acquisition of operational and maintenance skills by the local work force, the diffusion to other lines of production, and, finally, the adaptation and research necessary for the making of new technology (Santikarn 1981: 6–7; cf. Shiowattana 1991: 175–6). Such a classification makes clear that moving technologically sophisticated lines of production overseas is not enough. In the initial stages much depends on the readiness of the foreign firm to part with its knowledge whereas at a later stage the absorptive capacity of the host country economy becomes decisive.

Santikarn's in-depth analysis shows how actual transfers were impaired by extensive use of packaged technology as well as a high degree of specialization between foreign and local partners in joint ventures. Employment displacement was more important than the generation of new skills. Substantial payments were done for the technology used but almost one-half of these payments accrued to monopolistic advantages of the foreign company such as brand names and trademarks. The author recommended the Board of Investment should evaluate applications for promotional status on the grounds of skills generation rather than new employment (Santikarn 1981: 114, 143–254).

The well-balanced judgement of Santikarn has been reiterated by others. Effective management was seen as a necessary precondition for a successful unpackaging of imported technology in chemical and paper manufacturing whereas local capabilities in car assembly operations only improved significantly after much had been invested in the training of local staff. The price of technology stayed high with fees on occasion exceeding 5% of gross sales (ESCAP/UNCTC 1984: 184–233; cf. Khanthachai *et al.* 1987: 73–6; ESCAP/UNCTC 1987a: 240–90). It is increasingly argued that the recent 'new wave' type of Japanese investment has brought substantially greater benefits in terms of technology transfer than preceding joint ventures with Japanese multinationals. Examples are cited from Sony's newly established assembly of semiconductors and Toyota's modernized carassembly. Some observers go as far as to speak of a 'new wave of technology transfer from Japan' (Takeuchi 1991: 212-13). Yet remaining bottlenecks with absorbing new technology should not be underrated. There is a need for more case studies on technology transfers based on comparisons of experiences elsewhere in the region, especially in Malaysia and Indonesia.

A more favourable assessment as compared to the 1970s and 1980s also applies to the increasing sophistication of FDI involvement in the service sector, notably telecommunications, trading and financial services (United Nations 1995b: 249–79). Here, the emphasis lies more on foreign firms leading the way and serving as a source of inspiration for domestic producers. More in general, little crowding-out of domestic competitors appears to have taken place in Thailand in the wake of the influx of FDI (Lim and Pang 1991: 46; Jansen 1995; cf. Pongpissanupichit 1985: 343). Actual connections between domestic entrepreneurs and foreign capital vary considerably and are especially weak in regional economic centres outside Bangkok as is shown in an interesting recent case study of local entrepreneurship in Nakhon Ratchasima in eastern Thailand (Ueda 1995: 40–41).

Both economic growth and FDI have changed character in Thailand during the last generation. Import substitution has given way to an export-oriented industrialization just as American and conventional low technology investment is increasingly replaced by more technology-intensive endeavours in manufacturing. Two hypotheses have been advanced in this section. First, that the FDI entering Thailand in the 1970s and early 1980s was of a type that had limited effects in terms of promoting economic growth and industrial restructuring. Second, that the changing character of FDI since the late 1980s has resulted in significantly improved effects of FDI. The best results are seen in a general diversification of manufacturing. The prospects are increasingly bright for backward linkages and technology transfers. Today's industrial transformation in Thailand has more to learn and less to lose from FDI than at any other time.

7.4   THE NEED TO RESTRUCTURE

Professor B.J. Habibie is possibly the most controversial figure among technocrats and economists in Indonesia today. The flamboyant Minister of State Research enjoys the special protection of the ageing President Suharto in his ambitious scheme for domestic aircraft production through the state enterprise IPTN (Industri Pesawat Terbang Nusantara). This promotion of high technology in a country which has only recently entered the world's middle income economies has at least reactivated the discussion about the direction of restructuring necessary to make Indonesia less dependent on oil revenues. The appropriate slot for Indonesia has to be found within the 'flying geese'-type of industrial division of labour in the East and Southeast Asian region (Soesastro 1992). This section is specifically concerned with the role of FDI in the current drive towards non-oil export production in Indonesia.

Much writing about FDI in Indonesia since 1967 sticks to a standard format of recapitulating official figures from the investment coordinating board BKPM, broken down by investor and industry, before moving on to the successive liberalization of the investment climate and trade regime. Details on specific industries, let alone individual firms, are scarcely incorporated. The following analysis does not deviate from this tradition in the sense that it does leave oil out and relies on relatively general assessments rather than detailed firm analysis.[10] However, the theme of industrial strategy is used as a convenient device to link FDI with the pattern of economic development in Indonesia. In addition, reference to BKPM data is made only sparingly and with great caution. Finally, the discussion explicitly incorporates both the quantitative and qualitative sides of the FDI impact on industrial restructuring.

The oil boom in Indonesia was accompanied by a highly restrictive trade regime designed to offer a protective umbrella for import-substituting manufacturing. The extreme degree of effective protection allowed inefficiencies in production to develop. This led to a 'Dutch disease'-type of problem with manufacturing exports, i.e. the oil-based exchange rate of the Indonesian rupiah was too high considering the competitive capacity of non-oil export production (although not too high in terms of causing a deficit on the balance of payments). From 1982 falling oil prices induced a strategy of industrialization but the trade regime remained inward-looking. The deficit on the current account of the balance of payments was to be alleviated through reducing imports rather than by bolstering exports. This was a so-called 'structuralist' approach aiming at a deepening of manufacturing production for the domestic market. Its weak spot was that international differences in costs of production were largely ignored (Ariff 1977: 156; Thee 1990: 72–3).

The further decline of oil prices from 1986 occasioned a radical switch to an export-oriented outward-looking strategy. Significantly this coincided with more deregulation of the FDI climate in Indonesia. The intention was clear. Manufacturing exports should reduce the dependence on oil and FDI was to provide the advanced technology required for the technological upgrading of production in manufacturing. The late 1980s and early 1990s witnessed a spectacular increase in manufacturing output and exports. The total value of manufactured exports climbed from \$4.5 billion in 1986 to \$11.1 billion in 1989 only to double again between 1989 and 1993 (Thee 1990: 77; Hill 1994: 82–3; Pangestu and Azis 1994: 16). The current five-year development plan REPELITA (Rencana Pembangunan Lima Tahun) VI which runs up to 1998/99 postulates non-oil manufacturing exports as the engine of rapid economic growth, enabling Indonesia to catch up with neighbouring countries on the road towards near-NIC status.

Hill offers the most succinct general appraisal of the current process of industrialization in Indonesia. He enumerates several salient features including a continuous diversification, a deepening of the industrial structure, much new employment, rising quality standards and an increasing application of foreign technologies (Hill 1994: 80–84). In his authoritative overview of Indonesian industrialization, Thee directs attention especially to bottlenecks in terms of the human and institutional capital investment needed to attain the kind of sustained productivity growth which is absolutely essential to assure the competitiveness of Indonesian goods in international markets (Thee 1994: 217–32). The shift from oil to non-oil products as the prime source of export growth is now firmly entrenched in the economic structure of Indonesia. But economic restructuring is more than a larger share of manufacturing in GDP and a higher degree of export orientation in the secondary sector. It also has a third dimension, technological upgrading of manufactured exports, and this is where the potential contribution of FDI comes in.

When examining the link connecting FDI and manufacturing it is important to distinguish between the share of FDI in manufacturing and the share of manufacturing in FDI. It is acknowledged that foreign firms do not dominate Indonesian manufacturing. Domestic conglomerates and state-run enterprises prevail in several industries where foreign firms and multinationals are likely to possess a comparative advantage on account of their higher capital intensity of production. The importance of FDI must be sought along more qualitative lines. FDI does occupy significant positions in certain selected industries, e.g. aluminium smelting, chemicals, glass, tyres and beer breweries, as well as in some technology-intensive subsectors of otherwise domestic-controlled industries. Much FDI involvement takes the shape of licensing agreements rather than equity shares which makes it difficult to infer its importance from ownership statistics alone. Traditionally non-oil FDI in Indonesia has been strongly motivated by the segregative system of import protection with excessively high effective rates for major consumer goods such as footwear and electronics (Hill 1988: 84–97).

The BKPM data are difficult to use to ascertain the precise position of manufacturing in total FDI. In the first place, BKPM data never include investment in the oil and LNG sector since such projects must register with another agency of the Indonesian administration. BKPM data by definition thus give an incomplete coverage of total FDI in Indonesia. Elaborate additional estimates are necessary to gain a full picture. Second, the BKPM data consist of approvals rather than realized FDI. The BKPM data give an exaggerated impression of FDI entering Indonesia as numerous projects are included that may never survive beyond the planning stage (Hill 1988: 157–64; see also section 2.2 above). Uncritical use of BKPM data has, in the past, even resulted in gross misconceptions about the primacy of Japanese capital in accumulated FDI in Indonesia and easily makes future prospects look far too bright.

The shortcomings in the BKPM data can be alleviated for manufacturing alone by using Indonesian industrial census figures and for all FDI by relying on external estimates (Hill 1992: 232). According to the survey conducted by the United Nations Centre for Transnational Corporations, the non-oil share in total accumulated FDI in Indonesia declined from 55% in 1970 to 25% in 1990 (United Nations 1992: 146). It is highly unlikely that this trend was continued during the dramatic increase in incoming FDI since the late 1980s. Total approvals as registered with the BKPM rose above $10 billion on a yearly basis in 1992 reaching $23.7 billion in 1994 and $38.4 billion in 1995 (Thee 1996). Non-oil FDI is clearly becoming the key portion of new FDI in Indonesia.

Wide discrepancies between intended and implemented FDI mean that the BKPM data provide little more than a global hint about trends. Average realization rates differ by nationality of the investor and by sector. The average has been estimated at 32% for all non-oil FDI and 37–38% for manufacturing alone. These averages apply both to the initial decade of rebounding FDI in Indonesia, 1967–1976, and the entire period from 1967 up to 1993 (McCawley and Manning 1976: 33; Saad 1995: 202). The impression of a relatively constant relationship between approved and implemented FDI is, however, misleading. Other percentages have been calculated for shorter periods of observation while the differences by investor and industry become of importance as well when FDI patterns change (Rosendale 1980: 30–31; Healey 1981: 24–5; Hobohm 1987: 18; BKPM 1994: 13, 23–5). A realization rate of almost 40% was reported for new manufacturing FDI added to stock between 1987 and 1991 but it is uncertain whether that level could be maintained also during the most recent upsurge of new FDI.[11]

Manufacturing is the most important destination for non-oil FDI and its importance has been enhanced over time even if the change has been less than spectacular in the long run. According to the BKPM data, manufacturing corresponded to 58–59% of the non-oil total prior to 1978 but rose to 67% when calculated over the period 1967–1985. The share of manufacturing averaged 63–64% in the years 1987–1992 occasionally, in 1988 and 1989, even climbing above the 80% (Anwar 1980: 219; Hill 1988: 81; Bank Indonesia 1993: 150). Since the late 1980s the share has been said to fall slightly, towards 60%, as a result of increasing FDI in the service sector (Saad 1995: 201). This trend reflects recent achievements in industrialization perhaps even anticipating a further shift towards a post-industrial economy based more on services.

The composition of FDI in manufacturing has undergone much change since 1967, at least as may be inferred from BKPM data while assuming that differences in implementation rates would not distort general trends too much (Figure 7.7; Bank Indonesia 1993: 150; BKPM 1994: 37). The shift towards a strategy of export-oriented industrialization from the mid-1980s coincided with a strengthening of the foreign base in chemicals, textiles and the paper industry whereas metals, both base metals and metal goods, were relatively less favoured. At a later stage, in 1993 and 1994, these developments were reversed for textiles, now losing importance, and base metals manufacturing which recovered some of its previous position.

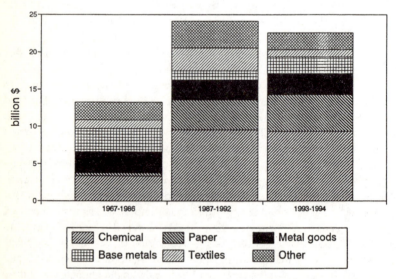

Figure 7.7   Manufacturing FDI in Indonesia: approvals by industry, 1967–1994

Significantly, metal goods, including electrical machinery and electronics, stayed at the same position within the hierarchy and did not expand at more than an average pace. The FDI contribution to industrial restructuring is thus above all channelled through rather conventional types of processing industries. This may not be exactly what Habibie has in mind. It certainly is a different situation as compared to Malaysia and Thailand.

Once the position of FDI in the industrial structure of Indonesia has been determined, it is necessary to look at actual FDI effects in greater detail. In doing so it is essential to distinguish between quantitative and qualitative contributions of FDI to the current economic transformation in this host country. The large size of the domestic economy, the huge labour force and the still very powerful base of oil and LNG revenues in the export trade all tend to downplay the contributions made by FDI when measured in purely quantitative terms. The highly selective participation of foreign capital in manufacturing, for whatever reason, has already been noted. It is the hope of the Indonesian government, as indeed in many industrializing recipients of foreign investment capital, that a disproportionate qualitative contribution may act as a multiplier in raising the ultimate impact of FDI.

The share of FDI in gross domestic capital formation in Indonesia is very low. In most years during the recent period it has amounted to less than 4% (Hill 1996: 78). It has, however, been demonstrated that the FDI share in capital formation should be doubled if we include also reinvestment of profits, i.e. foreign capital flows not showing up in the balance of payments figures. Finally, and here we already encounter a qualitative side of the argument, FDI has been shown to be strongly correlated to domestic investment which may be interpreted that more of the one also means more of the other (Ramstetter 1993; Saad 1995: 208).

The share of FDI looks entirely different when viewed within the framework of new investment in non-oil productive capacity which is admittedly a far more restricted concept than gross domestic capital formation. The accumulated total approved by the BKPM between 1967 and 1994 displayed a division of 60–40% between domestic and foreign capital respectively. Capital intensities were on average significantly higher on the foreign side of the investment balance sheet, $29.2 million per project against $15.3 million for domestic projects (BKPM 1994: 37). High capital intensities have in turn been associated with larger debts to the foreign investor as is suggested by a positive rank correlation between capital/labour ratios in manufacturing and debt/equity ratios among Japanese-affiliated firms starting out during the first decade of the more liberal FDI climate in Indonesia (Langhammer 1988: 108–9).

Capital intensities obviously have implications for the generation of new employment. Japanese investment in manufacturing had a rather bad reputation on this score in the 1970s and much of the 1980s compared to American competitors whereas the still infrequent NIC investment projects grew famous because of their relatively low ratios between capital and labour. All averages in manufacturing, however, were dwarfed by the extreme capital intensities in oil and LNG (Wells and Warren 1979: 74–7; Khong 1986: 102). A well known example of very limited employment effects due to an excessively high capital intensity in production is the prestigious aluminium smelter at Asahan in northern Sumatra. The total cost of construction of this joint venture between a Japanese consortium and the Indonesian state rose to $1.6 billion but only 2700 new jobs materialized in direct connection with the production line (Barlow and Thee 1988: 63–8; see also Ginting and Daroesman 1982: 68–9).

Total employment creation outside the oil sector has been estimated at slightly less than 400,000 for the entire period 1967–1993. Sizeable employment effects have only been recorded from about 1986. The annual increment in employment due to FDI is dwarfed by the increase in the domestic labour force, more than two million people each year (Saad 1995: 203). Some reservations need to be made with respect to this very harsh verdict on the employment effects of FDI in Indonesia. First, it appears that the dramatic enlargement of the very scale of FDI in the most recent years has brought a more than proportionate increase in the number of jobs created, e.g. an increase by 165% between 1993 and 1994 (BKPM 1994: 10). Second, only direct employment effects are counted, not those materializing in adjoining industries. Third and finally, the higher capital intensity in foreign-controlled production is also likely to ensure a higher skills level of the employment created than elsewhere which, again, brings us to the verge of a qualitative appendix to a basically quantitative argument.

Indonesia is a special case among Southeast Asian host countries with respect to FDI effects on the balance of trade. Any estimate of foreign-induced export earnings should include all oil and LNG exports since the entire output is brought forward by the partnership between foreign multinationals and the state oil company Pertamina. This was obviously far less the case with manufacturing output, at any rate up to the shift towards an export-oriented industrial strategy in 1986. In 1987 FDI was said to account for only 14% of total non-oil export revenue but the foreign contribution climbed above 30% in 1989 and averaged 39% in the years 1991/93 (Thee 1996: 58). A strong export orientation has come to characterize the majority of FDI in manufacturing and there are bright prospects for future substantial gains from FDI on the balance of trade (cf. Saad 1995: 203). Further study of the full effects on the balance of payments would have to incorporate the import intensities of foreign-controlled production and rising remittances as the investment climate becomes more liberal.

The qualitative side has so far been largely introduced in the form of modifications to general quantitative assessments. Linkages and technology transfers, however, do not easily lend themselves for quantification in the first place. The available evidence is rather fragmented and less than conclusive. There is frequent mention of intended linkages arising from major FDI projects, even including the Asahan smelter. The literature abounds with complaints about the limited absorptive capacity of Indonesian labourers as a result of the weaknesses of the educational system, particularly in the vocational and tertiary segments (Ozawa 1979: 98–100; World Bank 1991).

Next to environmental issues, the observers of the timber boom in Kalimantan and Sumatra from the early 1970s also paid attention to linkages with other activities in the local economy. Even if employment rose substantially, it was argued that few linkages with local industry would emerge as long as the production remained limited to logging for purposes of immediate exports (Koehler 1972: 128–9; Sumitro 1975: 110–11). The question of forward linkages also has a regional dimension. Provinces outside Java with a foreign-controlled extraction of natural resources do not fully benefit from these operations since revenues are distributed throughout the country according to the priorities of Indonesian fiscal policy (Hill 1996: 235–8).

Another concern refers to backward linkages in manufacturing where the assembly content of production is usually very high and much of the raw materials and parts indeed have to be imported from abroad. The reason for this lack of local procurement is simple. The foreign firms do not deem local producers capable of supplying the volume and quality required and therefore turn to either the parent company overseas or other foreign firms operating in Indonesia. This is particularly outspoken in an industry using advanced technology such as electronics. The problem is not really alleviated by the plans to manufacture the required components in Indonesia recently launched by leading Japanese electronics firms as Hitachi, Toshiba and Sanyo (*FEER* 28/4 1994; United Nations 1995a: 130–74).

The importance of transmitting skills can scarcely be too much emphasized when discussing FDI effects in Indonesia, in particular in the rapidly changing manufacturing sector. Already in the early 1980s the skills component was found to determine labour productivity in foreign-controlled firms to a significantly higher extent than the capital intensity of production. Skill intensity further counts as one of the statistically significant variables explaining interindustry variations in the share of FDI in manufacturing (Balasubamanyam 1984; Aswicahyono and Hill 1993).

Indonesian employees in foreign-held firms are frequently sent on training programmes in for instance Japan or Korea. This represents a kind of technology transfer which is essential but still restricted to operational capability and maintenance of existing facilities. The development of further-reaching mastery, e.g. in project execution, depends entirely on local effort. It has even been suggested that licensing agreements may occasion more actual technology transfers than joint ventures with foreign multinationals (ESCAP/UNCTC 1987a: 79–145). There is a general consensus that the main bottleneck in implementing technology transfers lies in the limited absorption capacity of the Indonesian partners of the joint ventures which in turn is only reinforced when the technical requirements of the production process itself remain low (Saad 1995: 212–13). The much-publicized recent emphasis on investment in human capital does, however, give grounds for a cautious optimism, especially when seen in conjunction with a slow movement in the direction of a higher level of technological sophistication in new manufacturing FDI.

The distance between Jakarta and Seoul is considerable, not only in air miles but above all in terms of industrial development and technological sophistication. Korea and the other NICs foreshadow a path of economic growth that is especially attractive to Indonesia since it does not depend on depletable oil and gas reserves. Manufacturing is gaining importance in Indonesia. So is FDI in manufacturing. The potential contribution of FDI in aiding industrial restructuring in Indonesia should be sought more on the qualitative side than in absolute volumes of investment expenditure, employment and export revenue. Linkages with local industry and technology transfers hold the greatest promises but also face the most stubborn bottlenecks.

7.5 HOPES FOR THE FUTURE

Confidence in the future is very gradually returning in the Philippines. When the Hong Kong concern First Pacific paid 19.6 billion pesos ($1.6 billion) for the Fort Bonifacio property in downtown Manila in early 1995 it was acclaimed as a sure sign that foreign investors were ready to return to the Philippines after having been away for so long (*Asia Yearbook* 1996: 196). FDI in the Philippines has experienced the strongest cyclical movement in the region starting out from an exceptional continuity with the colonial past that gave way to a protracted slowdown which has only been cautiously reversed since Marcos' flight from the country in 1986. The current section is about the effects of FDI in the light of this cyclical movement.

Foreign-controlled firms in the Philippines have traditionally displayed distinct characteristics separating them from domestic corporations (cf. section 6.1). The orientation towards exports is professed to be high, especially in manufacturing. Almost two out of every five firms receiving export incentives in the early 1970s had a sizeable foreign ownership. Much of the foreign capital is concentrated to a limited number of industries. In the 1980s more than three-quarters of all manufacturing FDI ended up in one of six leading industries: chemicals, food processing, basic metals, textiles, transport equipment and oil (Snow 1983: 88; UNIDO 1988: 27). Foreign firms were larger than domestic ones and capital intensities were usually higher. In the 1960s already more than half of the top 25 manufacturing corporations had a foreign ownership whereas the foreign share was only one-third if calculated over the 250 largest manufacturing firms in the country (Lindsey 1976: 136; Yoshihara 1985: 40; see also Alburo and Sicat 1983: 104–5).

These features of FDI had ramifications both for the efficiency of operations and the profits pocketed by owners, ultimately also for the effects on the Philippine economy. In 1970 the average rate of profit was calculated to be 22% in foreign-held firms against only 7% in companies owned by Filipino's, a somewhat larger difference as compared to the figures cited in the well known Tsuda report. Significantly, no explanation for this differential could be found by applying conventional regression analysis to the relevant cost variables (Lindsey 1976: 201; Tsuda *et al.* 1978: III, 65). Later time series analysis has revealed that both capital utilization and total factor productivity in Philippine manufacturing in fact declined systematically throughout the 1960s and 1970s (Hooley 1985: 24, 33; Hooley 1988: 353–4). Oligopoly profits may have been amassed on an appreciable scale but productivity gains to be transmitted to the host country economy were disappointing, to say the least.

The Philippines was the first host country of FDI in Southeast Asia to become subjected to attempts at rigorously measuring the consequences of the participation of foreign capital in the economy. Regrettably, however, this line of research did not grow as comprehensive as in the case of Malaysia nor was it adequately followed up in later years. Dasari's early study from 1972 was restricted to the effects on the balance of payments whereas a simultaneous calculation by the Board of Investment in Manila focused on income and employment effects. Dasari argued that the net contribution of FDI to export revenue was marginal. The resulting increase in exports even amounted to less than the simultaneous import substitution due to more production for the domestic market. The Board of Investment ascribed about 8% of Net Domestic Product to FDI. Foreign-induced employment was only 1.2%, 143,000 out of a total labour force in excess of 11.8 million (Dasari 1972: 167–9; Study 1972). These findings were less than encouraging.

Export incentives were very popular with foreign investors but in actual fact sales grew ever more oriented towards the domestic market. By the late 1970s foreign firms were even responsible for a larger share of imports than of exports, i.e. foreign firms were running a relatively larger trade deficit in their commercial relations with the outside world than domestic firms (McDougald 1981: 180). The Philippine government attempted to further enhance the export-earning capacity of foreign firms by establishing EPZs where foreign producers were surrounded by high walls of protection and newly erected infrastructural facilities. The Mariveles EPZ in Bataan was founded already in 1972 precisely at the time when the nearing expiration of the Laurel-Langley agreement made American firms worry about future possibilities for overseas sales. Bataan was eventually followed by several other EPZs, including those at Baguio, Mactan and Cavite. The four EPZs mentioned were all still in operation in the early 1990s.

The EPZ on the Bataan peninsula gained a notoriously bad reputation among EPZs in Southeast Asia, both on account of its social conditions and its meagre benefits. The location was wrong, in an isolated backward region 170 km north of Manila. Much of the labour had to be imported and working hours were excessively long. The costs of the physical infrastructure outweighed new incomes by far. Net export earnings by the foreign firms, i.e. after deduction of required imports, amounted to $82 million during the entire first decade of operations, 1973–1982, representing 43% of the total initial outlays by the Philippine government. Employment at Bataan climbed towards a peak at 23,000 persons in 1983 but then declined below 14,000 (Yamada 1978: 103; ESCAP/UNCTC 1985a: 224–42; Warr 1987: 235; United Nations 1994: 90–91). Prospects for positive FDI effects through such EPZs deteriorated further still during the early 1980s when foreign export markets were affected by the world recession and the general political and economic climate in the Philippines went from bad to worse.

A non-discriminatory legislation with respect to foreign ownership was defended on the grounds that foreign participation would result in a sound competition in the Philippine economy. Yet this presupposed that foreign firms would adjust to the specific supply conditions prevailing in the host country by, for instance, not applying excessively capital-intensive technologies of production (Cagampang-de Castro 1977: 162–3; Bautista *et al.* 1979: 77). Empirical studies, however, reaffirmed that the oligopolistic structure in much of manufacturing was retained also when Japanese multinationals started replacing their American predecessors in the 1970s. Japanese big business favoured a small group of Filipino giants and capital intensities rather increased than the other way around (Alburo 1981: 25–6; de Dios 1986). There was clearly a discrepancy between expectations and reality with respect to the structural impact of FDI on the Philippine economy.

The record was not much better for other FDI effects. A careful assessment of operations at 28 foreign manufacturing firms in the early 1980s made clear that the production was largely confined to the last stage and that little development of skills occurred (Lindsey 1986; 1989: 87–91). Linkages with local industry and technology transfers often failed to materialize which was, as we have seen, no uncommon experience in Southeast Asia during the 1970s and much of the 1980s. The Philippines stood out among the ASEAN member states because of the poor score, both in attracting FDI and benefiting from its presence. FDI effects were above all unimportant because so little FDI materialized in the first place.

The political upheaval in 1986 brought immediate change thus inaugurating a second phase in the development of FDI in the Philippines since the 1960s (Figure 7.8; Philippine 1992: 6.32–6.35).[12] New investment commitments, as measured by initial paid-out capital, rose almost fivefold between 1986 and 1989 but, more significantly, the share of foreign capital in total new investment increased almost tenfold. FDI had become utterly marginal by the final days of the Marcos regime and it accounted for a very substantial proportion of the increase under Aquino. At the end of the 1980s almost one-half of total new investment in corporate equity came from sources abroad.

Foreign involvement was greater still in manufacturing. The share of FDI in new manufacturing investment climbed from more than 10% before the fall of Marcos to two-thirds by 1989 and a staggering 88% by 1991. Manufacturing as a whole at first expanded at about the same pace as total new investment so that its share in the general total, embracing both foreign and domestic capital, stayed the same at about one-quarter until around 1990. This development suggests a certain gestation for large-scale FDI projects in manufacturing. The share of manufacturing in total FDI thus first fell, then rose again, from 77% in 1985 to 25% in 1988 and back to the level of 74% in 1991 (Philippine 1992: 6.32–6.35). Even if FDI positions are strengthened also in the service sector of the Philippine economy, e.g. finance and real estate, it appears that the largest potential for positive FDI effects on the rehabilitation of the domestic economy may emanate from manufacturing.

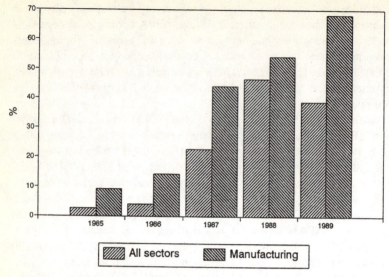

Figure 7.8   New FDI in the Philippines: foreign share in equity, 1985–1989

In 1988 the Japanese electronics firm Uniden set up a subsidiary in the Philippines for manufacturing mobile telephones thereby benefiting from low wages, a cheap currency and still existing preferences in gaining access to the American market (*FEER* 3/1 1991). Such an initiative is illustrative of new technological possibilities opening up in the wake of the recent influx of FDI. The electronics industry is likely to perform a pivotal function in this process. In 1992 this industry generated 28% of total export earnings whereas employment in the manufacturing of semiconductors alone rose to 65,000 (Aquino & Bolaños 1995: 184–5). Transfers of technology are still relatively limited but clearly improving. The increasing involvement of FDI in the service sector is also expected to have a positive impact through a higher efficiency and more linkages between subsectors (United Nations 1994: 73–111; United Nations 1995b: 151–203).

The evolution from misgivings and pessimism to new hopes for the future in the experience of the Philippines with FDI underscores better than anything else the importance of breaking with the past and creating entirely new conditions for FDI and its effects on the host country economy. This obviously applies to the political situation dictating the division of the development of the past decades into two sharply distinct phases. But it also applies to the very nature of FDI. The effects remained limited irrespective of the deteriorating investment climate and subsequent low levels of FDI. Awaiting more detailed analysis, it can be tentatively concluded that today's FDI seems to possess more potential for beneficial effects, not only on account of its greater magnitude but also because of its more competitive character and higher technological content.

It is still a bit early to pass judgement on the effects of the rebounding FDI on the economic development of Vietnam, let alone Myanmar, Laos and Cambodia. Suffice it to say that prospects for positive structural effects are improving, especially in Vietnam. Here the initial emphasis on resource-intensive FDI has given way to massive influx of foreign capital into manufacturing. By 1994 manufacturing already accounted for more than 40% of accumulated FDI in Vietnam. The rapidly increasing domestic market in particular attracts much fresh FDI into manufacturing (Gates 1995: 389; UNCTAD 1995: 54–5).

This Chapter has examined the record in the five major host countries of FDI in the region, thereby positioning FDI in its appropriate macro-economic context and reviewing FDI effects with the experiences before the Pacific War in the background. A whole host of FDI effects was reviewed, both quantitative ones such as contributions to capital formation, employment and export earnings and those of a more qualitative nature such as linkages and technology transfers. The quantitative side of the FDI impact was only consistently positive and sizeable in Singapore. Elsewhere the qualitative effects of FDI predominated. Actual results were initially limited or even negative in Malaysia, Thailand, Indonesia and the Philippines. The turn for the better came in the late 1980s. Even if important bottlenecks still remain with regard to linkages with local industry and technology transfer, prospects have become relatively bright for an effective positive contribution of FDI to the current process of industrialization in virtually every major host country of Southeast Asia.

We have emphasized in our discussion the unique development of each host country. In Singapore the bargaining power of the self-confident government in bending FDI activities to its own purposes has been crucial. For Malaysia it was technology which defined its special niche within the hierarchy between NICs and those wanting to become near-NICs soon. Thailand appeared not fundamentally different from Malaysia. Here it also boiled down to sustaining rapid economic growth. In Indonesia restructuring and industrialization appeared the only way to escape from an over-dependence on oil revenues. For the Philippines it was primarily a matter of a changing climate and changing expectations of FDI and the gains to be had from it. Self-assertive Singaporeans, technology-minded Malaysians, growth-obsessed Thais, restructuring Indonesians and optimistic Filipinos. That is how FDI links up with industrialization in Southeast Asia today.

This chapter has considered FDI in the broader context of economic growth. The literature abounds with statistical information about the recent economic performance in Southeast Asia. Table 7.9 highlights economic growth and industrial expansion in the five major host countries of the region during the 1980s and early 1990s and sums up the growth across those years.

8 Conclusion

When violence flared up in the streets of Jakarta in late July 1996 one of the first worries of the Suharto government was whether this would affect the attractiveness of Indonesia as the foremost recipient of foreign investment capital in Southeast Asia. Indeed, two out of three Korean executives in a small fax poll were immediately prepared to reconsider making new investments in Indonesia (*FEER* 22/8 1996). Both reactions underscore the sensitivities surrounding FDI in Southeast Asia today. Official concern about incoming FDI readily seems entirely out of proportion considering the relatively small role it plays in all host countries except Singapore. Yet in this region it fits into a long tradition of preoccupation, albeit with varying emotional undertones, with foreign involvement in domestic economic affairs. It forms an integral part of the heritage of colonialism in all host countries in the region except Thailand with its intimate link between the presence of foreign capital and the colony's economic development, or rather lack of such progress. This book is about FDI in Southeast Asia in the twentieth century. It argues that FDI was important in the economic life of the region during the late colonial period and that it has today, at long last, become important again in most parts of the region.

But FDI in Southeast Asia does not look the same today as yesterday. The line of continuity was broken by the radical disruption in mid-century due to warfare and Japanese occupation, decolonization and the assertion of newly independent nation states. A full generation of disruption had irrevocable consequences for both appearance and substance of FDI in the region. Such changes, it is maintained here, also mean changes in effects of FDI on domestic economic development in the host country. This book has identified prevalent patterns of FDI and indicated the impact of FDI by contrasting the late colonial era and the contemporary period. This was done both in general terms (Chapter 2), by more detailed discussions of the situation prior to the Pacific War (Chapters 3 and 4) and the resurgence of FDI in the region since the 1960s (Chapters 6 and 7). The latter two were separated by a brief interlude in the transitionary phase including the changes in investment climate necessary to condition the return of large-scale FDI to the region (Chapter 5).

A conspicuous difference in the pattern of today's FDI as compared to the late colonial past concerns the nationality of the investor. Investors from the metropolitan mother countries predominated strongly in the colonies, to varying degrees, whereas the resurgence after decolonization brought an influx of first American, then Japanese and finally NIC capital. Another important difference refers to the sectoral composition of FDI. The traditional combination of resource-oriented FDI with tropical cash crop production for exports reached the highest degree of perfection in colonial Indonesia and Malaya while there was a stronger tendency towards diversification in French Indochina and the Philippines. The resurgence since the 1960s has witnessed a sharp shift in favour of manufacturing, increasingly also in the direction of services.

The contrast with the past is less pronounced when it comes to both the relative attractiveness of individual host countries within the region and the relative position of FDI within the host country economy. The hierarchy of host countries, as revealed by accumulated FDI rather than professed preferences, has to a large extent remained the same with Indonesia in the first rank followed by first Singapore/Malaysia, then Thailand and the Philippines although the order between the latter two has been reversed. The order of magnitude of FDI in the domestic economy, here expressed as real FDI per capita, has stayed strikingly similar over time while showing much variation across host countries. Two of the latest trends, finally, deserving to be mentioned include West European investors jumping on the bandwagon of opportunities in a region of rapid growth as well as the gradual opening-up of host countries like Vietnam and Myanmar that for decades were effectively sealed off from incoming FDI.

The pattern of FDI was not determined in the same fashion under colonialism as today. The supply side, i.e. private foreign capital seeking investment outlets, was decisive in the first period whereas FDI in the later period emerges as the outcome of a bargaining process between the supply side and the demand side, i.e. governments of independent host countries wishing to employ foreign capital for purposes of domestic economic development. An overwhelming majority of suppliers of overseas investment capital in the earlier period came from the colonial powers in Western Europe and North America. There was little variation in outlook and motives among Western pioneers seeking to enhance comparative advantages and profit opportunities by securing access to vital raw materials and new markets. FDI in the late colonial period was primarily geared to fit the specific resource endowment and economic structure in the recipient host country.

The resurgence of FDI in the region since the 1960s, however, has been accompanied by an increasing variegation on the supply side including Japanese 'new wave' and NIC investors. Such FDI is possibly best described in terms of a relocation of stages of the production process according to the 'flying geese'-model of stepwise industrialization throughout the East and Southeast Asian region. FDI then materializes in conjunction with the specific strategy of industrial restructuring in the host country in question. The need to relocate manufacturing production out of countries higher up on the ladder of regional industrialization thus coincides with the wish of those further down to gain access to foreign-controlled technology. The great change in FDI patterns since the colonial period refers to the orientation of the host countries. A global shift has taken place from the northwest–southeast orientation defined by the colonial relationship towards a north–south orientation based on differences in advancement along the same path of industrialization. FDI in the colonial period was primarily geared to fit conditions in the host country. Today the nationality of the investor has gained importance in determining the final pattern of FDI. The colonial link has vanished and FDI has become more footloose.

The impact of FDI can only be fully understood within the context of domestic development and here we encounter the most critical divide between the two situations under study, i.e. between the colonial state in operation in all host countries but Thailand against the current thrust for industrialization and rapid economic growth throughout the region. This difference in terms of the broader setting has repercussions for both the investment climate and the degree to which FDI is incorporated into domestic economic life. The investment climate under colonialism was favourable but not equally favourable to all investors. Investors from the metropolitan mother countries occupied such privileged positions and entertained such long-run expectations about staying in business in the colony that the very distinction between 'foreign' and 'domestic' gets blurred. The colonial state produced one kind of dualism, a dichotomy between the alien perspective from headquarters in the mother country and a fair degree of local entrenchment in the colony.

The ideals of industry possess an irresistible appeal to economic policy-makers in contemporary Southeast Asia and all host country governments, with the exception of Singapore, have needed much time to strike the appropriate balance between priorities of economic nationalism and using foreign capital to further industrialization. Rankings by investment climate usually put Singapore first, followed by Malaysia, Thailand, Indonesia and the Philippines, in that order. Meanwhile, foreign investors have become more 'multinational' and FDI more footloose. This book suggests that the differentiation in the impact of FDI refers today to attitudes of individual host countries and before the Second World War to the nationality of those shaping the colonial state.

FDI served to substitute for domestic savings and to generate additional export revenue and some new employment. This applies to both the colonial period and today. But, from the perspective of the recipient country, the final effect on the external balance was disappointing, first because of the large outflow of profits under colonial rule, then because of the high import propensity of foreign-controlled production little adjusted to domestic conditions. Singapore alone formed an exception to the rule. Elsewhere signals of a more positive contribution only became clearly discernible since the late 1980s. In no colony did FDI trigger off the transition to self-sustained economic growth. Since independence such a contribution was only unequivocally made in Singapore. In all other major host countries the impact of FDI on economic growth was not impressive when measured in quantitative terms.

One similarity in the impact of FDI on the host country economy in the colonial period and today concerns structural change. The foremost contribution of FDI under the aegis of colonial rule, apart from the sheer inauguration of a fuller utilization of natural riches, was the creation of physical infrastructure and corporate networks. There was more emphasis on the erection and improvement of the physical infrastructure in French Indochina and more emphasis on corporate networks in colonial Indonesia and Malaya. Such networks can be considered as extended backward linkages. The most important forward linkage was the immediate connection of export production to world markets as such. Other kinds of forward linkages were, however, lacking altogether. Scarcely any development of skills took place except perhaps, to a limited extent, in the Philippines where American business stimulated domestic participation.

The scope for structural change today embraces both forward and backward linkages and above all the eagerly awaited transfer of technology. Actual transfers remained disappointing for a considerable time. Signs of improvement are mostly of a comparatively recent date. Contributions of this kind are potentially of great significance in the light of the current restructuring of the economies in several major host countries of the region. Effective linkages and technology transfer may safeguard the near-NIC status of Malaysia and aid Thailand and Indonesia, later possibly also the Philippines, in the same direction. This book argues that the impact of FDI on the economic development of the host country is more profound and more favourable than in the colonial period. This may be ascribed to the qualitative side of the FDI impact rather than the quantitative one. This implies that today's host country governments have been more successful in reaping the benefits from FDI than their predecessors in the colonial era.

The FDI impact has been considered here in its most immediate form, i.e. it is easily identified and changes may be directly linked to the preceding influx of FDI. The overall development impact of FDI, however, poses a far broader question including the way in which FDI shaped the process of long-run economic development in host countries. A full treatment of such broad matters lies beyond the scope of an analysis as the present one which focuses on comparisons across countries in a large region and over a protracted period of time.

Southeast Asia has regained its attraction as a major recipient of FDI and FDI has reconquered its key position in the region's economic development. This represents a long-run continuity bridging the first four decades with the final one-third of the twentieth century. The combined study of these two interlinked periods is especially rewarding because it makes us better appreciate how much has changed with respect to FDI in the meantime. Appearance has changed with new investors moving in looking for other targets. Substance has changed too with other reasons to invest and FDI occupying a different position in the domestic economy. Ramifications have changed as well with partly other effects materializing and improving prospects for substantial positive contributions to future growth. These are, as it were, the changing faces of foreign investment in Southeast Asia during the twentieth century.

Notes

2 THE HISTORICAL PERSPECTIVE

1. A slightly different version of this chapter is published as Lindblad 1997.

3 PIONEERS AND PROFITS

1. Excerpts from this chapter were also presented in Lindblad 1996a.
2. The emphasis on the masculinity of the pioneer in this example does not imply that women played no role whatsoever in implementing FDI projects in Southeast Asia during the colonial period. In fact, however, the overwhelming majority of pioneers were male.
3. The business archives of the Østasiatiske Kompagni are kept at the headquarters of the concern in Copenhagen in Denmark but are not available to researchers.
4. The information on Guthrie derives from University of London, School of Oriental and African Studies library collection: Guthrie & Co. Archive. Sign. G/MIN. Minute Book.
5. Letter from the auditors, dated 8 January 1913.
6. The business archives of Harrisons & Crosfield are not at the public's disposal. No pre-war company reports are available even at the British Library Science Reference and Information Service in London.
7. Sources to Figures 3.1 and 3.2: Company reports consulted in National Archives at The Hague: Direktie-archief van de N.V. Billiton Maatschappij 1852–1970, vols. 41–4, 89; Archieven van de N.V. Deli Maatschappij en de daarmee gefuseerde bedrijven 1869–1967, vol. 39; Archief van de N.V. Cultuur- en Handel-Maatschappij Michiels-Arnold 1887–1957, vols. 109, 126; Archief van de N.V. Cultuur-Maatschappij Wonolangan 1895–1963, vols. 113–21.
8. The information on results given in the annual reports of Wonolangan is not sufficiently detailed to allow a calculation of profits. The profits calculated for Billiton and Michiels-Arnold include dividend payments, additions to reserves and bonuses.
9. Solvability is calculated as total liabilities divided by non-equity capital. Liquidity equals liquid assets plus credits divided by outstanding debts.

4 INSIDE THE COLONIAL STATE

1. An earlier version of this section was included in Lindblad 1991.
2. 'Other' in Figure 4.4 refers to additional benefits accruing to directors and allocations for special purposes, including tax reserves and the like.

5 LOW TIDE AND HIGH HOPES

1. University of London, School of Oriental and African Studies library collection: Guthrie & Co. Archive. Sign. G/UT/24. Shareholders' meeting, 29 December 1959.
2. The nationality of a firm is derived from the ethnic origin of the majority of the members of the board. Joint ventures are companies with two groups of board members of similar size but of different ethnic origin. The data represented in Figure 5.1 are from two Thai language sources, *Prachum-kotmai Pracham-sok*, vol. 18–26 [1901-1913] and *Racha-kichanubeksa*, vol. 29–48 [1912–1932]. This information was transcribed and translated into Japanese, partly also into English, by Dr Suehiro Akira of Tokyo University (formerly at Osaka City University) and kindly put at my disposal.
3. University of London, School of Oriental and African Studies library collection: Guthrie & Co. Archive. Sign. G/UT/24. 48th general meeting, 2 January 1959.
4. The data represented in Figure 5.2 are from University of London, School of Oriental and African Studies library collection: Guthrie & Co. Archive. Sign. G/UT/24. Annual reports. The book year runs from 1 August–31 July.

6 THE NEW INVESTORS

1. The survey covered 1057 individual Japanese-affiliated companies in Southeast Asia of which 831 (79%) stated objectives. Percentages may add up to more than 100 since multiple responses were given.
2. The stated nominal equity figures of the subsidiaries are likely to grossly understate the true magnitude of Japanese capital actually invested. These equity figures merely serve as a rough indication of the degree of capitalization in the production line or firm in question and are only used in conjunction with data on employment at the subsidiary.
3. Data from the Bank of Thailand compiled in February 1996 and kindly put at my disposal by the United Nations/ESCAP in Bangkok.
4. Preliminary statistics on NIC direct investment in Southeast Asia during the years 1989–1991 were compiled by the Institute of Developing Economies in Tokyo and kindly put at my disposal.
5. The Institute of Developing Economies at Tokyo played an intermediary role in gaining access to the English-language edition of the 1986 issue.

7 THE IDEALS OF INDUSTRY

1. The 'Singapore 500' list is published by a private firm, Datapool. Financial institutions are excluded. Details are given on gross revenue, net profits (after tax but before extraordinary items), total assets ('shareholders' funds' including accumulated profits and reserves). No information is given on types of activities, dates of establishment or employment.

2. Electrical and electronics products are combined in Figure 7.2 so as to ensure comparability over the entire period.
3. The data underlying Figure 7.3 were provided by the Hitachi Semiconductor (Malaysia) Sdn. Bhd. office at Penang during my visit to the company in August 1994. The cooperation of the firm and its employees is gratefully acknowledged.
4. I gladly acknowledge the cooperation I received when I visited the head office of Hitachi at Tokyo in August 1994.
5. 'Other' includes NIC investors.
6. Unpublished statistics on applications, approvals and start-ups prepared by the International Division of the Bank of Thailand. This information was kindly put at my disposal by the Institute of Developing Economies in Tokyo.
7. The following information was given for each firm: company name, year of establishment, employment, type of business, distribution of equity between Thai and foreign shareholders.
8. The category 'Other manufacturing' includes very diverse types of industries, *e.g.* iron and steel, jewellery, furniture, food processing, toys, even Christmas tree decorations.
9. Information from the Bank of Thailand compiled in July–September 1990.
10. In a future study I hope to look more carefully into recent Korean investment, in particular in Indonesian manufacturing.
11. This draws on information contained in an unpublished memorandum entitled 'The Republic of Indonesia' and prepared by the financial advisors Lazard Frères, Lehman Bros. and S.G. Warburg & Co. in March 1993.
12. The values in Figure 7.8 are in million pesos. The exchange rate with the dollar stayed roughly the same. One dollar was worth 19.03 pesos in 1985 and 21.74 pesos in 1989.

Bibliography

Alburo, F.A. 1981. *Some Aspects of Japanese Investments in the Philippines*, Quezon City: University of Philippines.

Alburo, F.A. and L.M. Sicat 1983. 'Philippine–Japan Economic Relations: Investment', in Sekiguchi Sueo (ed.), *ASEAN–Japan Relations: Investment*, Singapore: Institute of Southeast Asian Studies, 93–148.

Ali, A. 1994. 'Japanese Industrial Investments and Technology Transfer in Malaysia', in K.S. Jomo (ed.), *Japan and Malaysian Development: In the Shadow of the Rising Sun*, London: Routledge, 102–26.

Ali, A. and H. Osman-Rani 1987. 'The Malaysian Experience with the MNCs in the Industrial Sector', in F. Shahadan and N.A.H. Idris (eds), *Financing for Development, with Special Reference to ASEAN*, Singapore: Oxford University Press, 167–95.

Allen, G.C. and A.G. Donnithorne 1957. *Western Enterprise in Indonesia and Malaya: A Study in Economic Development*, London: Allen & Unwin.

Allen, T. 1974. *Policies of ASEAN Countries towards Direct Foreign Investment*, New York: Asia Society.

Andrus, J.R. 1948. *Burmese Economic Life*, Palo Alto: Stanford University Press.

Annual Report 1951. *Annual Report of the Federation of Malaya 1950*, London: HM Stationery.

Anwar, M.A. 1980. 'Trade Strategies and Industrial Development in Indonesia', in R. Garnaut (ed.), *ASEAN in a Changing Pacific and World Economy*, Canberra: Australian National University Press, 207–31.

Aquino, Th.G. and A.B. Bolaños 1995. 'Foreign Investment Inflows and Political Stability in the Philippines', in *The New Wave of Foreign Direct Investment in Asia*, Tokyo/Singapore: Nomura Research Institute/Institute of Southeast Asian Studies, 174–96.

Ariff, M. 1977. 'Trade Policies and ASEAN Industrial Cooperation', in M. Ariff and Fong Chang Onn (eds), *ASEAN Cooperation in Industrial Projects*, Kuala Lumpur: Malaysian Economic Association, 151–63.

Ariff, M. 1992. 'Foreign Direct Investment in Malaysia: Trends, Determinants and Implications', in M. Ariff and Hirashi Yokoyama (eds), *Foreign Direct Investment in Malaysia*, Tokyo: Institute of Developing Economies, 1–24.

Ariff, M. and H. Hill 1985. *Export-oriented Industrialization: The ASEAN Experience*, Sydney: Allen & Unwin.

Ariff, M. and Hirashi Yokoyama (eds) 1992. *Foreign Direct Investment in Malaysia*, Tokyo: Institute of Developing Economies.

Arndt, H.W. 1967. 'Survey of Recent Developments', *Bulletin of Indonesian Economic Studies*, 3 (7), 1–37.

Arndt, H.W. 1974. 'Professor Kojima on the Macroeconomics of Foreign Direct Investment', *Hitotsubashi Journal of Economics*, 15 (1), 26–35.

Arndt, H.W. 1989. 'Industrial Policy in East Asia', *Industry and Development*, 22, 1–66.

ASEAN 1990. *ASEAN Selected Statistics, 1982–1988*, Jakarta: ASEAN Secretariat.

213

ASEAN 1994. *ASEAN Macro-economic Outlook 1994–1995*, Jakarta: ASEAN Secretariat.

ASEAN-U.S. Initiative 1989. *ASEAN-U.S. Initiative: Assessment and Recommendations for Improved Economic Relations*, Honolulu: East–West Centre.

Asia Yearbook 1996. *Asia 1996 Yearbook: A Review of the Events of 1995*, Hong Kong: Far Eastern Economic Review.

Aswicahyono, H.H. and H. Hill 1993. 'Explaining Foreign Investment Shares in LDC Industry: Incorporating the Policy Factor', *Economics Letters*, 41, 167–70.

Athukorala P. and J. Menon 1996. 'Foreign Investment and Industrialization in Malaysia: Exports, Employment and Spillovers', *Asian Economic Journal*, 10, 29–44.

Aung Tun Thet 1989. *Burmese Entrepreneurship: Creative Response in the Colonial Economy*, Stuttgart: Steiner Wiesbaden.

Balance of Payments 1977. *Balance of Payments Manual*, Washington, D.C.: International Monetary Fund.

Balasubramanyam, V.N. 1984. 'Factor Proportions and Productive Efficiency of Foreign–owned Firms in the Indonesian Manufacturing Sector', *Bulletin of Indonesian Economic Studies*, 20 (3), 70–94.

Baltussen, J.H.L.M. 1993. 'Het investeringsklimaat in de ASEAN, 1985–1990', unpublished M.A. thesis, University of Leiden, The Netherlands.

Bank Indonesia 1993. *Statistik ekonomi-keuangan Indonesia/Indonesian Financial Statistics*, Jakarta: Bank Indonesia.

Barlow, C. and Thee Kian Wie 1988. *The North Sumatran Regional Economy: Growth with Unbalanced Development*, Singapore: Institute of Southeast Asian Studies.

Baudet, H. 1975. 'Nederland en de rang van Denemarken', *Bijdragen en Mededelingen betreffende de Geschiedenis der Nederlanden*, 90, 430–43.

Bautista, R.M. 1981. *Capital Utilization in Manufacturing: Columbia, Israel, Malaysia and the Philippines*, New York: Oxford University Press.

Bautista, R.M. *et al.* 1979. *Industrial Promotion Policies in the Philippines*, Manila: Philippine Institute for Development Studies.

Beredjick, N. and T. Waelde 1988. *Petroleum Investment Policies in Developing Countries*, London: Graham & Trotman.

BKPM 1994. *Perkembangan investasi tahun 1994 dan prospek investasi tahun 1995*, Jakarta: BKPM.

Blake, M.L. 1982. *The Participation of Female Factory Workers in Voluntary Associations: Case Studies of Electronics Factory Workers in Malaysia and Thailand*, Ph.D. dissertation, Universiti Sains Malaysia, Penang.

Boomgaard, P. and A.J. Gooszen 1991. *Changing Economy in Indonesia: XI. Population Trends, 1795–1942*, Amsterdam: Royal Tropical Institute.

Booth, A. 1990. 'Foreign Trade and Domestic Development in the Colonial Economy', in A. Booth, W.J. O'Malley and A. Weidemann (eds), *Indonesian Economic History in the Dutch Colonial Era*, New Haven: Yale University, 267–95.

Booth, A. 1991. 'The Economic Development of Southeast Asia, 1870–1985', in G.D. Snooks, A.J.S. Reid and J.J. Pincus (eds), *Exploring Southeast Asia's Economic Past* [= *Australian Economic History Review*, 31], Canberra: Australian National University, 20–52.

Booth, A. 1995. 'Sources of Investment and Technological Change in Colonial and Post-colonial Indonesia', paper prepared for the EUROSEAS Conference 'Keys to Southeast Asia', Leiden, the Netherlands, 29 June – 1 July.

Bowe, M. and J.W. Dean 1990. 'Voluntary Debt Relief and the Philippines, *ASEAN Economic Bulletin*, 7 (1), 11–38.

Brief Information 1960. *Brief Information Concerning Investment in Thailand*, Bangkok: Board of Investment.

Brittan, L. 1995. 'Investment Liberalization: The Next Great Boost to the World Economy', *Transnational Corporations*, 4 (1), 1–10.

Broersma, K.E. 1985. *Eene Zaak van Regt en Billijkheid: Enkele episoden uit de enerverende Billitongeschiedenis, 1865–1985*, Leidschendam.

Brown, I. 1988. *The Elite and the Economy in Siam, c. 1890–1920*, Singapore: Oxford University Press.

Brown, I. 1993. 'Imperialism, Trade and Investment in the Late Nineteenth and Early Twentieth Centuries', in J. Butcher and H.W. Dick (eds), *The Rise and Fall of Revenue Farming: Business Elites and the Emergence of the Modern State in Southeast Asia*, New York: St. Martin's, 80–88.

Brown, R.A. 1994. *Capital and Entrepreneurship in Southeast Asia*, Basingstoke: Macmillan.

Burke, G. 1990. 'The Rise and Fall of the International Tin Agreements', in K.S. Jomo (ed.), *Undermining Tin: The Decline of Malaysian Pre-eminence*, Sydney: University of Sydney, 43–70.

Business and Investment 1987. *Business and Investment Environment in Thailand*, Kuala Lumpur: Asian and Pacific Development Centre and South Pacific Bureau for Economic Cooperation.

Cable, V. and B. Persaud 1987. *Developing with Foreign Investment*, London: Croom Helm.

Cagampang-de Castro, S.M. 1977. *Foreign Business Enterprise in the Philippines: A Study of the Legal Framework in a Developing Economy*, Quezon City: Multiplex Publamark.

Cain, P.J. and A.G. Hopkins 1993. *British Imperialism: I. Innovation and Expansion, 1688–1914; II. Crisis and Deconstruction, 1914–1990*, London/New York: Longman.

Callis, H.G. 1942. *Foreign Capital in Southeast Asia*, New York: Institute of Pacific Relations.

Campo, J.N.F.M. à 1992. *Macht, markt en ruimte: Stoomvaart en staatsvorming in de Indonesische archipel 1850–1914*, Hilversum: Verloren.

Campo, J.N.F.M. à 1995. 'Strength, Survival and Success: A Statistical Profile of Corporate Enterprise in Colonial Indonesia, 1883–1913', *Jahrbuch für Wirtschaftsgeschichte*, (1), 45–74.

Campo, J.N.F.M. à 1996. 'The Rise of Corporate Enterprise in Colonial Indonesia, 1893–1913', in J.Th. Lindblad (ed.), *Historical Foundations of a National Economy in Indonesia, 1890s–1990s*, Amsterdam: North-Holland, 71–94.

Carr, D.W. 1978. *Foreign Investment and Development in the Southwest Pacific with Special Reference to Australia and Indonesia*, New York: Praeger.

Caves, R.E. 1982, 1996. *Multinational Enterprise and Economic Analysis*, Cambridge: Cambridge University Press.

Chang, Y.S. 1971. *The Transfer of Technology; Economics of Offshore Assembly:The Case of Semiconductor Industry*, New York: UNITAR.

Chapman, A. 1946. 'American Policy in the Philippines', *Far Eastern Survey*, 15, 164–9.

Chee Peng Lim and Lee Poh Ping 1979. *The Role of Japanese Direct Investment in Malaysia*, Singapore: Institute of Southeast Asian Studies.

Chee Peng Lim and Lee Poh Ping 1983. 'Japanese Direct Investment in Malaysia, with Special Reference to Japanese Joint Ventures', in S. Sekiguchi (ed.), *ASEAN–Japan Relations: Investment*, Singapore: Institute of Southeast Asian Studies, 61–92.

Chen, E.K.Y. 1992. 'Changing Pattern of Financial Flows in the Asia–Pacific Region and Policy Responses', *Asian Development Review*, 10 (2), 41–65.

Chen Tain-Jy 1995. 'Economic Effects of Taiwanese FDI on Host Countries', paper prepared for seminar on 'Taiwanese FDI in Southeast Asia' at Kuala Lumpur, Jakarta, Manila, Ho Chi Minh City, Bangkok, 6–15 March.

Chen Tain-Jy, Chen Yi-Ping and Ku Ying-Hua 1995. 'Taiwan's Outward Direct Investment; Has the Domestic Industry Been Hollowed Out?', in *The New Wave of Foreign Direct Investment in Asia*, Tokyo/Singapore: Nomura Research Institute/Institute of Southeast Asian Studies, 87–110.

Cheong, K.C. and K.C. Lim 1981. 'Implications of the Transfer of Technology and Primary-ancillary Linkages: A Case Study of the Electronics and Electrical Industries in Malaysia', in H. Osman-Rani *et al.* (eds), *Development in the Eighties, with Special Emphasis on Malaysia* [=*Jurnal Ekonomi Malaysia*, 3 (4)], 119–46.

Chia Siow Yue 1980. 'Singapore's Trade and Development Strategy and ASEAN Economic Cooperation, with Special Reference to the ASEAN Common Approach to Foreign Economic Relations', in R. Garnaut (ed.), *ASEAN in a Changing Pacific and World Economy*, Canberra: Australian National University Press, 241–72.

Chia Siow Yue 1982. 'EC Investment in ASEAN', in N. Akrasanee and H.C. Rieger (eds), *ASEAN–EEC Economic Relations*, Singapore: Institute of Southeast Asian Studies, 256–313.

Chia Siow Yue 1983. 'Codes of Conduct for MNCs and Governments in ASEAN', *Contemporary Southeast Asia*, 5, 219–36.

Chia Siow Yue 1984. 'Export Processing and Industrialization: The Case of Singapore', in F. Lee (ed.), *Export Processing Zones and Industrial Employment in Asia*, Bangkok: ILO/ARTEP, 95–156.

Chia Siow Yue 1985. 'The Role of Foreign Trade and Investment in the Development of Singapore', in W. Galenson (ed.), *Foreign Trade and Investment: Economic Development in the Newly Industrializing Asian Countries*, Madison: University of Wisconsin Press, 259–300.

Chia Siow Yue 1986. 'Direct Foreign Investment and the Industrialization Process in Singapore', in Lim Chong-Yah and P.J. Lloyd (eds), *Singapore: Resources and Growth*, Singapore: Oxford University Press, 79–117.

Chia Siow Yue 1990. 'Japanese Foreign Direct Investment in ASEAN and Asia NIEs', unpublished report, Tokyo: Institute of Developing Economies.

Chinwanno, C. and S. Tambunlertchai 1983. 'Japanese Investment in Thailand and Its Prospects in the 1980s', in S. Sekiguchi (ed.), *ASEAN–Japan Relations: Investment*, Singapore: Institute of Southeast Asian Studies, 181–226.

Chong Li Choy 1986. 'Singapore's Development: Harnessing the Multinationals', *Contemporary Southeast Asia*, 8, 56–69.

Chowdhury, A. and I. Islam 1993. *The Newly Industrializing Economies of East Asia*, London: Routledge.

Chunanunthatham, S. *et al.* 1987. *Trade and Financing Strategies for Thailand in the 1980s*, London: Overseas Development Institute.

Clad, J. 1989. *Behind the Myth: Business, Money and Power in Southeast Asia*, London: Grafton.

Clapham, M. 1970. 'Some Difficulties of Foreign Investors in Indonesia', *Bulletin of Indonesian Economic Studies*, 6 (1), 73–80.

Conrad, J. 1947[2]. *Almayer's Folly: A Story of an Eastern River*, London: Dent.

Country Report 1990. *Country Report for Seminar on Investment Promotion: I. Asian Nations*, Tokyo: Japan International Cooperation Agency.

Creutzberg, P. 1977. *Changing Economy in Indonesia: III. Expenditure on Fixed Assets*, The Hague: Nijhoff.

Cribb, R. 1994. 'Introduction; The Late Colonial State in Indonesia', in R. Cribb (ed.), *The Late Colonial State in Indonesia: Political and Economic Foundations of the Netherlands Indies, 1880–1942*, Leiden: KITLV, 1–10.

Cunyngham–Brown, S. 1971. *The Traders: A Story of Britain's Southeast Asian Commercial Adventure* [Guthries], London: Newman Neame.

Dasari, D. 1972. *Balance of Payments Effects of Direct Foreign Investment: A Case Study of the Philippines*, Ph.D. dissertation, New York University.

Davies, G. 1969. 'United Kingdom Investment', in H. Hughes and P.S. You (eds), *Foreign Investment and Industrialization in Singapore*, Canberra: Australian National University, 46–61.

Davis, L.E. and R. Huttenback 1986. *Mammon and the Pursuit of Empire: The Political Economy of British Imperialism, 1860–1912*, Cambridge: Cambridge University Press.

Deli Maatschappij 1919. *Gedenkschrift bij gelegenheid van het vijftigjarig bestaan*, Amsterdam: Deli.

Deli Maatschappij 1929. *Gedenkschrift bij gelegenheid van het zestigjarig bestaan*, Amsterdam: Deli.

Derksen, J.B.D. and J. Tinbergen 1945. 'Berekeningen over de economische betekenis van Nederlandsch-Indië voor Nederland', *Maandschrift van het Centraal Bureau voor de Statistiek*, 40, 210–16.

Detailed Benchmark 1983. *Detailed Benchmark Definition of Foreign Direct Investment*, Paris: OECD.

Dick, H.W. 1993. 'Oei Tiong Ham', in J. Butcher and H.W. Dick (eds), *The Rise and Fall of Revenue Farming: Business Elites and the Emergence of the Modern State in Southeast Asia*, New York: St. Martin's, 272–80.

Dick, H.W. 1996. 'The Emergence of a National Economy, 1808–1990s', in J.Th. Lindblad (ed.), *Historical Foundations of a National Economy in Indonesia, 1880s–1990s*, Amsterdam: North-Holland, 21–51.

Dickie, R.B. and T.A. Layman 1988. *Foreign Investment and Government Policy in the Third World: Forging Common Interests in Indonesia and Beyond*, Basingstoke: Macmillan.

Dios, E.S. de 1986. 'Protection, Concentration and the Direction of Foreign Investments', *Philippine Review of Economics and Business*, 29, 57–82.

Directory 1993. *Directory of Potential Joint Venture Partners in Thailand*, Tokyo: ASEAN Centre.

Dixon, C. 1991. *Southeast Asia in the World-economy: A Regional Geography*, Cambridge: Cambridge University Press.

Doner, R. 1987. *Domestic Coalitions and Japanese Auto Firms in Southeast Asia: A Comparative Bargaining Study*, Berkeley: University of California Press.

Doronila, A. 1992. *The State, Economic Transformation, and Political Change in the Philippines, 1946–1972*, Singapore: Oxford University Press.

Doshi, T. 1989. *The Singapore Petroleum Industry: Houston of Asia*, Singapore: Institute of Southeast Asian Studies.

Drabble, J.H. 1972. 'Investment in the Rubber Industry in Malaya, *c.* 1900–1922', *Journal of Southeast Asian Studies*, 3, 247–61.

Drabble, J.H. 1973. *Rubber in Malaya 1876–1922: The Genesis of the Industry*, Kuala Lumpur: Oxford University Press.

Drabble, J.H. and P.J. Drake 1981. 'The British Agency Houses in Malaysia: Survival in a Changing World', *Journal of Southeast Asian Studies*, 12, 297–328.

Dunning, J.H. 1994. 'Re-evaluating the Benefits of Foreign Direct Investment', *Transnational Corporations*, 3 (1), 23–52.

Dunning, J.H. and J. Cantwell 1987. *IRM Directory of Statistics of International Investment and Production*, Basingstoke: Macmillan.

ECAFE 1949. *Economic Survey of Asia and the Far East 1948*, Lake Success, NY: United Nations.

Elson, R.E. 1992. 'International Commerce, the State and Society: Economic and Social Change', in N. Tarling (ed.), *The Cambridge History of Southeast Asia: II. The Nineteenth and Twentieth Centuries*, Cambridge: Cambridge University Press, 131–95.

Eng, P. van der 1993. 'The "Colonial Drain" from Indonesia, 1823–1990', *Economics Division Working Paper Southeast Asia* [Australian National University: Research School of Pacific Studies], 93/2.

Eng, P. van der 1994. 'Assessing Economic Growth and Standards of Living in Asia, 1870–1990', in A.J.H. Latham and H. Kawakatsu (eds), *The Evolving Structure of the East Asian Economic System since 1700: A Comparative Analysis*, Milan: Università Bocconi, 95–108.

Ernst, P.G. 1937. *Det store eventyr: Om H.N. Andersen og Østasiatiske Kompagni*, Copenhagen: Pedersen.

ESCAP 1991. *Statistical Yearbook for Asia and the Pacific 1991*, Bangkok: United Nations.

ESCAP/UNCTC 1984. *Costs and Conditions of Technology Transfer through Transnational Corporations*, Bangkok: United Nations.

ESCAP/UNCTC 1985a. *An Evaluation of Export Processing Zones in Selected Asian Countries*, Bangkok: United Nations.

ESCAP/UNCTC 1985b. *Transnational Corporations from Developing Asian Economies*, Bangkok: United Nations.

ESCAP/UNCTC 1987a. *Technology Transfer under Alternative Arrangements with Transnational Corporations*, Bangkok: United Nations.

ESCAP/UNCTC 1987b. *Transnational Corporations and the Electronics Industries of ASEAN Economies*, Bangkok: United Nations.

ESCAP/UNCTC 1988. *Transnational Corporations from Developing Asian Economies: Host Country Perspectives*, Bangkok: United Nations.

ESCAP/UNCTC 1990. *Environmental Aspects of Transnational Corporation Activities in Pollution-intensive Industries in Selected Asian and Pacific Developing Countries*, New York: United Nations.

Esmara, H. 1975. 'An Economic Survey of Riau', *Bulletin of Indonesian Economic Studies*, 11 (3), 25–49.

Euh Yoon-Dae and H. Min Sang 1986. 'Foreign Direct Investment from Developing Countries: The Case of Korean Firms', *Developing Economies*, 24, 149–68.

European Companies 1987. *European Companies in the Philippines*, London: Catholic Institute of International Relations.

Faaland, J., J.E. Parkinson and R. Sanisman 1990. *Growth and Ethnic Inequality: Malaysia's New Economic Policy*, London: Hurst.

Facts 1924. *Facts about the Philippines*, New York: Philippine–American Chamber of Commerce.

Falkus, M. 1989. 'Early British Business in Thailand', in R.P.T. Davenport–Hines and G. Jones (eds), *British Business in Asia since 1860*, New York: Cambridge University Press, 117–56.

Fallows, J. 1994. *Looking at the Sun: The Rise of the New East Asian Economic and Political System*, New York: Pantheon.

Fong Chan Onn 1990. 'Multinational Corporations in ASEAN: Technology Transfer and Linkages with Host Countries', in Soon Lee Ying (ed.), *Foreign Direct Investment in ASEAN*, Kuala Lumpur: Malaysian Economic Association, 254–84.

Foreign Equity 1992. *Foreign Equity Investment in Singapore, 1980–1989*, Singapore: Department of Statistics.

Fry, M.J. 1993. *Foreign Direct Investment in Southeast Asia: Differential Impacts*, Singapore: Institute of Southeast Asian Studies.

Fukushima Kiyohiko and C.H. Kwan 1995. 'Foreign Direct Investment and Regional Industrial Restructuring in Asia', in *The New Wave of Foreign Direct Investment in Asia*, Tokyo/Singapore: Nomura Research Institute/Institute of Southeast Asian Studies, 3–39.

Furnivall, J.S. 1944. *Netherlands India: A Study of Plural Economy*, Cambridge: Cambridge University Press.

Gates, C.L. 1995. 'Foreign Direct Investment, Institutional Change and Vietnam's Gradualist Approach to Reform', *Southeast Asian Affairs*, 382–400.

Gevers, F.P.A. 1991. 'Koloniale bedrijfsvoering in het Interbellum: De N.V. Deli Maatschappij aan Sumatra's Oostkust, 1918–1940', *Jaarboek voor de Geschiedenis van Bedrijf en Techniek*, 8, 136–59.

Gibson, J. 1966. 'Production-Sharing: Part II', *Bulletin of Indonesian Economic Studies*, 3 (4), 75–100.

Ginting, M. and R. Daroesman 1982. 'An Economic Survey of North Sumatra', *Bulletin of Indonesian Economic Studies*, 18 (3), 52–83.

Gleeck, L.E., Jr. 1975. *American Business and Philippine Economic Development*, Manila: Carmelo & Bauermann.

Godée Molsbergen, E.C. 1937. *Maatschappij tot exploitatie van rijstlanden op Java 'Michiels-Arnold' N.V. 1887–1939*, The Hague: Michiels-Arnold.

Goedkoop, J.A.M. 1990. 'Handelsvereeniging "Amsterdam", 1945–1958: Herstel en heroriëntatie', *Jaarboek voor de Geschiedenis van Bedrijf en Techniek*, 7, 219–40.

Golay, F.H. 1983. 'Taming the American Multinationals', in N.G. Owen (ed.), *The Philippine Economy and the United States: Studies in Past and Present Interactions*, Ann Arbor, MI: Centre of South and Southeast Asia Studies, 131–76.

Goodman, G.K. 1983. 'America's "Permissive" Colonialism: Japanese Business in the Philippines, 1899–1941', in N.G. Owen (ed.), *The Philippine Economy and the United States: Studies in Past and Present Interactions*, Ann Arbor, MI: Centre of South and Southeast Asia Studies, 37–62.

Gould, J.W. 1961. *Americans in Sumatra*, The Hague: Nijhoff.

Grist, D.H. 1933. *Nationality of Ownership and Nature of Constitution of Rubber Estates in Malaya*, Kuala Lumpur: Caxton.

Gruythuysen, M.W.M.M., R.T.M. Guleij and A.M. Tempelaars 1988. *Inventaris van de archieven van de N.V. Deli Maatschappij en daarmee gefuseerde bedrijven, 1869–1967*, The Hague: National Archives.

Gruythuysen, M.W.M.M. and R. Kramer 1990. *Inventaris van het direktiearchief van de N.V. Billiton-Maatschappij 1852–1970: I. Nederlands-Indische/Indonesische aktiviteiten*, The Hague: National Archives.

Guisinger, S. 1991. 'Foreign Direct Investment Flows in East and Southeast Asia: Policy Issues', *ASEAN Economic Bulletin*, 8 (1), 29–46.

Gull, E.M. 1943. *British Economic Interests in the Far East*, London: Oxford University Press.

Gurney, P.B. 1983. 'Joint–venture Investments in Indonesia', *Contemporary Southeast Asia*, 4, 522–37.

Halim, B. 1988. 'The Deregulation Package of December 24, 1987 and its Impact on the Indonesian Capital Market', *Ekonomi dan Keuangan Indonesia*, 36, 191–208.

Hamzah, B.A. 1981. 'Oil and Independence in Brunei: A Perspective', *Southeast Asian Affairs*, 93–102.

Handboek 1914, 1930, 1940. *Handboek voor cultuur- en handelsondernemingen in Nederlands-Indië*, Amsterdam: De Bussy.

Hardy, A. 1994. 'The Economics of French Rule in Indochina: Paul Bernard (1892–1960)', unpublished article, Canberra: Australian National University.

Harrisons & Crosfield 1943. *East India Merchant House: 100 Years as India Merchants*, London.

Hartendorp, A.V.H. 1958. *History of Industry and Trade of the Philippines*, Manila: American Chamber of Commerce of the Philippines.

Hauser, E.O. 1937. 'Britain's Economic Stake in Southeast Asia', *Far Eastern Survey*, 6, 283–8.

Healey, D.T. 1981. 'Survey of Recent Developments', *Bulletin of Indonesian Economic Studies*, 17 (1), 1–35.

Heinberg, A. 1943. *En dansk världserövrare: Sagan om H.N. Andersen*, Stockholm: Natur & Kultur.

Hicks, G.L. (ed.) 1993. *Overseas Chinese Remittances from Southeast Asia, 1910–1940*, Singapore: Select Books.

Hiemenz, U. 1987. 'Foreign Direct Investment and Industrialization in ASEAN Countries', *Weltwirtschaftliches Archiv*, 123, 121–38.

Hill, H. 1988. *Foreign Investment and Industrialization in Indonesia*, Singapore: Oxford University Press.

Hill, H. 1990. 'Foreign Investment and East Asian Economic Development', *Asian-Pacific Economic Literature*, 4 (2), 21–58.

Hill, H. 1992. 'Manufacturing Industry', in A. Booth, (ed.), *The Oil Boom and After: Indonesian Economic Policy and Performance in the Soeharto Era*, Singapore: Oxford University Press, 204–57.

Hill, H. 1994. 'The Economy', in H. Hill (ed.), *Indonesia's New Order: The Dynamics of Socio-economic Transformation*, Honolulu: University of Hawaii Press, 54–122.

Hill, H. 1996. *The Indonesian Economy since 1966: Southeast Asia's Emerging Giant*, Cambridge: Cambridge University Press.

Hill, H. and B. Johns 1985. 'The Role of Foreign Direct Investment in Developing East Asian Countries', *Weltwirtschaftliches Archiv*, 121, 355–81.

Hirschman, A.O. 1977. 'A Generalized Linkage Approach to Development, with Special Reference to Staples', *Economic Development and Cultural Change*, 25 (1) (supplement), 67–98.

Hlaing, A. 1964. 'Trends of Economic Growth and Income Distribution in Burma, 1870–1940', *Journal of the Burma Research Society*, 47, 89–147.

Hobohm, S. 1987. 'Survey of Recent Developments', *Bulletin of Indonesian Economic Studies*, 23 (2), 1–37.

Hock, T. 1990. 'Singapore', in E.K.Y. Chen (ed.), *Foreign Direct Investment in Asia*, Tokyo: Asian Productivity Organization, 105–25.

Hoffman, L. and Tan Siew Ee 1980. *Industrial Growth, Employment and Foreign Investment in Peninsular Malaysia*, Kuala Lumpur: Oxford University Press.

Holloway, N. *et al.* 1991. *Japan in Asia*, Hong Kong: Far Eastern Economic Review.

Hooley, R. 1985. *Productivity Growth in Philippine Manufacturing: Retrospect and Future Prospects*, Manila: Philippine Institute for Development.

Hooley, R. 1988. 'A Comparative Study of Manufacturing Productivity among ASEAN Countries', in M. Dutta (ed.), *Research in Asian Economic Studies: IA. Asian Industrialization: Changing Economic Structures*, Greenwich, CT/London: JAI Press, 346–59.

Horaguchi Haruo and B. Toyne 1990. 'Setting the Record Straight: Hymer, Internalization Theory and Transaction Cost Economics', *Journal of International Business Studies*, 21, 487–94.

Huff, W.G. 1994. *The Economic Growth of Singapore: Trade and Development in the Twentieth Century*, Cambridge: Cambridge University Press.

Hughes, H. 1969. 'Conclusions', in H. Hughes and P.S. You (eds), *Foreign Investment and Industrialization in Singapore*, Canberra: Australian National University, 177–210.

Hunter, A. 1971. 'Oil Developments', *Bulletin of Indonesian Economic Studies*, 7 (1), 96–113.

IMF 1991. *International Financial Statistics*, Washington, D.C.: International Monetary Fund.

Indikator 1996. 'Indikator ekonomi', *Bulan Statistik Bulanan*, Jakarta: Biro Pusat Statistik.

Ingram, J.C. 1971. *Economic Change in Thailand 1850–1970*, Palo Alto: Stanford University Press.

Inoue Ryuichiro 1993. 'An East Asian Industrial Policy Model', in Ryuichiro Inoue, Hirohisa Kohama and Shujiro Urata (eds), *Industrial Policy in East Asia*, Tokyo: JETRO, 2–27.

Intarathai, K. 1974. *The Impact of Direct Foreign Private Investment on the Industrialization of Thailand*, Ph.D. dissertation, University of Illinois, Urbana, IL.

Investing 1991. *Investing in ASEAN*, Jakarta: ASEAN Secretariat.

Jackson, J.C. 1968. *Planters and Speculators: Chinese and European Agricultural Enterprise in Malaya, 1786–1921*, Kuala Lumpur: University of Malaya Press.

Jansen, K. 1995. 'The Macroeconomic Effects of Direct Foreign Investment: The Case of Thailand', *World Development*, 23, 193–210.

Japanese Overseas Investment 1986. *Japanese Overseas Investment: A Complete Listing by Firms and Countries*, Tokyo: Toyo Keizai Shinposha.

Jenista, F. 1971. 'Conflict in the Philippine Legislature: The Commission and the Assembly from 1907 to 1913', in N.G. Owen (ed.), *Compadre Colonialism: Studies on the Philippines under American Rule*, Ann Arbor: University of Michigan, 77–102.

Jesudason, J.V. 1989. *Ethnicity and Economic Rationality: The State, Chinese Business and Multinationals in Malaysia*, Singapore: Oxford University Press.

JETRO 1994. *Directory of Japanese-affiliated Companies in Asia: 1994–95*, Tokyo: JETRO.

Johnson, M. 1977. 'Oil I: Recent Developments', *Bulletin of Indonesian Economic Studies*, 13 (3), 34–48.

Jomo K.S. 1986. *A Question of Class: Capital, the State and Uneven Development in Malaysia*, Singapore: Oxford University Press.

Jomo K.S. 1990. *Growth and Structural Change in the Malaysian Economy*, London: Macmillan.

Jomo K.S. 1994. 'The Proton Saga: Malaysian Car, Mitsubishi Gain', in K.S. Jomo, (ed.), *Japan and Malaysian Development: In the Shadow of the Rising Sun*, London: Routledge, 263–90.

Jun, Kwang W. *et al.* 1993. 'Japanese Foreign Direct Investment: Recent Trends, Determinants and Prospects', unpublished report, Washington, D.C.: World Bank.

Jungnickel, R., A. Gerberding and U. Maenner 1986. *Investitionsbedingungen in der ASEAN-Region*, Hamburg: Weltarchiv.

Kamp, A.F. 1960. *De standvastige tinnen soldaat 1860–1960: N.V. Billiton Maatschappij*, The Hague: Billiton.

Kano Hiroyoshi 1989. 'Indonesian Business Groups and Their Leaders', *East Asian Cultural Studies*, 28, 145–72.

Katano Hikoji 1981. *Japanese Enterprises in ASEAN Countries: Statistical Outlook*, Kobe: Kobe University Press.

Kato Tsuyoshi 1991. 'When Rubber Came: The Negeri Sembilan Experience', *Tonan Ajia Kenkyu [Southeast Asian Studies]*, 29 (2), 109–57.

Kebschull, D. and O.G. Mayer 1974. *Deutsche Investitionen in Indonesien*, Hamburg: Weltarchiv.

Keiko Saruwatari 1991. 'Malaysia's Localization Policy and Its Impact on British-owned Enterprises', *Developing Economies*, 29, 371–86.

Keller, A.S. 1940. 'Netherlands India as a Paying Proposition', *Far Eastern Survey*, 9, 11–18.

Khanthachai, N. *et al.* 1987. *Effective Mechanisms for the Enhancement of Technology and Skills in Thailand*, Singapore: Institute of Southeast Asian Studies.

Khin Maung Kyi U 1970. 'Western Enterprise and Economic Development in Burma', *Journal of the Burma Research Society*, 53 (1), 25–52.

Khong Cho Oon 1986. *The Politics of Oil in Indonesia: Foreign Company–Host Government Relations*, Cambridge: Cambridge University Press.

Khor Kok Peng 1983. *The Malaysian Economy: Structures and Dependence*, Kuala Lumpur: Institut Masyarakat Malaysia.

King, F.H.H. 1987–1991. *The History of the Hong Kong and Shanghai Banking Corporation*, Cambridge: Cambridge University Press.

Kirchbach, F. von 1983. *Economic Policies towards Transnational Corporations: The Experience of the ASEAN Countries*, Baden–Baden: Nomos.

Kitagawa Hiroshi 1995. 'Financial Liberalization in Asian Countries', in Kawagoe Toshihiko and S. Sekiguchi, (eds), *East Asian Economies: Transformation and Challenges*, Singapore: Institute of Southeast Asian Studies, 139–71.

Knickerbocker, F.T. 1973. *Oligopolistic Reaction and Multinational Enterprise*, Cambridge, MA: Harvard University Press.

Knight, G.R. 1996. 'Did "Dependency" Really Get It Wrong? The Indonesian Sugar Industry, 1880–1942', in J.Th. Lindblad (ed.), *Historical Foundations of a National Economy in Indonesia, 1880s–1990s*, Amsterdam: North-Holland, 155–74.

Koehler, K.G. 1972. 'Wood Processing in East Kalimantan: A Case Study of Industrialization and Foreign Investment in Indonesia', *Bulletin of Indonesian Economic Studies*, 8 (3), 93–129.

Kojima Kiyoshi 1973. 'A Macro-economic Approach to Foreign Direct Investment', *Hitotsubashi Journal of Economics*, 14 (2), 1–21.

Kojima Kiyoshi 1977. *Japan and a New World Economic Order*. Boulder, CO: Westview Press.

Kojima Kiyoshi 1978. *Direct Foreign Investment: A Japanese Model of Multinational Business Operations*, London: Croom Helm.

Kojima Kiyoshi 1985/86. 'Japanese-Style Direct Foreign Investment', *Japanese Economic Studies*, 14, 52–82.

Kommer, A. van 1989. 'De Deli Maatschappij aan de Oostkust van Sumatra gedurende de jaren 1900–1940', in A.H.P. Clemens and J.Th. Lindblad (eds), *Het belang van de Buitengewesten: Economische expansie en koloniale staatsvorming in de Buitengewesten van Nederlands–Indië, 1870–1942*, Amsterdam: NEHA, 97–122.

Korthals Altes, W.L. 1987. *Changing Economy in Indonesia: VII. Balance of Payments, 1822–1939*, Amsterdam: Royal Tropical Institute.

Kroef, J.M. van der 1955. 'Indonesia's Economic Difficulties', *Far Eastern Survey*, 24, 17–24.

Kroef, J.M. van der 1960. 'Indonesia's Economic Dilemma', *Far Eastern Survey*, 29, 49–63.

Kusumautmadja, M. 1974. 'Mineral Resources Exploration and Exploitation and the Law in the Southeast Asian Region', *Ekonomi dan Keangan Indonesia*, 22, 3–73.

Kwan Kuen–Chor and Lee Soo Ann 1983. 'Japanese Direct Investment in the Singapore Manufacturing Industry', in S. Sekiguchi (ed.), *ASEAN–Japan Relations: Investment*, Singapore: Institute of Southeast Asian Studies, 149–80.

Lachica, E. 1984. *Ayala: The Philippines' Oldest Business House*, Makati: Filipinas Foundation.

Langeveld, H.J. 1978. 'Arbeidstoestanden op de ondernemingen ter Oostkust van Sumatra tussen 1920 en 1940 in het licht van het verdwijnen van de poenale sanctie in de arbeidscontracten', *Economisch- en Sociaal-Historisch Jaarboek*, 41, 294–368.

Langhammer, R.J. 1988. 'Financing of Foreign Direct Investment and Trade Flows: The Case of Indonesia', *Bulletin of Indonesian Economic Studies*, 24 (1), 97–114.

Lauwerier, O.L.J. and A.D. Schermer 1987. *The Oriental Challenge: Investigations on Business Opportunities in Thailand, Singapore and Indonesia*, Delft: Eburon.

Lee Chung H. 1984. 'On Japanese Macro-economic Theories of Direct Foreign Investment', *Economic Development and Cultural Change*, 32, 713–23.

Lee Honggue 1995. 'Globalization, Foreign Direct Investment, and Competitive Strategies of Korean Electronics Companies', in *The New Wave of Foreign Direct Investment in Asia*, Tokyo/Singapore: Nomura Research Institute/Institute of Southeast Asian Studies, 64–86.

Li Dun Jen 1982; 1955. *British Malaya: An Economic Analysis* [1895–1938], Kuala Lumpur: INSAN.

Liem Tjwan Ling 1989. 'Sugar King: Oei Tiong Ham', in Yoshihara Kunio (ed.), *Oei Tiong Ham Concern: The First Business Empire of Southeast Asia*, Kyoto: Centre for Southeast Asian Studies.

Lim Chong-Yah 1967. *Economic Development of Modern Malaya*, Kuala Lumpur: Oxford University Press.

Lim, D. 1983. 'Foreign Investment', in D. Lim (ed.), *Further Readings on Malaysian Economic Development*, Kuala Lumpur: Oxford University Press, 207–53.

Lim Joo-Jock 1977. *Foreign Investment in Singapore: Economic and Socio-political Ramifications*, Singapore: Institute of Southeast Asian Studies.

Lim, L.Y.C. and Pang Eng Fong 1977. *The Electronics in Singapore: Structure, Technology and Linkages*, Singapore: Economic Research Centre, University of Singapore.

Lim, L.Y.C. and Pang Eng Fong 1991. *Foreign Direct Investment and Industrialization in Malaysia, Singapore, Taiwan and Thailand*, Paris: OECD.

Lim Mah Hui and Teoh Kit Fong 1986. 'Singapore Corporations Go Transnational', *Journal of Southeast Asian Studies*, 17, 336–65.

Limlingan, V.S. 1986. *The Overseas Chinese in ASEAN: Business Strategies and Management Practices*, Manila: Vita.

Lindblad, J.Th. 1988. *Between Dayak and Dutch: The Economic History of Southeast Kaïimantan, 1880–1942*, Dordrecht/Providence: Foris.

Lindblad, J.Th. 1989a. 'Economic Aspects of the Dutch Expansion in Indonesia, 1870–1914', *Modern Asian Studies*, 23 (1), 1–23.

Lindblad, J.Th. 1989b. 'The Petroleum Industry in Indonesia before the Second World War', *Bulletin of Indonesian Economic Studies*, 25 (2), 53–77.

Lindblad, J.Th. 1991. 'Foreign Investment in Late-colonial and Post-colonial Indonesia', *Economic and Social History of the Netherlands*, 3, 183–208.

Lindblad, J.Th. 1992. 'Regional Patterns in the Foreign Trade of Java, 1911–1940', in A.H.P. Clemens, J.Th. Lindblad and L.J. Touwen, *Changing Economy in Indonesia: XIIB. Regional Patterns in Foreign Trade, 1911–1940*, Amsterdam: Royal Tropical Institute, 19–32.

Lindblad, J.Th. 1994. 'Foreign Trade and Economic Growth in Late Colonial Indonesia, 1900–1940', in A.J.H. Latham and H. Kawakatsu (eds), *The Evolving Structure of the East Asian Economic System since 1700: A Comparative Analysis*, Milan: Università Bocconi, 57–68.

Lindblad, J.Th. 1996a. 'Business Strategies in Late Colonial Indonesia', in J.Th. Lindblad (ed.), *Historical Foundations of a National Economy in Indonesia, 1880s–1990s*, Amsterdam: North-Holland, 207–28.

Lindblad, J.Th. 1996b. 'The Economic Relationship between the Netherlands and Colonial Indonesia, 1870–1940', in J.L. van Zanden (ed.), *The Economic Development of the Netherlands since 1870*, Cheltenham: Elgar, 109–19.

Lindblad, J.Th. 1997. 'Foreign Investment in Southeast Asia in Historical Perspective', *Asian Economic Journal*, 11, 61–80.

Lindenberg, M.M. 1973. *Foreign and Domestic Investment in the Pioneer Industry Program: Malaysia 1965–1970*, Ph.D. dissertation, University of Southern California, Los Angeles.

Lindsey, C.W. 1976. *Concentration in Philippine Manufacturing, 1960–1970*, Ph.D. dissertation, University of Texas, Austin.

Lindsey, C.W. 1986. 'Transfer of Technology to the ASEAN Region by US Transnational Corporations', *ASEAN Economic Bulletin*, 3, 225–47.

Lindsey, C.W. 1989. 'Commodities, Technology and Trade: Transnational Corporations and Philippine Economic Development', *Philippine Review of Economics and Business*, 26, 67-108.

Locher-Scholten, E.B. 1994. *Sumatraans sultanaat en koloniale staat: De relatie Djambi–Batavia (1830–1907) en het Nederlandse imperialisme*, Leiden: KITLV.

Lockwood, W.W. 1936. 'America's Stake in the Far East: II. Investments', *Far Eastern Survey*, 5, 175–85.

Loh Kok Wah, F. 1988. *Beyond the Tin Mines: Coolies, Squatters and New Villagers in the Kinta Valley, Malaysia, 1880–1980*, Singapore: Oxford University Press.

Lukman, N. and J.M. McGlinchey 1986. 'The Indonesian Petroleum Industry: Current Problems and Future Prospects', *Bulletin of Indonesian Economic Studies*, 22 (3), 70–92.

Macaulay, R.H. 1934. *History of the Bombay–Burma Trading Corporation*, London: Spottis Woode & Ballantyne.

McCawley, P. and C. Manning 1976. 'Survey of Recent Developments', *Bulletin of Indonesian Economic Studies*, 12 (3), 1–49.

McDougald, C.C. 1981. *Multinational Corporations in the Philippines, 1978*, Manila: American Chamber of Commerce.

McKern, R.B. and P. Koomsup 1987. *The Minerals Industries of ASEAN and Australia: Problems and Prospects*, Sydney: Allen & Unwin.

Macmillan, A. 1923. *Seaports of the Far East: Historical and Descriptive, Commercial and Industrial Facts, Figures and Resources*, London: Collingridge.

Maddison, A. 1989. 'Dutch Income in and from Indonesia, 1700–1938', *Modern Asian Studies*, 23, 645–70.

Manarungsan, S. 1989. *Economic Development of Thailand, 1850–1950: Response to the Challenge of the World Economy*, Ph.D. dissertation, University of Groningen, the Netherlands.

Manasan, R.G. 1988. *A Review of Investment Incentives in ASEAN Countries*, Manila.

Marappan, A. and K.S. Jomo 1994. 'Japanese Multinational Intra-firm Trade: Transfer Pricing Practices in Malaysia', in K.S. Jomo (ed.), *Japan and Malaysian Development: In the Shadow of the Rising Sun*, London: Routledge, 127–53.

Marseille, J. 1984. *Empire colonial et capitalisme français: Histoire d'un divorce*, Paris: Albin Michel.

Meijer, H. 1994. *Den Haag–Djakarta: De Nederlands-Indonesische betrekkingen, 1950–1962*, Ph.D. dissertation, University of Utrecht, the Netherlands.

Million Baht Business 1991. *Million Baht Business Information: Thailand 1991*, Bangkok: Industrial Business Research.

Mirza, H. 1986. *Multinationals and the Growth of the Singapore Economy*, London: Croom Helm.

Mollema, J.C. 1922. *De ontwikkeling van het eiland Billiton en van de Billiton Maatschappij*, The Hague: Billiton.

Montiel, P.J. 1994. 'Capital Mobility in Developing Countries: Some Measurement Issues and Empirical Estimates', *World Bank Economic Review*, 8, 311–50.

Morgan, K. and A. Sayer 1988. *Microcircuits of Capital: 'Sunrise' Industry and Uneven Development*, Boulder CO.: Westview.

Murray, M.J. 1980. *The Development of Capitalism in Colonial Indochina (1870–1940)*, Berkeley: University of California Press.

Natarajan, S. and Tan Juay Miang 1992. *The Impact of MNC Investments in Malaysia, Singapore and Thailand*, Singapore: Institute of Southeast Asian Studies.

Nørlund, I. 1991. 'The French Empire, the Colonial State in Vietnam and Economic policy, 1885–1940', in G.D. Snooks, A.J.S. Reid and J.J. Pincus (eds), *Exploring Southeast Asia's Economic Past* [= *Australian Economic History Review* 31 (1)], Melbourne: Oxford University Press Australia, 72-89.

O'Connor, D. 1989. 'Transnational Corporations and Free Trade Zones: A Case Study of the Malaysian Experience with Special Reference to the Electronics Industry', in T. Carino (ed.), *Transnationals and Special Economic Zones: The Experience of China and Selected ASEAN Countries*, Manila: De la Salle University Press, 87–116.

OECD 1993. *International Direct Investment Statistics Yearbook 1993*, Paris: OECD.

Oei, H.L. 1969. 'Implications of Indonesia's New Foreign Investment Policy for Economic Development', *Indonesia*, 7, 33–66.

Ohta Hideaki, Tokuno Akihiro and Takeuchi Ritsuko 1995. 'Evolving Foreign Investment Strategies of Japanese Firms in Asia, in *The New Wave of Foreign Direct Investment in Asia*, Tokyo/Singapore: Nomura Research Institute/Institute of Southeast Asian Studies, 43–63.

Ooi Jin Bee 1982. *The Petroleum Resources of Indonesia*, Kuala Lumpur: Oxford University Press.

Osman-Rani, H., Toh Kin Woon and A. Ali 1986. *Effective Mechanisms for the Enhancement of Technology and Skills in Malaysia*, Singapore: Institute of Southeast Asian Studies.

Ostry, S. & F. Harianto 1995. 'The Changing Pattern of Japanese Foreign Direct Investment in the Electronics Industry in East Asia', *Transnational Corporations*, 4 (1), 11–43.

Owen, N.G. 1971. 'Introduction: Philippine Society and American Colonialism', in N.G. Owen (ed.), *Compadre Colonialism: Studies on the Philippines under American Rule*, Ann Arbor, MI: University of Michigan Press, 1–12.

Owen, N.G. 1984. *Prosperity without Progress: Manila Hemp and Material Life in the Colonial Philippines*, Berkeley: University of California Press.

Ozawa, T. 1979. *Multinationalism, Japanese Style: The Political Economy of Outward Dependency*, Princeton: Princeton University Press.

Panchareon, W. 1990. 'Thailand', in E.K.Y. Chen (ed.), *Foreign Direct Investment in Asia*, Tokyo: Asian Productivity Organization, 153–87.

Pang Eng Fong 1995. 'Staying Global and Going Regional: Singapore's Inward and Outward Direct Investments', in *The New Wave of Foreign Direct Investment in Asia*, Tokyo/Singapore: Nomura Research Institute/Institute of Southeast Asian Studies, 111–29.

Pangestu, M. 1986. 'The Pattern of Direct Foreign Investment in ASEAN: The United States vs. Japan', *ASEAN Economic Bulletin*, 3, 301–28.

Pangestu, M. and I.J. Azis 1994. 'Survey of Recent Developments', *Bulletin of Indonesian Economic Studies*, 30 (2), 3–47.

Pangestu, M. and A.D. Habir 1989. 'Trends and Prospects in Privatization and Deregulation in Indonesia', *ASEAN Economic Bulletin*, 5 (3), 224–41.

Pangestu, M. and I.N. Hasni 1991. 'The EC Internal Market and the ASEAN Textile and Clothing Industry', in N. Wagner (ed.), *ASEAN and the EC: The Impact of 1992*, Singapore: Institute of Southeast Asian Studies, 190–240.

Panglaykim, J. 1977. *Indonesia's Economic and Business Relations with ASEAN and Japan*, Jakarta: Centre of Strategic and International Studies.

Panglaykim, J. 1979. 'Memahami usaha-usaha patungan penting dalam pembinaan hubungan Indonesia–Jepang', *Ekonomi dan Keuangan Indonesia*, 27, 83–102.

Philippine 1992. *Philippine Statistical Yearbook 1992*, Manila: National Statistical Coordination Board.

Phipatseritham, K. and Kunio Yoshihara 1983. *Business Groups in Thailand*, Singapore: Institute of Southeast Asian Studies.

Phongpaichit, P. 1990. *The New Wave of Japanese Investment in ASEAN*, Singapore: Institute of Southeast Asian Studies.

Pointon, A.C. 1964. *The Bombay–Burmah Trading Corporation Limited, 1883–1963*, Southampton: Millbrook.

Pongpissanupichit, J. 1985. *Private Direct Foreign Investment and Thai Economy*, Ph.D. dissertation, Cornell University, Ithaca, NY.

Pornavalai, S. 1989. *Japanese Enterprise and the Strategy of Thailand to be NIC*, Bangkok: Thammasat University Press.

Porter, C. 1938. 'Philippine Industries Today and Tomorrow', *Far Eastern Survey*, 7, 143–49.

Potting, C.J. 1987. 'De muntvoorziening in Nederlands–Indië, 1877–1914', *Economisch- en Sociaal-Historisch Jaarboek*, 50, 111–44.

Primo Braga, C.A. and G. Bannister 1994. 'East Asian Investment and Trade: Prospects for Growing Regionalization in the 1990s', *Transnational Corporations*, 3 (1), 97–136.

Pugh, P. *et al.* 1990. *Great Enterprise: A History of Harrisons & Crosfield*, London: Harrisons & Crosfield.

Pupphavesa, W. and B. Pussarungsri 1995. 'Foreign Direct Investment and Industrial Restructuring in Thailand', in *The New Wave of Foreign Direct Investment in Asia*, Tokyo/Singapore: Nomura Research Institute/Institute of Southeast Asian Studies, 160–73.

Puthucheary, J.J. 1960. *Ownership and Control in the Malayan Economy*, Singapore: Eastern Universities Press.

Rajaghanttam 1991. *Kajian perletakan industri eletronik di kawasan Bayan Lepas*, Ph.D. dissertation, Universiti Sains Malaysia, Penang.

Ramstetter, E.D. 1993. 'Recent Trends in Direct Foreign Investment in the Asian Developing Economies', paper presented at the seminar on 'Trade Policy and the Investment Climate in Indonesia', Centre for Strategic and International Studies, Jakarta, 25 June.

Rana, P.B. & J.M. Dowling, Jr. 1988. 'The Impact of Foreign Capital on Growth: Evidences from Asian Developing Countries', *Developing Economies*, 26, 3–11.

Ranken, E.A. 1989. 'De niet-Europese bijdrage tot de economische ontwikkeling van West-Borneo, 1900–1940', in A.H.P. Clemens and J.Th. Lindblad, (eds), *Het belang van de Buitengewesten: Economische expansie en koloniale staatsvorming in de Buitengewesten van Nederlands–Indië, 1870–1942*, Amsterdam: NEHA, 177–209.

Rasiah, R. 1987. 'Pengantarabangsaan pengeluaran dan pembahagian buruh antarabangsa: Kajian kes industri separa konduktor di Pulau Pinang', unpublished M.Sc. thesis, Universiti Sains Malaysia, Penang.

Rasiah, R. 1988. 'The Semiconductor Industry in Penang: Implications for the New International Division of Labour Theories', *Journal of Contemporary Asia*, 18, 24–46

Rasiah, R. 1991. 'Foreign Firms in Penang's Industrial Transformation', *Jurnal Ekonomi Malaysia*, 23, 91–117.

Razak Abdul, A. 1984. 'Joint Venture between Malaysian Public Corporations and Foreign Enterprises: An Evaluation', in Lim Lin Lean and Chee Peng Lim (eds), *The Malaysian Economy at the Crossroads: Policy Adjustment or Structural Transformation*, Kuala Lumpur: Malaysian Economic Association, 263–99.

Reid, A.J.S. 1979. *The Blood of the People: Revolution and the End of Traditional Rule in Northern Sumatra*, Kuala Lumpur: Oxford University Press.

Reid, A.J.S. 1992. 'Economic and Social change, *c*. 1400–1800', in N. Tarling (ed.), *The Cambridge History of Southeast Asia: I. From Early Times to c. 1800*, Cambridge: Cambridge University Press, 460–507.

Reinhardt, J. 1993. 'Industrial Restructuring and Industrial Policy in Vietnam', in Mya Than and J.L.H. Tan (eds), *Vietnam's Dilemmas and Options: The Challenge of Economic Transition in the 1990s*, Singapore: Institute of Southeast Asian Studies, 71–96.

Report 1951. *Report of the Registrar of Companies: Singapore 1950*, Singapore: Government Printing Office.

Robequain, C. 1944. *The Economic Development of French Indo-China*, London: Oxford University Press.

Robinson, K.M. 1986. *Stepchildren of Progress: The Political Economy of Development in an Indonesian Mining Town*, Albany: State University of New York Press.

Rodan, G. 1989. *The Political Economy of Singapore's Industrialization: National State and International Capital*, London: Macmillan.

Rosendale, P. 1974. 'Survey of Recent Developments', *Bulletin of Indonesian Economic Studies*, 10 (3), 1–25.

Rosendale, P. 1980. 'Survey of Recent Developments', *Bulletin of Indonesian Economic Studies*, 16 (1), 1–33.

Ruzicka, I. 1979. 'Rent Appropriation in Indonesian Logging: East Kalimantan, 1972/3–1976/7', *Bulletin of Indonesian Economic Studies*, 15 (2), 45–74.

Saad, I. 1995. 'Foreign Direct Investment, Structural Change and Deregulation in Indonesia', in *The New Wave of Foreign Direct Investment in Asia*, Tokyo/Singapore: Nomura Research Institute/Institute of Southeast Asian Studies, 197–219.

Saham, J. 1980. *British Industrial Investment in Malaysia, 1963–1971*, Kuala Lumpur: Oxford University Press.

Salleh, I.M. 1992. 'Electronics and Electrical Machinery Industry', in M. Ariff and Hirashi Yokoyama (eds), *Foreign Direct Investment in Malaysia*, Tokyo: Institute of Developing Economies.

Salleh, I.M. 1995. 'Foreign Direct Investment and Technology Transfer in the Malaysian Electronics Industry', in *The New Wave of Foreign Direct Investment in Asia*, Tokyo/Singapore: Nomura Research Institute/Institute of Southeast Asian Studies, 133–59.

Santikarn, M. 1981. *Technology Transfer: A Case Study*, Singapore: Singapore University Press.

Sarkar, N.K. 1976. *Foreign Investment and Economic Development in Asia*, Bombay: Longmans Orient.

Sarraut, A. 1923. *La mise en valeur des colonies françaises*, Paris: Payot.

Schlosssstein, S. 1991. *Asia's New Little Dragons: The Dynamic Emergence of Indonesia, Thailand and Malaysia*, Chicago: Contemporary Books.

Segers, W.A.I.M. 1988. *Changing Economy in Indonesia: VIII. Manufacturing Industry, 1870–1942*, Amsterdam: Royal Tropical Institute.

Sekiguchi Sueo and L.B. Krause 1980. 'Direct Foreign Investment in ASEAN by Japan and the United States', in R. Garnaut (ed.), *ASEAN in a Changing Pacific and World Economy*, Canberra: Australian National University Press, 421–47.

Shakow, A. 1962. *Foreign Economic Assistance in Indonesia, 1950–1961*, Ph.D. dissertation, London School of Economics, London.

Shepherd, J. 1941. *Industry in Southeast Asia*, New York: Institute of Pacific Relations.

Shiowattana, P. 1991. 'Technology Transfer in Thailand's Electronics Industry', in: Shoichi Yamashita (ed.), *Transfer of Japanese Technology and Management to the ASEAN Countries*, Tokyo: University of Tokyo Press, 169-93.

Sibunruang, A. and P. Brimble 1988. *The Employment Effects of Manufacturing Multinational Enterprises in Thailand*, Geneva: ILO.

Sieh-Lee, M.L. 1979. 'Effects of Type of Industry on Share Ownership Distribution in Malaysian Manufacturing Companies', *Malayan Economic Review*, 24, 63–84.

Simandjuntak, D.S. 1989. 'Recent Changes in Indonesia's Policy on Foreign Direct Investment', *Indonesian Quarterly*, 17, 316–25.

Singapore 1989. *Singapore 500*, Singapore: Datapool.

Skougaard, H. 1943. *H.N. Andersen og det Østasiatiske Kompagni*, Copenhagen: Olsen.

Snow, R.T. 1983. 'Export-minded Industrialization, the International Division of Labour and the Rise of the Subcontract Bourgeoisie in the Philippines', in N.G. Owen (ed.), *The Philippine Economy and the United States: Studies in Past and Present Interactions*, Ann Arbor, MI: Centre of South and Southeast Asia Studies, 77–108.

Soesastro, H. 1992. 'Teknologi dan keunggulan komparatif', in M.A. Anwar, Thee Kian Wie and I.J. Azis (eds), *Pemikiran, pelaksanaan dan perintisan pembangunan ekonomi*, Jakarta: Gramedia, 547–74.

Somers Heidhues, M.F. 1992. *Bangka Tin and Mentok Pepper: Chinese Settlement on an Indonesian Island*, Singapore: Institute of Southeast Asian Studies.

Steinberg, D.J. 1981. 'Burmese Economics: The Conflict of Ideology and Population', in F. Lehman (ed.), *Military Rule in Burma since 1962: A Kaleidoscope of Views*, Singapore: Maruzen Asia, 29–50.

Steven, R. 1988. 'Japanese Foreign Direct Investment in Southeast Asia: From ASEAN to JASEAN', *Bulletin of Concerned Asian Scholars*, 20(4), 34–57.

Study 1972. *Study of Private Foreign Investment in the Philippines*, Manila: Board of Investment.

Subido, C. 1974. 'Determinants of Direct Foreign Investment', *Philippine Economic Journal*, 13, 231–59.

Subido, C. 1975. *Determinants of Direct Foreign Investment in the Philippines*, Ph.D. dissertation, University of Philippines, Quezon City.

230   *Bibliography*

Suehiro Akira 1989. *Capital Accumulation in Thailand, 1885–1985*, Tokyo: Centre of East Asian Cultural Studies.

Sumitro, A. 1975. *Foreign Investment in the Forest-based Sector of Indonesia: Increasing Its Contribution to Indonesian Development*, Ph.D. dissertation, University of Minnesota, Minneapolis.

Svedberg, P. 1978. 'The Portfolio-Direct Comparison of Private Foreign Investment in 1914 Revisited', *Economic Journal*, 88, 763–77.

Svedberg, P. 1981. 'Colonial Enforcement of Foreign Direct Investment', *Manchester School of Economic and Social Studies*, 49, 21–38.

Takeuchi, J. 1991. '"Technology Transfer" and Japan–Thai Relations', in Shoichi Yamashita (ed.), *Transfer of Japanese Technology and Management to the ASEAN Countries*, Tokyo: University of Tokyo Press, 199–233.

Tambunlertchai, S. 1975. *Foreign Direct Investment in Thailand's Manufacturing Industries*, Ph.D. dissertation, Duke University, Chapel Hill, NC.

Tambunlertchai, S. 1977. *Japanese and American Investments in Thailand's Manufacturing Industries*, Tokyo: Institute of Developing Economies.

Tambunlertchai, S. 1980. 'Attitudes and Experiences in Japanese-Thai Joint Venture Investments', in M. Krongkaew (ed.), *Current Development in Thai-Japanese Economic Relations: Trade and Development*, Bangkok: Thammasat University Press, 270–314.

Tambunlertchai, S. 1991. 'The Changing Pattern of Japanese Direct Investment in Thailand', in: Tran Van Tho (ed.), *Japan's Direct Investment in Thailand: Patterns and Issues*, Tokyo: Japan Centre for Economic Research.

Tambunlertchai, S. 1993. 'Manufacturing', in P.G. Warr (ed.), *The Thai Economy in Transition*, Cambridge: Cambridge University Press, 118–50.

Tambunlertchai, S. and S. Chirathivat 1990. 'Management of Thailand's International Economic and Trade Relations', in S. Prasith-rathsint (ed.), *Thailand on the Move: Stumbling Blocks and Breakthroughs*, Bangkok: Thai University Research Association, 189–231.

Tan Cheng Leong and T.S. Lim 1992. *Malaysia: Business and Investment Opportunities*, Singapore: Cassia Communications.

Tan, G. 1978. 'Foreign Investment, Employment Generation and the Profit–wage Ratio in the Manufacturing Sector of West Malaysia', *UMBC Economic Review*, 14, (2), 26–9.

Tate, D.J.M. 1979. *The Making of Modern Southeast Asia*, Kuala Lumpur: Oxford University Press.

Taylor, M. and M. Ward 1994. 'Industrial Transformation since 1970: The Context and the Means', in H. Brookfield (ed.), *Industrial Transformation with Industrialization in Peninsular Malaysia*, Kuala Lumpur: Oxford University Press, 95–121.

Than, M. 1990. 'The Union of Burma Foreign Investment Law: Prospects of Mobilizing Foreign Capital for Development', in M. Than and J.L.H. Tan (eds), *Myanmar Dilemmas and Options: The Challenge of Economic Transition in the 1990s*, Singapore: Institute of Southeast Asian Studies, 186–218.

Thee Kian Wie 1977. *Plantation Agriculture and Export Growth: An Economic History of East Sumatra, 1863–1942*, Jakarta: LEKNAS-LIPI.

Thee Kian Wie 1984. 'Japanese and American Direct Investment in Indonesian Manufacturing Compared', *Ekonomi dan Keuangan Indonesia*, 32, 89–105.

Thee Kian Wie 1990. 'Indonesia's Manufactured Exports: Performance and Prospects', in Sanjoto Sastromihardjo and Norio Mihira (eds), *Indonesia's*

Non-oil Exports: Performance and Prospects, Tokyo: Institute of Developing Economies, 69–99.

Thee Kian Wie 1991. 'The Surge of Asian NIC Investment into Indonesia', *Bulletin of Indonesian Economic Studies*, 27 (3), 55–88.

Thee Kian Wie 1993. 'Foreign Investment and the ASEAN Economies, with Special Reference to Indonesia', *Indonesian Quarterly*, 21, 434–49.

Thee Kian Wie 1994. *Industrialisasi di Indonesia: Beberapa Kajian*, Jakarta: LP3ES.

Thee Kian Wie 1995. 'Foreign Direct Investment in Indonesia since Independence', paper prepared for the EUROSEAS Conference 'Keys to Southeast Asia', Leiden, the Netherlands, 29 June – 1 July.

Thee Kian Wie 1996. 'Penanaman modal asing langsung di Indonesia sejak kemerdekaan', unpublished paper, Jakarta: LIPI.

Thoburn, J.T. 1981. *Multinationals, Mining and Development: A Study of the Tin Industry*, Farnborough: Gower.

Thompson, V. 1937. 'Indochina: France's Great Stake in the Far East', *Far Eastern Survey*, 6, 15–22.

Thompson, V. 1938. 'Siam Manoeuvring towards Self-sufficiency', *Far Eastern Survey*, 7, 289–95.

Tin Htoo 1959. 'Rubber Industry in Mergui District', *Journal of the Burma Research Society*, 42 (2), 153–70.

Todd, D. 1990. *The World Electronics Industry*, London/New York: Routledge.

Toh Mun Heng and L. Low 1990. 'An ASEAN Trade Model: Trade Flows, Linkages and Multipliers', in Yoichi Nakamura and J.T. Yap (eds), *ASEAN Link: An Econometric Study*, Singapore: Longman.

Tourret, R. *et al.* 1989. *Thailand*, London: Euromoney.

Tsuda M. *et al.* 1978. *The Impact of TNCs in the Philippines*, Quezon City: University of Philippines Law Centre.

Ueda Yoko 1995. *Local Economy and Entrepreneurship in Thailand: A Case Study of Nakhon Ratchasima*, Kyoto: Kyoto University Press.

UNCTAD 1994. 'World Investment Report 1994: Transnational Corporations, Employment and the Workplace: A Summary', *Transnational Corporations*, 3 (2), 73–114.

UNCTAD 1995. *World Investment Report: Transnational Corporations and Competitiveness*. New York/Geneva: United Nations.

UNIDO 1988. *Philippines: Sustaining Industrial Recovery through Privatization and Foreign Investment*, Vienna: UNIDO.

United Nations 1992. *World Investment Directory 1992: I. Asia and the Pacific*, New York: United Nations.

United Nations 1994. *Transnational Corporations and Technology Transfer in Export Processing Zones and Science Parks*, New York: United Nations.

United Nations 1995a. *Transnational Corporations and Backward Linkages in Asian Electronics Industries*, New York: United Nations.

United Nations 1995b. *Transnational Corporations and Selected Service Industries in Asia and the Pacific*, New York: United Nations.

Valdepenas, V.B., Jr. and G.M. Bautista 1977. *The Emergence of the Philippine Economy*, Manila: Papyrus.

Vernon, R. 1966. 'International Investment and International Trade in the Product Cycle', *Quarterly Journal of Economics*, 80, 190–207.

Vietnam Opportunities 1992. Vietnam Opportunities: The Official Vietnamese Business Guide, Hong Kong/London.

Viravan, A. 1972. 'Foreign Investment in Developing Countries: Thailand', in P. Drysdale (ed.), *Direct Foreign Investment in Asia and the Pacific*, Canberra: Australian National University Press, 227–41.

Voon Phin Keong 1973. 'The Rubber Industry of Burma, 1876–1964', *Journal of Southeast Asian Studies*, 4, 216–28.

Vries, J. de 1989. *Geschiedenis van de Nederlandsche Bank: V. De Nederlandsche Bank van 1914 tot 1948: Visserings tijdvak 1914–1931*, Amsterdam: NIBE.

Wagner, N. 1989. *ASEAN and the EC: European Investment in ASEAN*, Singapore: Institute of Southeast Asian Studies.

Walinsky, L.J. 1962. *Economic Development in Burma, 1951–1960*, New York: Twentieth-century Fund.

Warr, P.G. 1987. 'Export Promotion via Industrial Enclaves: The Philippines' Bataan Export Processing Zone', *Journal of Development Studies*, 23, 220–41.

Warr, P.G. 1993. 'The Thai Economy', in P.G. Warr (ed.), *The Thai Economy in Transition*, Cambridge: Cambridge University Press, 1-80.

Weisfelt, J. 1972. *De Deli Spoorweg Maatschappij als factor in de economische ontwikkeling van de Oostkust van Sumatra*, Ph.D. dissertation, Erasmus University, Rotterdam.

Wells, L.T. and V.E. Warren 1979. 'Developing Country Investors in Indonesia', *Bulletin of Indonesian Economic Studies*, 15 (1), 69–84.

Wong, J. 1979. *ASEAN Economies in Perspective: A Comparative Study of Indonesia, Malaysia, the Philippines, Singapore and Thailand*, Basingstoke: Macmillan.

Wong Lin Ken 1965. *The Malayan Tin Industry to 1914*, Tucson: Arizona University Press.

Wong Poh Kam 1991. 'The EC Internal Market and the ASEAN Electronics Industry', in N. Wagner (ed.), *ASEAN and the EC: The Impact of 1992*, Singapore: Institute of Southeast Asian Studies, 153–89.

Wong Tai Chee 1990. 'Industrial Development, the New Economic Policy in Malaysia and the International Division of Labour', *ASEAN Economic Bulletin*, 7 (1), 106–19.

World Bank 1991. *Indonesia: Employment and Training; Foundations for Industrialization in the 1990s*, Washington, D.C.: World Bank.

World Bank 1996. *Atlas 1996*, Washington, D.C.: World Bank.

Yamada, T. 1978. 'Foreign Investment in the ASEAN Region', in L.R. Vasey (ed.), *ASEAN and a Positive Strategy for Foreign Investment*, Honolulu: Pacific Forum, 97–117.

Yamashita Shoichi 1991. 'Economic Development of the ASEAN Countries and the Role of Japanese Direct Investment', in Shoichi Yamashita (ed.), *Transfer of Japanese Technology and Management to the ASEAN Countries*, Tokyo: University of Tokyo Press, 3–22.

Yeung, W.C.H. 1994. 'Hong Kong Firms in the ASEAN Region; Transnational Corporations and Foreign Direct Investment', *Environment and Planning*, 26, 31–56.

Yew Siew Yong 1988. 'Employment Effects of Multinational Enterprises in Malaysia', unpublished report, Geneva: ILO.

Yip Yat Hong 1969. *The Development of the Tin Mining Industry of Malaya*, Kuala Lumpur: University of Malaya Press.

Yoder, A. 1957. 'Patterns of Foreign Investment in Thailand', *Far Eastern Survey*, 26, 170–5.

Yokoyama Hirashi 1992. 'The Production Structure of Manufacturing Industries with Foreign Direct Investment: Production Function Perspectives', in M. Ariff and Hirashi Yokoyama (eds), *Foreign Direct Investment in Malaysia*, Tokyo: Institute of Developing Economies, 45-66.

Yoshida Masami *et al.* 1994. 'Regional Economic Integration in East Asia: Special Features and Policy Implications', in V. Cable and D. Henderson (eds), *Trade Blocs? The Future of Regional Integration*, London: Royal Institute of International Affairs, 59–108.

Yoshihara Kunio 1976. *Foreign Investment and Domestic Response: A Study of Singapore's Industrialization*, Singapore: Eastern Universities Press.

Yoshihara Kunio 1978. *Japanese Investment in Southeast Asia*, Honolulu: University Press of Hawaii.

Yoshihara Kunio 1985. *Philippine Industrialization: Foreign and Domestic Capital*, Manila: Oxford University Press.

Yoshihara Kunio 1988. *The Rise of Ersatz Capitalism in Southeast Asia*, Singapore: Oxford University Press.

Yoshino, M.Y. 1976. *Japan's Multinational Enterprises*, Cambridge, MA: Harvard University Press.

Zyll de Jong, E. van 1940. 'The American Stake in Netherlands India', *Far Eastern Survey*, 9, 145–53.

Index

The index does not include individual countries in Southeast Asia, other countries appearing very frequently or general economic concepts such as growth, equity and profits. Full explanations of abbreviations are found in the List of Abbreviations above (page xii).

234